WHAT WORKS
IN
DEVELOPMENT?

WHAT WORKS
IN
DEVELOPMENT?

Thinking Big
and
Thinking Small

JESSICA COHEN AND WILLIAM EASTERLY
EDITORS

BROOKINGS INSTITUTION PRESS
Washington, D.C.

Library of Congress Cataloging-in-Publication data
What works in development? : thinking big and thinking small / Jessica L. Cohen and
William Easterly, editors.
    p.   cm.
  Includes bibliographical references and index.
  ISBN 978-0-8157-0282-5 (pbk. : alk. paper)
  1. Economic development. 2. Social planning. 3. Development economics.
I. Cohen, Jessica L. II. Easterly, William Russell.
  HD75.W485 2009
  338.9—dc22   2009039932

9 8 7 6 5 4 3 2 1

Contents

WHAT WORKS
IN
DEVELOPMENT?

1

Introduction:
Thinking Big versus Thinking Small

JESSICA COHEN AND WILLIAM EASTERLY

The starting point for the contributions to this volume, and the conference for which they were prepared, is that there is no consensus on "what works" for growth and development. The ultimate goal of development research—a plausible demonstration of what has worked in the past and what might work in the future—remains elusive. As Martin Ravallion points out in his comment on chapter 2, we are beyond "policy rules" such as the Washington Consensus, and "thinking big" on development and growth is in crisis. The "big" triggers for economic growth have not been shown to work, either because they in fact did not work or because it was impossible to demonstrate their impact persuasively.

As a result, many in development have turned to "thinking small." For the most part—but not exclusively—the focus has shifted from macro- to micropolicy questions. This type of research commonly seeks the most effective method for delivering public goods such as education and vaccines. A growing methodology for analyzing micropolicy questions is randomized controlled trials (also known as Randomized Evaluations, REs). Much of this volume is about the merits and drawbacks of REs in elucidating what works in development. The specific arguments—we say more on them later in this chapter—revolve around several nagging questions. What kind of development policy research yields "hard" evidence? Are some types of evidence "harder" than others? Is there a trade-off between the scope of the questions researchers ask and the quality of the evidence they generate? What questions and what quality of evidence matter most for development policy and aid effectiveness? In exploring these issues, it is essential to first ask how the crisis in thinking big transpired and whether thinking small is indeed a solution.

The Collapse of "Thinking Big"

The failure of thinking big—elsewhere described as "the panaceas that failed"— has been widely acknowledged.[1] Many would agree with Arnold Harberger that "there aren't too many policies that we can say with certainty . . . affect growth."[2] Some, like those behind the Barcelona Development Agenda, would go even further: "There is no single set of policies that can be guaranteed to ignite sustained growth."[3] Even the universally revered dean of growth theory, Robert Solow, believes that "in real life it is very hard to move the permanent growth rate; and when it happens . . . the source can be a bit mysterious even after the fact."[4]

Where did this pessimism come from? As both Abhijit Banerjee, and William Easterly in his comment on Banerjee, discuss later in the volume, several contributing factors readily come to mind: despite concerted attempts, macroeconomists were unable to deliver higher growth; the credibility of the growth regression literature waned; extremely volatile growth rates could not be explained; and growth analysis neglected to do enough long-run regressions.

The Failure of Big Pushes to Raise Growth

Three unsuccessful pushes are particularly notable:

1. The early big push in foreign aid (especially in the most aid-intensive continent, Africa).

2. Structural adjustment (also known as the Washington Consensus) in the 1980s and 1990s.

3. "Shock therapy" in the former Communist countries.

All of these episodes are far from natural experiments, of course, with adverse selection posing a severe problem for the interpretation of policy impact. However, all three had such poor outcomes that the counterfactual—that growth would have been even worse without the macroeconomic intervention—was hardly plausible.

---

1. Easterly (2001).

2. Harberger (2003).

3. The Barcelona Development Agenda was the consensus document resulting from Forum Barcelona 2004, Barcelona, Spain, September 24–25 (www.barcelona2004.org/esp/banco_del_conocimiento/docs/CO_47_EN.pdf). Those involved in this exercise included Olivier Blanchard, Guillermo Calvo, Stanley Fischer, Jeffrey Frankel, Paul Krugman, Dani Rodrik, Jeffrey D. Sachs, and Joseph E. Stiglitz.

4. Solow (2007).

The Failure of the Growth Regression Literature

The pessimism surrounding big pushes intensified as the credibility of the cross-country growth literature declined, with its endless claims for some new "key to growth" (regularly found to be "significant") and probably well-deserved reputation for rampant data mining. As the Easterly comment on Banerjee notes, the number of variables claimed to be significant right-hand-side (RHS) determinants approached 145, which is probably an undercount.[5] Having a long list of possible controls to play with, researchers found it easy enough to arrive at significant results, and using the abundant heuristic biases that make it possible to see patterns in randomness, convinced themselves that the significant results were from the "right" specification, and that the others (usually unreported) were from the "wrong" ones.[6]

The growth literature was also criticized for its inability to address causality. In the absence of clear evidence that growth outcomes can be attributed to specific levers, development research has severely limited utility for policy. This deficiency was probably due to the infeasibility of instrumenting for multiple RHS variables. Any such attempts usually relied on the Arellano-Bond or Arellano-Bover dynamic panel techniques, which (essentially using lagged RHS variables as instruments) became a kind of magical machine churning out causal econometric results. Unfortunately, the identifying assumptions were so implausible as to leave most outside observers unconvinced. This left the causality question unresolved.

Not to overstate the inevitability of the collapse of growth knowledge, neither data mining nor causality was a completely hopeless cause in aggregate regressions. Data mining can be held in check with a well-known methodology: estimating slight variants of the original specification that are as plausible as the original; or, better yet, adding new data that were unavailable at the time of the original estimation to the exact specification. As far as causality was concerned, occasionally there would be a reasonably plausible instrument for a RHS variable of particular interest.

Both remedies can be explored in the hotly debated literature on the effect of aid on growth. Since it is hard for researchers to hold themselves aloof from the strong vested interests in and political biases for or against aid, there was enormous scope for data mining in aid and growth regressions. One very simple test of data mining is to add new data that were not available at the time of the original regression specification and see if the results still hold. The famous result of Craig Burnside and David Dollar that "aid raises growth in a good policy environment" did not pass this test.[7]

---

5. Durlauf, Johnson, and Temple (2005).

6. Kahneman and Tversky (2000); Kahneman and others (1982); Gilovich and others (2002).

7. See Burnside and Dollar (2000); Easterly, Levine, and Roodman (2004).

As for causality, one promising instrument for aid was population size, because of the quirk that the aid donor bureaucracy does not fully increase aid dollars one for one with recipient population size. Log of population is thus an excellent predictor of aid/gross domestic product (GDP), thankfully unrelated to the economic motivations for aid, and has been used in many studies. Another original strategy for identifying the impact of aid on growth has been to instrument aid from the Organization of Petroleum Exporting Countries (OPEC) to their poor Muslim allies with the interaction between oil price and a Muslim dummy variable.[8] This approach uncovered a short-term effect of aid on output, but also a zero effect on medium-term growth. The generalizability problems of such identification strategies are much like those of REs. Does small-population-induced aid have the same effect as other aid? Does intra-Muslim aid have the same effect as aid from the United Kingdom to Africa? Another problem, which REs typically do not have, is serious doubt about the excludability of the instrument in cross-country growth regressions.

But even when establishing causality was not possible, it would have been equally extreme to say that strong partial correlations would or should have no effect on priors about causal policy effects. Researchers were also probably influenced by the established body of theory, which tended to predict causal effects of policies on growth without much reason to think that growth would feed back into policies.

The Volatility of Growth Rates

By and large, the growth literature has also failed to establish even robust partial correlations between growth and country characteristics. One reason is that growth rates are extremely volatile while country characteristics are persistent. A crude way of showing growth volatility is to do a random effects regression on a panel of annual per capita growth rates between 1960 and 2005. This reveals that only 8 percent of the cross-time, cross-country variation in growth is due to permanent country effects; the other 92 percent is transitory. The annual standard error of the pure time-varying component of growth is an amazing 5.06 percentage points.[9] In the latest successive decades, 1985–95 and 1995–2005, there is virtually zero correlation between a country's performance in one decade and its performance in the next (hence virtually 100 percent mean reversion). This is very bad news when almost all of the plausible determinants of growth are relatively permanent country factors. It was like trying to explain differences in this week's batting averages of baseball players by differences in long-run fundamentals such as training regimens (or steroids!). The noise-to-signal ratio is so high with both

8. Werker, Ahmed, and Cohen (2009).

9. This was documented more than fifteen years ago by Easterly and others (1993), and in another form by Pritchett, Rodrik, and Hausmann (2005), who showed high-growth episodes to be almost always temporary.

weekly batting averages and decade growth rates that any such attempt is largely futile.

Long-Run versus Short-Run Development and Growth Literature

When asked about the impact of the French Revolution, Zhou En-Lai reportedly said it was "too soon to tell." So with growth performance. A *very* long-run average of growth rates is needed to lower the noise-to-signal ratio enough to have something interesting to relate. To put it another way, growth analysis has suffered from what Daniel Kahneman and Amos Tversky sarcastically call the Law of Small Numbers problem: reading too much into growth differences over one or two decades when they were mostly transitory.[10] The obvious answer was to go to more long-run analysis, which is in fact the direction the macro literature took, doing regressions for log *levels* of per capita income as a function of long-run characteristics such as institutions.[11]

The lack of persistence of growth rates made data mining easy—and easy to catch. As new growth observations came in, almost uncorrelated with past observations, the data miners would keep finding new variables that "explained" growth. As yet more new data came along, country factors would be the same, but the growth rates would get scrambled again, and the results would vanish. In an amusing nonacademic example, countries in which people ate fast were found to grow more rapidly over 2001–08 than countries in which people ate slowly.[12] Fast-Food USA has been growing faster than slow-eating Japan. The culture on eating presumably is persistent, so this result would not have held in the old days of rapid Japanese and slow U.S. growth, and any slow-eating French boom would make the result disappear again.

Those who reject such chicanery currently hold the field in empirical growth research. This position itself may not be sustainable, however. For the consumers of academic research, just saying "it's too soon to tell" about a matter as visible as economic growth differences is almost impossible to accept. So the nearly universal debunking of growth knowledge has not stopped attempts to explain growth.

The latest attempts appear to embrace a theory on the order of

$$\textit{Growth (country i, period t)} = \textit{Coefficient (country i, period t)} *$$
$$\textit{Policy (country i, period t)}.$$

This equation finally fits the data very well! Alas, tautological and nonfalsifiable theories are not usually allowed. Lest we appear to exaggerate, consider a statement by the World Bank Growth Commission in the aftermath of $4 million

---

10. Kahneman and Tversky (1982).

11. Acemoglu and others (2001, 2004); Easterly and Levine (2003); Rodrik, Subramanian, and Trebbi (2004).

12. See Floyd Norris, "Eat Quickly, for the Economy's Sake," *New York Times*, May 8, 2009.

worth of conferences and consultants: "It is hard to know how the economy will respond to a policy, and the right answer in the present moment may not apply in the future."[13] In chapter 2 of this volume, Dani Rodrik also seems to flirt with this extreme at times, although he avoids nonfalsifiable tautology by laying claim to independent knowledge with growth diagnostics exercises that would give insights into the coefficient (i,t)'s.[14]

Ricardo Hausmann in chapter 6 notes the complexity of public policy and institutions and suggests that the search for which policy is "the answer" only makes sense if there was a "central planner" implementing policies, which is no more feasible for public policy than for private goods markets. He argues for decentralized public policymaking to address such complexity.

The unpopular but well-justified focus on the long term can also generate insights into development from long-run stylized facts. A long tradition in development is to establish robust stylized facts in levels that guide development thinking—examples are the positive correlation between democracy and per capita income (which has stimulated thinking about causal channels in both directions), the negative correlation between per capita income and fertility (often interpreted causally as "development is the best contraceptive"), the relationship between life expectancy and income, and how that relationship (the "Preston curve") has shifted over time (suggesting that major changes in health technology can improve health without income growth), and so on.[15] The neoclassical production function model of development has come into question because of its violation of many stylized facts about development (such as capital flows, brain drain, and the failure of absolute convergence).[16] New growth models have also been guided by macro stylized facts. For example, idea models that stress R&D efforts as a determinant of growth have run afoul of the stationarity of growth rates and the nonstationarity of R&D efforts,[17] although they would fit the very long run of world development as a whole.[18] Another stylized fact in many analyses is the surprising significance of very long-run history for determining today's outcomes, which may lend support to some growth theory models with increasing returns and sensitivity to initial conditions. As David Weil notes, commenting on chap-

13. World Bank Growth Commission on Development (2008).

14. Of course, parameter heterogeneity is indeed a problem, and econometrics can at least discuss what the estimated coefficients mean when there is such heterogeneity. The coefficients will mean something very much like what the analogous situation in micro experiments means, with the estimate signifying something like a "local average treatment effect" (Deaton [2009]). The difference in macro regressions is that the "local" is averaging over a lot of very varied experiences across countries, while the "local" in micro is averaging over a specific population within a small treatment site.

15. On life expectancy and income, see Deaton (2006).

16. As discussed in Klenow and Rodríguez-Clare (1997); Easterly and Levine (2001).

17. Jones (2005).

18. Kremer (1993); Galor and Weil (2000).

ter 4, scientific experiments are not the only means of learning about development; historians do not do experiments, but most economists think that they learn something from historians (including economic historians such as Stanley Engerman and Kenneth Sokoloff analyzing why North America is richer than South).

So thinking big is not dead. However, sixty-year-old hopes that thinking big would translate into clear guidance on how to move immediately into rapid growth and development have been repeatedly disappointed.

The New Promise of "Thinking Small"

The macro literature is not alone in lacking decisive evidence. REs, "natural experiments," and other methodologies prioritizing transparency and clean identification became popular because of the great vacuum of microevidence on development projects. As Lant Pritchett has eloquently put it, nearly all World Bank discussion of policies or project design had the character of "ignorant armies clashing by night."[19] Despite the heated debate among advocates of various activities, they rarely presented any firm evidence or considered the likely impact of those actions. As far as we know, there was never any definitive evidence that would inform decisions of funding one instrument versus another (such as vaccinations versus public education about hygiene to improve health, or textbook reform versus teacher training to improve educational quality).

Even a World Bank handbook was quick to note that "despite the billions of dollars spent on development assistance each year, there is still very little known about the actual impact of projects on the poor."[20] The RE literature made a clear case for basing aid policy on evidence rather than prejudice and special interests. This methodology holds tremendous promise for improving aid effectiveness (and cost-effectiveness) by helping policymakers, donors, and nongovernmental organizations (NGOs) choose between a nearly infinite range of development program possibilities. While REs have some drawbacks—and doing them well is often an art—they have the undeniable strength of transparency and usability. A simple comparison of means between treatment and control groups can persuasively illustrate the impact of many different types of development policies and NGO programs.

But has the RE literature managed to solve the problems that afflicted the thinking big literature? There is already some backlash against REs, in some ways reminiscent of the backlash against aggregate macrowork, although many of the issues are quite different.

19. Pritchett (2009, p. 121).
20. Baker (2000).

Arguments for and against REs

The view that REs are a major advance over cross-country empirics has drawn strong support as well as criticism. We do not try to resolve that debate here. Instead we simply summarize some of the arguments on both sides regarding RE identification, external validity, RE links to theory, data mining, RE effect on implementing agencies, its effect on policy, and the underlying ethical and social engineering concerns. The order in which we present them should *not* be taken to imply that one side or the other has a decisive last word on the matter.

RE IDENTIFICATION. The most important claim of RE supporters is that they have solved the identification problem. Controlling the assignment mechanism through randomization allows a causal ("treatment") effect (usually of a development program or policy) to be estimated by removing selection bias. If the great majority of people offered the treatment in an RE accept it or (in the less likely case) there is no selective compliance with the randomization, REs allow one to estimate average program impact through a simple comparison of means across treatment and control.

When compliance with the program or policy is selective (for example, when only the sickest people take up a health product or the smartest children use new textbooks in a school), a common approach is to instrument the actual treatment with the treatment assignment. This is an advance over using standard instrumental variables (IVs) since (as long as the randomization was not compromised somehow) one can be sure that the instrument is exogenous and that the causal effect on outcomes is being identified. In sum, REs deliver an internally valid estimate of the causal effect of a policy or program on outcomes, something that is unattainable with observational studies.

A primary criticism with RE identification (when the treatment effect is instrumented), however, is the ambiguity about *what* is being identified. If the impact of the policy or program varies across members of the treatment group (that is, there are heterogeneous treatment effects), the parameter being identified is a Local Average Treatment Effect (LATE). Specifically, it is the impact for the subset of people who were induced to adopt the treatment because it was offered to them ("compliers") and excludes those who would never adopt the treatment, or who would have adopted it in the absence of the intervention.[21] Although this contains much useful information, it omits important details about the effect of the treatment on individuals who are not "local." As Ravallion points out later in the volume, this poses a problem for generalizability. If the program has a very different impact on the "compliers" than on others in the population, how can a policymaker determine its possible impact on a national level? Further, the average estimate that LATE delivers has limited usefulness. How valuable is LATE rel-

---

21. Imbens and Angrist (1994).

ative to the median effect of a program? And is LATE useful for the case in which a program has a positive average impact but causes a small share of people to suffer very negative consequences?

EXTERNAL VALIDITY. Can an RE finding be generalized to other settings? Among the skeptics, Angus Deaton and Dani Rodrik might concede RE's internal validity but would seriously question its external validity.[22] Like many others, they wonder whether the particular outcome of a particular program carried out on a particular population in a particular country by a particular implementing organization would be found in other circumstances. One of the main objectives of REs is to guide policy decisions, but how can policymakers be sure whether a program that worked well in one country would have similar effects in another? Or, if it worked with an urban population, that it would work with a rural one? Equally important, how can one tell that the program would be as effective if implemented by the government rather than by an NGO? According to Nancy Cartwright, REs do "not tell us what the overall outcome on the effect in question would be from introducing the treatment in some particular way in an uncontrolled situation, even if we consider introducing it only in the very population sampled. For that we need a causal model."[23]

One possible solution is to replicate the program in many different settings to confirm a general result.[24] However, the incentives for researchers to do replications fall off very rapidly with the number of replications already performed. Moreover, it is unclear how many are needed or how to choose the right sample of environments (with what factors varying?) to validate a result from the original study. Replication is often mentioned as a solution to the external validity problem without guidance on *how many* or *what kind* of replications are "enough" to establish generalizability. The problems in generalizing from a small slice of experience are analogous to those for the Law of Small Numbers in aggregate growth analysis mentioned earlier.

For some, the biggest problem is the lack of a model to clarify why, when, and where the treatment is expected to work.[25] In other words, an RE is most useful when it sheds light on some behavioral response (such as the price elasticity of demand for health inputs)—although even then it may not extrapolate to other settings. REs are less useful when they issue a blanket claim that "*X* works but not *Y*" on the basis of one very small sample in a particular context, without any clear intuition as to why *X* is more likely to work than *Y*. As Rodrik points out in chapter 2, the progression from RE results to policy often involves the same kinds of appeals to theoretical priors, common sense, casual empirics about similarity of the new policy setting to the original research setting in some (but not all) aspects,

22. See Deaton (2009); and Rodrik's discussion in chapter 2.
23. Cartwright (2007) in Deaton (2008).
24. Duflo, Glennester, and Kremer (2008); Banerjee and Duflo (2008).
25. See, for example, Deaton (2009).

and other more casual sources of evidence as does using aggregate econometric results and stylized facts to influence policy.

In their defense, however, REs are not alone in facing a trade-off between internal validity and generalizability. Although cross-country macrostudies are widely thought to be more generalizable than REs because they estimate averages over time, space, and population (see chapter 2), some would counter that observational studies of program impact covering large temporal and cross-sectional dimensions are equally prone to this trade-off.[26] Such studies must often control for multiple covariates (or use matching) to estimate a treatment effect, but, once covariates are controlled for, the estimate will be dominated by groups with overlapping covariates. In other words, cross-temporal/cross-sectional studies do not estimate an average treatment effect for an entire population—but only for a certain subpopulation—just as in the case of REs and IV studies. The advantage of REs here is that they often produce detailed microdata that can help in understanding this population and assessing its generality.

Furthermore, previous theoretical and empirical research, as well as plain common sense, provides some intuitive grounds for determining which characteristics would really affect program impact (and which would be inconsequential or secondary) and hence could provide guidance for a manageable number of replications. In an evaluation of a school intervention that tries to reduce student-teacher ratios, for example, the main concern would be whether the results extend to a context in which teachers' contracts are different, not the color of the school walls. This sense of what should matter and what should not pervades today's increasingly thorough and careful research into REs and external validity. As Banerjee points out in chapter 7, the significant advantage of REs lies in replicability, since hypotheses about external validity are *testable* with this methodology. Ideally, one uses theory to decide what factors would matter for replicability, but absent that theory, REs can be repeated as frequently as necessary. Atheoretical replication is clearly not ideal from a social science perspective, but to policymakers or NGOs wanting to know how to improve education or reduce poverty in their country, this feature of REs is a great help.

Of course, it is also important to consider "confounding" factors in assessing external validity, as illustrated in a study of subsidized bed nets in Kenya.[27] The larger policy question that motivated this investigation was whether bed nets should be free or highly subsidized for pregnant women. Two factors suggested that the study's results might not hold for other populations: (1) social marketing of bed nets had taken place recently, and (2) only pregnant women were targeted with bed nets. Although these factors were likely to have influenced the behavioral response to bed-net pricing, they are not necessarily a problem for external validity. From a

26. See Imbens and Woolridge (2008); Banerjee and Duflo (2008).
27. See Cohen and Dupas (2009); Rodrik (chapter 2).

policy perspective, this is the relevant environment and population to consider: social marketing of bed nets is exceedingly common in Africa, and pregnant women and their babies are the target groups for malaria prevention.

In any case, exact replication of REs in different contexts is not required to draw broad lessons about development, as demonstrated by Michael Kremer and Alaka Holla in chapter 4, in their discussion of RE literature dealing with education and public health and with price sensitivity in these areas. They find that a number of REs actually explore program variation within different treatment arms of the same experiment.[28] Furthermore, a number of studies have used randomization to estimate structural models.[29] A better grounding of REs in economic theory could no doubt elucidate the environmental and behavioral factors behind the results being reported in the program evaluation literature.

Another possibility is to use qualitative research to explore the results of an RE more closely and to give direction for future research. Anne Case (this volume) argues that REs miss out on important information by focusing only on quantitative variables. She suggests a mix of qualitative and quantitative analysis. Of course, macrostudies would benefit from this mix as well, and one advantage of REs is that they routinely collect very detailed microdata that could be combined with a qualitative analysis. Nava Ashraf goes a step further, arguing that qualitative analysis should be combined with theory to help use REs more systematically in a search for what works in development. Responding to Hausmann's claim in chapter 6 that REs cannot possibly guide complex and multidimensional policies, Ashraf argues that qualitative evidence can shed some light on the many ways in which quantitative RE results may vary across contexts and then theory can be used to predict which types of variation would meaningfully affect the estimated program impact.

Another way forward for REs is to make better use of macrodata. Using the example of determinants of child mortality, Peter Boone and Simon Johnson argue in chapter 3 that—in the absence of a theory that is being tested—correlations observed in macrodata can be very useful for motivating the design of an RE. Klenow (commenting on chapter 7) points out that a divide between "micro" (controlled, laboratory work) and "macro" (data analysis of trends, for example) exists in most areas of the natural sciences, but that it is routine for macrostudies to motivate and guide micro ones. He uses the example of macrostudies of trends in obesity guiding lab experiments on diet and exercise, or the correlation between smoking and lung cancer spurring more controlled microwork on carcinogenic triggers.

RE LINKS TO THEORY. Should REs stop making general "X works"–type statements and instead try to estimate parameters in a theoretical model of human behavior, as critics suggest? For Deaton, "heterogeneity is not a technical problem,

---

28. See Banerjee and Duflo (2008).
29. See Imbens (2009).

but a symptom of something deeper, which is the failure to specify causal models of the processes we are examining."[30] The shift toward such models is already under way in the RE literature but is not reflected much in this volume. The extensive discussion of the free provision of bed nets and water purification tablets, for example, provides little theoretical analysis and instead jumps immediately to policy: bed nets should be given away free to avoid reduction in uptake; on the other hand, a fee for water purification tablets would help to screen out likely nonusers (see chapters 3 and 4 and the comments by Jessica Cohen and David Weil).

In chapter 4, Kremer and Holla do identify an interesting theoretical anomaly: poor people seem remarkably price-sensitive toward goods that should presumably pay for themselves in the form of health and lost income. They consider two explanations—(1) a behavioral anomaly (such as commitment problems or hyperbolic discounting, "procrastination"), and (2) a lack of knowledge of the payoff from these goods—and appear to favor the first. David Weil notes how problematic this conclusion is: are the same people also procrastinating on getting their crops into the ground or harvested? If not, why is this behavioral anomaly focused on health?

These alternatives have very different policy implications, since zero pricing might "nudge" the behavior in the right direction under the first hypothesis but would just mean a lot of the goods would go unused under the second. Anecdotes exist of malaria bed nets being used as wedding veils and fishing nets, for example, and even more systematic evidence reveals that free insecticide-treated bed nets donated by an NGO have been diverted for drying and catching fish on Lake Victoria in western Kenya. Given the drastically different implications of the two explanations, the debate surrounding them has attracted surprisingly little attention, as attested by the underdevelopment of theory in the RE literature. Hypothesis 2 creates even more puzzles: why do poor people not have accurate knowledge of the payoff to health goods when there is a strong incentive to acquire such knowledge and the knowledge seems readily available? Efforts to address this question could lead to even more interesting theory and empirics about knowledge acquisition. Do the poor in Africa not place much credence in scientific medicine because they have a malfunctioning health system that does not reliably deliver benefits from scientific medicine? Does more general education correlate with more knowledge of payoffs to health goods? As David Weil notes, maybe the customers do not believe the mosquito theory of malaria, doubt the quality of the bed net, or have trouble knowing whom to believe between bed-net promoters and traditional healers.

The overall result of such efforts could shed light on the long-debated issue of whether poor people fit the rational *homo economicus* model (at a time when no

---

30. Deaton (2009).

one is even sure that highly educated rich people do). Perhaps the paucity of such discussion reflects a fear of political incorrectness, but it may also reflect an insufficient commitment to theoretical inquiry in the RE literature.[31] As Captain Von Trapp says in the *Sound of Music*, we all seem to be "suffering from a deplorable lack of curiosity." Kremer, for one, seems ambivalent on the issue of rational decisionmaking among the poor: although he presumes an extremely high degree of rationality and calculation among poor shopkeepers, from which he reaches an estimate of the return to capital, he questions rationality in usage of health services and fertilizer.[32]

Arguably, the weak links of REs to theory—and the consequences that might have for generalizability—are relevant for observational macrostudies as well. Sendhil Mullainathan (this volume) argues that the absence of theory compromises generalizability both when one is seeking to extrapolate "up" from a microstudy and "down" from a macrostudy. He uses the example of wanting to know what average wages are in Oklahoma. Which information is preferable: average wages in Kansas or average wages in the United States overall? Neither is sufficient for extrapolating wages in Oklahoma without some theory to guide that extrapolation.

While a better grounding in theory would benefit observational studies as well as REs, the latter do have several advantages in their links to theory: REs can test theories in a very controlled environment, generate parameter estimates with much more internal validity than other approaches, and deliver a body of evidence on which a theory can be developed. It is possible to get an accurate estimate of price sensitivity to bed nets or water purification because of RE methodology. Behavioral theories consistent with that evidence can be developed precisely because the RE methodology offers replicability and transparency. These behavioral theories can in turn be tested with REs. The circle from evidence generation to theory back to evidence—facilitated by the experimental methodology—occurs frequently within experimental economics. The early economic experiments such as the ultimatum game generated a body of evidence contradicting the rational actor model, which in turn led to a proliferation of theoretical models of fairness and reciprocal behavior.[33] These alternative models generate behavioral parameters that can be

---

31. Several issues could be discussed on this specific "human capital irrationality" result: (1) the effect of education on the ability to process other information about human capital, such as that on nutrition and transmission of malaria and diarrhea; (2) how "human capital irrationality" is related to what seems to be high rationality and resourcefulness in managing finances (Collins and others [2009]); and (3) whether the delivery of health and nutrition services to the poor can affect their acceptance of scientific theories of disease.

32. See Kremer, Lee, and Robinson (2008); Kremer and Holla (chapter 4); and Duflo, Kremer, and Robinson (2007).

33. See, for example, Duflo, Kremer, and Robinson (2009), who use early experimental evidence on the importance of perceived "fairness" in the context of moral hazard to design a principal-agent model incorporating fairness, which is then tested experimentally. (They then use all of these experimental results to motivate a model of "inequity aversion"!)

calibrated by future experiments. Thus although the criticism that REs ought to be tied more closely to theory is a valid one, it fails to recognize that REs are arguably the best-suited methodology for linking with theory.

Finally, pragmatically, one may not always want to link REs to theory. In many areas of development, one may simply want to know whether a policy or program works or does not work. Obviously it is optimal if this evidence feeds into a theory that can inform other research, but if it is used to reallocate many millions of dollars in foreign aid, that is not such a bad outcome.

DATA MINING. The pure RE design prevents data mining, for there is only one regression, of outcome on the treatment dummy, which is specified in advance. This sounds like a clear advantage for RE over growth regressions with almost infinitely flexible specifications.

However, as many have pointed out, the incentives for a "result" are still very strong, and the RE design is not quite as restrictive as just stated.[34] First, there are numerous possible outcome measures. Second, more than one site may be reporting results. Third, RE regressions usually include covariates, and the list could be almost as long as in growth regressions. If the randomization is successful, the inclusion of covariates should not change the coefficient but only increase precision. In the presence of budget and administrative constraints, however, RE samples are often small, which means it is more difficult to achieve a balance across treatment groups, and covariates can change the estimated treatment effect. Data mining is most likely to occur in the search for a significant program impact among different subpopulations. After all the expense and time of a randomized trial, not only is it is very hard to conclude "we found nothing," but with the aforementioned tendency to see patterns in randomness, it becomes difficult to resist the temptation to play with all these margins to get a result. Those who acknowledge these problems recommend full disclosure, but this is hard to enforce.[35] In chapter 3, Boone and Johnson argue that the current RE methodology used in development economics would not meet the standards of the medical literature largely because it fails to prespecify primary "endpoints" and typically lacks a statistical analysis plan.

All the same, REs are moving toward higher standards with regard to data mining. The majority of well-executed REs report the basic specification without covariates. Most REs use ex ante stratification as well, which allows them to include subgroup analyses that preserve the integrity of the randomization. Further, while the ex post search for significant program effects is not exactly kosher, it helps pave the way forward, by suggesting follow-up evaluations and hypotheses to be tested.[36] Even when REs are not done as carefully as they should be, the scope for data mining is likely to be less than in cross-country regressions.

34. See Deaton (2009); Duflo, Glennerster, and Kremer (2008).
35. See Duflo, Glennester, and Kremer (2008).
36. Imbens (2009).

Perhaps a larger problem is publication bias. If a researcher is so virtuous as to disclose a "no results" finding, the study will probably not get published (especially since such an outcome does not necessarily prove zero effect but may merely mean the estimated effect suffers from imprecision). Somebody later surveying the literature might then assume a positive and significant result of the intervention in question, unaware of the unpublished regressions with no results. It would be nice to see an aggregate test of the RE literature for data mining/publication bias, as has been done with other literatures. Of course, publication bias is a concern in all empirical literatures, not just the RE literature—in any context it can make it difficult to infer "what works" from published information. This problem could be ameliorated if institutions could conduct REs without an (academic) publication incentive.

THE EFFECT OF REs ON IMPLEMENTING AGENCIES. RE will inevitably be seen as an evaluation of, at the very least, whether *that* program by *that* NGO or aid agency (or specific department or even individual) worked on that occasion. This will in many circumstances reflect well or badly on those proposing and implementing the program. RE proponents such as Esther Duflo and Michael Kremer want to discourage this interpretation. Furthermore, they oppose any scheme that would reward or penalize particular aid actors for positive or negative results of evaluations, in part because implementing agencies might then be less likely to cooperate in an RE.[37] Or if the agency felt threatened by a negative result or perceived great rewards to a positive result, it might manipulate the results.

Even so, many RE proponents do think that aid systems could be redesigned to reward positive REs: "Positive results . . . can help build a consensus for the project, which has the potential to be extended far beyond the scale that was initially envisioned."[38] If this is true, it is hard to imagine that an implementing agency or its staff would be indifferent to a large increase in its budget from scaling up, or to kudos for having found a very successful intervention. Official aid agencies and NGOs are notoriously sensitive to good or bad press. It would be naïve to think that they are ever indifferent to how an evaluation comes out. Hence the incentive for implementing agencies to manipulate results already exists. REs in medicine (the gold standard for RE literature) have been criticized on these very grounds when private drugmakers finance RE studies of their drugs.[39] When agencies are already confident a program is working, notes Ravallion later in the volume, they selectively agree to REs, which could bias the probability of a positive evaluation upward. The RE literature obviously needs to

37. See the discussion on the Creative Capitalism website: "Holding Aid Agencies Accountable," an e-mail exchange between William Easterly, Esther Duflo, and Michael Kremer, July 31, 2008 (http://creativecapitalism.typepad.com/creative_capitalism/2008/07/exchange.html).
38. Duflo (2004).
39. Deaton (2009).

devote more attention to such manipulation of evaluations and ways to counter-act this threat.

Of course, not all REs are directed at existing programs—that is, ongoing pro-grams whose implementers may have a stake in finding positive results. Many evaluate existing government policies or new programs that are run by the re-searchers themselves.[40] When REs are involved with specific implementing agen-cies, they often deal with new variations on existing programs.[41] Although the desire for positive press may still be present in these cases, there is much less incentive to interfere with the study so as to influence outcomes. To assuage an implementing NGO's fear of negative results, an RE may evaluate several versions of a program simultaneously, shifting the focus to what works best from whether a program works at all. The testing of new variations can relieve the pressure of demonstrating that sunk resources were spent wisely.

If the anticipation of a negative evaluation of an existing program could influ-ence the validity of an RE, it would be sensible for REs to test programs or poli-cies prospectively. An evaluation of a prospective program's impact—rather than the time and money already spent—seems like something that RE researchers would be happy to advocate for.

RE EFFECTS ON POLICY. It has been said that since RE is "credibly establish-ing which programs work and which do not, the international agencies can coun-teract skepticism about the possibility of spending aid effectively and build long-term support for development. Just as randomized trials revolutionized medicine in the twentieth century, [REs] have the possibility to revolutionize social policy during the twenty-first."[42] Moreover, REs are thought to present a simple form of unambiguous evidence that is more likely to influence policy than other evidence connected with empirical development. Here, the great success story is PRO-GRESA in Mexico, which was scaled up and continued under two different administrations in part because of the positive results of REs.[43]

At the same time, some have doubts about RE's effects on policy, arguing that much of PROGRESA's success in Mexico, for example, was due to political fac-tors, particularly since municipalities that had previously voted for the party in power were more likely to be enrolled in the program, despite attempts to depoliticize it.[44] Even those who dispute that finding have observed that a nondis-cretionary PROGRESA/OPORTUNIDADES program paid off at the polls for the incumbent in both the 2000 and 2006 elections, and that President Vicente

---

40. For example, Ashraf and others (2009) introduce a new savings product and evaluate the impact, and Dupas (2009) introduces a new HIV education program and evaluates its impact.

41. For example, Cohen and Dupas (2009) explore the impact of increasing the prevailing subsidy level for bed nets in Kenya.

42. Duflo and Kremer (2008).

43. Levy (2006).

44. Green (2005).

Fox's decision to expand OPORTUNIDADES from rural areas to the cities made political sense since his party's political base was urban.[45]

In other instances, REs have clearly failed to translate into program adoption, a famous example being the evaluation of private school vouchers in Colombia.[46] Despite the accolades heaped on the program by the RE, it was discontinued and never revived. The RE literature itself may be less interested in influencing policy than RE proponents would like (the cancellation of the Colombian voucher program, for example, receives little mention in this huge literature). Moreover, many results in the literature are based on NGO endeavors, not government projects.

Some would even argue that REs can have a minimal impact on policy at best. In Hausmann's view, set forth in chapter 6, the policy environment is too "complex" to be informed by REs that can inevitably vary only several dimensions at once. In this sense, it is naïve to search for simple policy solutions to development. The issue of policy complexity is particularly problematic when spillover effects are likely to be present. Ravallion (this volume) notes that in most REs the control group cannot really be said to be untreated because limited government/ NGO resources and attention are likely to flow into control areas when the treated areas benefit from an intervention. Jessica Cohen (this volume) points out that REs focusing on whether a particular policy or program increases uptake of a public health product are likely to often miss behavioral spillover effects that could ultimately influence the overall morbidity or mortality impact.

Anne Case notes that the political receptivity to outsiders' intervening in social service delivery to the poor is very much an unresolved question. The solution of bypassing the government is also doubtful because of the uneven quality of private service delivery. Case points out that all of this seriously tempers Boone and Johnson's optimism that REs can lead the way to wiping out "pockets of poverty."

Paul Romer also criticizes the naïveté of RE-based policy advice that "fails to take into account what people know about why government policymakers do what they do" and does not recognize that "policymakers are constrained, but rarely ignorant." He predicts that "the experimentalists will overstate their conclusions if they too try to change what practitioners do." He recommends instead that researchers NOT try to be policymakers but just show those who are "how scientific tools like experiments can help them do their jobs."

Using education as an example, Lant Pritchett argues in chapter 5 that government behavior as driven by economists' normative recommendations performs very poorly as a positive model. He also points out that the policy effects of RE cannot themselves be identified using RE: "the randomization agenda as a methodological approach inherits an enormous internal contradiction—that all empirical

45. Diaz-Cayeros and others (2008).
46. Angrist and others (2002).

claims should only be believed when backed by evidence from randomization, excepting, of course, those enormous (and completely unsupported) empirical claims about the impact of randomization on policy."

On the other hand, notes Ben Olken, one cannot ignore the role of evidence in policymaking in general (see his comment on chapter 5). Even though knowledge about "what works" is not guaranteed to change policy, he argues it should more often than not move policymakers in the right direction, in part because they want to get reelected. If politicians can be convinced of the benefits of a particular policy or program for their constituents, they may be willing to adopt it, particularly if the results are presented as rigorous and transparent. Another reason that RE results could be adopted into policy, says Olken, is that they often inform the experts who are called in to consult with governments.

With so much of development policy and programming driven by fads, unproved hypotheses, and anecdotal evidence, a powerful but often overlooked benefit of REs is their ability to highlight not only what works but also what does not. REs can very transparently illustrate that money and effort are flowing in the wrong direction. A 2009 study of bed-net subsidies for pregnant women in Kenya (discussed by Rodrik, this volume) is a good example of an RE that directly influenced policy by illustrating that something of a development "fad" (social marketing) was neither effective nor cost-effective in this case. By illustrating that, contrary to conventional wisdom, usage of public health products given for free need not be lower than those sold for a positive price—and that social marketing funds were being misdirected—the study played an important role in the Kenyan government's decision to make bed nets free for pregnant women.

Even if there is often no direct link between evidence and implementation, it is hard to believe that a robust knowledge of effective development programs is not useful. Knowing what works should bring governments closer to effective programs than chaos and confusion can. This is becoming increasingly apparent as more and more institutions that hold the purse strings of foreign aid are linking funding to evidence. For better or worse, governments tend to have limited power over how foreign aid will be spent in their country. If a donor such as the World Bank or the Gates Foundation decides that it wants to fund a child health program on the basis of evidence generated from the types of REs advocated by Boone and Johnson in chapter 3, for example, recipient country governments are unlikely to refuse. Nancy Birdsall (this volume) discusses an example of how donors might compel governments to adopt programs that acquired evidence suggests are important for development. "Cash on Delivery" (COD) aid can link funds for development directly to the achievement of certain objectives, which could be measures of broad outcomes (such as graduation rates) or of more specific input (for example, student-teacher ratios). Linking aid to some broad objective (and remaining agnostic about how best to accomplish it) is appealing in that it resolves the problem of policy complexity that is raised by Hausmann and others in this volume.[47]

ETHICAL CONCERNS. Randomized experiments involve human subjects, which raises tricky ethical issues. Whereas most universities have review boards to address such issues, other bodies that undertake REs may not undergo this kind of scrutiny and thus may be unable to ensure that valuable (possibly life-saving) treatments are not being withheld for scientific research purposes, which is morally objectionable, of course. That such choices are made randomly is of little consolation to those denied the treatment in a community and may even heighten the sense of mystery and distrust surrounding the researchers and what these outsiders are really up to. When the treatment and control groups are in the same or adjacent communities, the RE may generate envy and resentment. RE implementation offers researchers little advice on how to engage local communities to address such issues together.

RE defenders would point out, however, that resources are never unlimited, so it is impossible to treat everybody. Random assignment is a well-accepted device for allocating scarce resources fairly. The RE can be designed in a way to minimize some of the problems just mentioned. Often the treatment is phased in, so the control group in one period becomes the treatment group in the next period. Control and treatment groups can also be spatially separated to minimize envy and resentment. Finally, it is certainly becoming the norm for REs to undergo ethical approval.

SOCIAL ENGINEERING AND THE LACK OF A HISTORICAL TRACK RECORD. What if REs were to succeed in influencing policies on a large scale—would that be a good thing? Needless to say, this question cannot be answered by RE methodology, but more casual empiricism would detect the lack of any obvious examples of countrywide escapes from poverty using policies determined by REs. So the large-scale application of REs to determine policy is an untested bit of social engineering, the outcomes of which would be hard to predict.

As David Weil notes later in this volume, there is insufficient discussion about why outsiders promoting REs to provide social services are doing what they are doing:

> Do economists know something that poor people in developing countries do not know and therefore plan to do something the poor would have done if they were more knowledgeable? Do economists have a different discount rate than they do? Do economists place a different value on the lives of their children or some such thing? Being explicit about why one wants to be in the business of providing social services might help in designing policies that achieve one's goals.

Another real-world consideration noted by Ross Levine is the importance of tacit knowledge for both macro- and micropolicy implementation. One could do

---

47. Although this raises some new concerns about negative spillover effects on other (nonincentivized) objectives.

rigorous experiments to confirm the physics of hitting a baseball and come up with detailed recommendations based on proven models of physics involving bat speed and location and responding to the speed and trajectory of the baseball. Or one could let a kid practice hitting baseballs for years, which would develop tacit knowledge that cannot be codified into written recommendations. Policy formulation and implementation must surely involve some tacit knowledge that REs cannot supply. It follows also, as Levine notes, that current policies and institutions exist for reasons partly based on such tacit knowledge. Even if they are not optimal, changing policies through RE operating on a presumed blank slate is unlikely to be optimal either.

What do societies do instead of RE? Presumably they rely on some kind of social knowledge and learning to inform their choice of economic institutions and policies. As Banerjee points out in chapter 7, there is little evidence that "growth policy experts" have played any role in making growth happen. Between 1960 and 2008—the period in which economists repeatedly failed to explain growth differences between countries and repeatedly failed in large-scale attempts to raise growth—developing countries grew at the highest rate in human history: 2.7 percent a year per capita, which implies a 3.5 times increase in income. It is also at least anecdotally interesting that East Asia had few academic economists with international reputations during its period of rapid growth, while slow-growing Latin America was awash in them.

Economic arguments still may get some credit. This was also the period in which development policy shifted away from state planning toward more market-friendly approaches, informed in part by big macrofacts, like the failure of planned systems compared with market systems over the long run. It helped that this failure had been predicted by economists like Friedrich Hayek and Milton Friedman even as the planned systems appeared to be doing well. Policy and growth regressions offer no evidence that any part of the growth just cited is due to this shift, but the long-run levels suggest that this shift will pay off sooner or later.

Historically, of course, today's rich countries managed to provide public goods without using REs at all. Alternative mechanisms worked, such as feedback from citizens to politicians through voting, interest group lobbying, decentralization of power to the local level appropriate for most of the public goods, competition between jurisdictions to attract mobile factors, or just "calling your congressman." And, even more obviously, the supply of private goods is not guided by RE testing of "which private goods work," but simply by the choices of consumers in competitive markets. The RE literature could give a little more recognition to these alternative mechanisms for deciding upon public or private goods.

Choice and research evidence need not merely be substitutes, however; they could also be complements. Economic research, both macro and micro, naturally aspires to make more knowledge available to those who make the choices (both leaders and citizens).

Evidence versus Prejudice

REs represent progress in having added to the kit of empirical research a tool that alters the priors of other academics as well as policymakers when there is a strong result (particularly if it helps test a behavioral model). The effect on priors is perhaps the real acid test of what this methodology has to contribute. One commonly cited benefit of REs is that they have raised the bar for what is considered plausible evidence about what works in development. While the highest standard for evidence may not always be an RE, and one may choose to ask questions that cannot be tackled with this methodology, the centrality of REs seems to have made policymakers take issues of endogeneity, selection bias, and sound causal estimation more seriously.

We close with the conciliatory thought that the most relevant divide in development may *not* be between micro and macro or between aggregate data and REs, but rather between those who value objective evidence and those who do not. The development policy discussion has been dominated to an astonishing degree by wishful thinking, baseless assertions, and logical and statistical fallacies. Equally amazing, development efforts keep trying the same thing over and over again, despite a long record of previous failures. By way of example, a computer kiosk program for the poor in India failed to work because of unreliable electricity and Internet connectivity, yet the World Bank's "Empowerment Sourcebook" noted "the success of the initiative." Responding to criticism of the sourcebook, Bank officials stated that the document was merely indicating that the institution intended to help achieve "greater empowerment." One may well ask, as does Banerjee: "Helped to achieve greater empowerment? Through non-working computers?"[48]

Development economists can continue to quarrel about what methodology produces respectable evidence, but they clearly agree on the much larger question of what is *not* respectable evidence, namely, most of what is currently relied on in development policy discussions. What unites us is larger than what divides us.

References

Acemoglu, Daron, Simon Johnson, and James A. Robinson. 2001. "The Colonial Origins of Comparative Development: An Empirical Investigation." *American Economic Review* 91 (December): 1369–1401.

———. 2004. "Institutions as a Fundamental Cause of Long-Run Growth." Working Paper 10481. Cambridge, Mass.: National Bureau of Economic Research.

Angrist, Joshua D., and others. 2002. "Vouchers for Private Schooling in Colombia: Evidence from a Randomized Natural Experiment." *American Economic Review* 92 (December): 1535–58.

Ashraf, Nava, Dean S. Karlan, and Wesley Yin. 2007. "Female Empowerment: Impact of a Commitment Savings Product in the Philippines." Discussion Paper DP6195. Center for Economic and Policy Research (March) (http:ssrn.com/abstract=1134236).

48. Banerjee (2007, pp. 77, 112).

Baker, Judy L. 2000. *Evaluating the Impact of Development Projects on Poverty: A Handbook for Practitioners.* Washington: LCSPR/PRMPO, World Bank

Banerjee, Abhijit. 2007. *Making Aid Work.* MIT Press.

Burnside, Craig, and David Dollar. 2000. "Aid, Policies, and Growth: Revisiting the Evidence." Policy Discussion Working Paper 3251. Washington: World Bank.

Cohen, Jessica, and Pascaline Dupas. 2009 (forthcoming). "Free Distribution or Cost-Sharing? Evidence from a Randomized Malaria Prevention Experiment." *Quarterly Journal of Economics.*

Collins, Daryl, and others. 2009. *Portfolios of the Poor: How the World's Poor Live on $2 a Day.* Princeton University Press.

Deaton, Angus. 2006. "Global Patterns of Income and Health: Facts, Interpretations, and Policies." Annual Lecture 10. World Institute for Development Economics. Helsinki (September).

———. 2009. "Instruments of Development: Randomization in the Tropics and the Search for the Elusive Keys to Economic Development." Working Paper 14690. Cambridge, Mass.: National Bureau of Economic Research.

Diaz Cayeros, Alberto, Federico Estévez, and Beatriz Magaloni. 2008. "Strategies of Vote Buying: Social Transfers, Democracy and Welfare in Mexico." Stanford Department of Political Science. Draft manuscript.

Duflo, Esther. 2004. "Scaling Up and Evaluation." In *Accelerating Development,* edited by Francois Bourguignon and Boris Pleskovic, pp. 342–67. Oxford University Press.

Duflo, Esther, Michael Kremer, and Jonathan Robinson. 2009. Nudging Farmers to Use Fertilizer: Theory and Experimental Evidence from Kenya, mimeo.

Duflo, Esther, Rachel Glennerster, and Michael Kremer. 2008. "Using Randomization in Development Economics Research: A Toolkit." In *Handbook of Development Economics,* vol. 4, edited by T. Paul Shultz and John Strauss. Amsterdam: North-Holland.

Duflo, Esther, and Michael Kremer. 2008. "Use of Randomization in the Evaluation of Development Effectiveness." In *Reinventing Foreign Aid,* edited by William Easterly, pp. 93–120. MIT Press.

Dupas, Pascaline. 2009. "Do Teenagers Respond to HIV Risk Information? Evidence from a Field Experiment in Kenya." Working Paper 14707. Cambridge, Mass.: National Bureau of Economic Research.

Durlauf, S., P. Johnson, and J. Temple. 2006. "Growth Econometrics," in *Handbook of Economic Growth,* edited by P. Aghion and S. Durlauf. Amsterdam: North-Holland.

Easterly, William. 2001. *The Elusive Quest for Growth: Economists' Adventures and Misadventures in the Tropics.* MIT Press.

Easterly, William, and others. 1993. "Good Policy or Good Luck? Country Growth Performance and Temporary Shocks." *Journal of Monetary Economics* 32, no. 3: 459–83.

Easterly, William, and Ross Levine. 2001. "It's Not Factor Accumulation: Stylized Facts and Growth Models." *World Bank Economic Review* 15, no. 2.

———. 2003. "Tropics, Germs, and Crops: The Role of Endowments in Economic Development." *Journal of Monetary Economics* 50, no. 1 (January): 3–39.

Easterly, William, Ross Levine, and David Roodman. 2004. "New Data, New Doubts: A Comment on Burnside and Dollar's 'Aid, Policies, and Growth' (2000)." *American Economic Review,* 94, no. 3 (June): 774–80.

Fehr, Ernst, and others. 2007. "Fairness and Contract Design." *Econometrica* 75, no. 1: 121–54.

Galor, Oded, and David N. Weil. 2000. "Population, Technology, and Growth: From Malthusian Stagnation to the Demographic Transition and Beyond." *American Economic Review* 90, no. 4: 806–28.

Gilovich, Thomas, Dale Griffin, and Daniel Kahneman. 2002. *Heuristics and Biases: The Psychology of Intuitive Judgment.* Cambridge University Press.

Green, Tina. 2005. "Do Social Transfer Programs Affect Voter Behavior? Evidence from Progresa in Mexico, 1997–2000." University of California, Berkeley. Photocopy.

Harberger, Arnold. 2003. "Sound Policies Can Free Up Natural Forces of Growth." *IMF Survey* 32, no. 13: 213–16.

Imbens, Guido W. 2009. "Better Late than Nothing: Some Comments on Deaton (2009) and Heckman and Urzua (2009)." Working Paper 14896. Cambridge, Mass.: National Bureau of Economic Research.

Imbens, Guido W., and Joshua D. Angrist. 1994. "Identification and Estimation of Local Average Treatment Effects." *Econometrica* 62 (March): 467–75.

Imbens, Guido W., and Jeffrey Woolridge. 2008. "Recent Developments in the Econometrics of Program Evaluation." Working Paper 14251. Cambridge, Mass.: National Bureau of Economic Research.

Jones, Chad. 2005. "Growth and Ideas." In *Handbook of Economic Growth*, edited by Philippe Aghion and Steven Durlauf (www.econ.berkeley.edu/~chad/handbook200.pdf).

Kahneman, Daniel, and Amos Tversky. 2000. *Choices, Values, and Frames.* Cambridge University Press.

Kahneman, Daniel, Paul Slovic, and Amos Tversky, eds. 1982. *Judgment under Uncertainty: Heuristics and Biases.* Cambridge University Press.

Kahneman, Daniel, and Amos Tversky. 1982. "Belief in the Law of Small Numbers." In *Judgment under Uncertainty: Heuristics and Biases*, edited by Daniel Kahneman, Paul Slovic, and Amos Tversky, pp. 23–31. Cambridge University Press.

Klenow, Peter J., and Andrés Rodríguez-Clare. 1997. "Economic Growth: A Review Essay." *Journal of Monetary Economics* 40 (December): pp. 597–617.

Kremer, Michael. 1993. "Population Growth and Technological Change: 1,000,000 B.C. to 1990." *Quarterly Journal of Economics* 108 (August): 681–716.

Kremer, Michael, Jean N. Lee, and Jonathan Robinson. 2008. "The Return to Capital for Small Retailers in Kenya: Evidence from Inventories," unpublished.

Levy, Santiago. 2006. *Progress against Poverty: Sustaining Mexico's Progresa-Oportunidades Program.* Brookings.

Pritchett, Lant. 2008. "It Pays to Be Ignorant: A Simple Political Economy of Rigorous Program Evaluation." In *Reinventing Foreign Aid*, edited by William Easterly, pp. 121–44. MIT Press.

Pritchett, Lant, Deepa Narayan, and Soumya Kapoor. 2009. *Moving Out of Poverty: Success from the Bottom Up.* New York: Palgrave/Macmillan for the World Bank.

Pritchett, Lant, Dani Rodrik, and Ricardo Hausmann. 2005. "Growth Accelerations." *Journal of Economic Growth* 10, no. 4: 303–29.

Rodrik, Dani, A. Subramanian, and F. Trebbi. 2004. "Institutions Rule: The Primacy of Institutions over Geography and Integration in Economic Development." *Journal of Economic Growth* 9, no. 2 (June).

Solow, Robert. 2007. "The Last 50 Years in Growth Theory and the Next 10." *Oxford Review of Economic Policy* 23, no. 1: 3–14.

Werker, Eric D., Faisal Z. Ahmed, and Charles Cohen. 2009. "How Is Foreign Aid Spent? Evidence from a Natural Experiment." *American Economic Journal: Macroeconomics* 1, no. 2 (July): 225–44.

World Bank Commission on Growth and Development. 2008. *The Growth Report: Strategies for Sustained Growth and Inclusive Development.* Washington.

2

The New Development Economics: We Shall Experiment, but How Shall We Learn?

DANI RODRIK

D evelopment economics has long been split between the study of *macro*-development (economic growth, international trade, and fiscal/macro-policies) and *micro*development (microfinance, education, health, and other social programs). Even though the central question animating both branches ostensibly is how to achieve sustainable improvements in living standards in poor countries, their concerns and methods have at times diverged so much that they seem at opposite extremes of the economics discipline.

I argue in this chapter that it is now possible to envisage a reunification of the field as these sharp distinctions are eroding in some key respects. Microdevelopment economists have become more interested in policy questions (as opposed to theory and hypothesis testing), and their experimental approach nicely dovetails with some of the current macropolicy trends on the ground. But there is also some basis for pessimism, related to the divergence in empirical methods.

The good news is the substantial convergence in the policy mind-set exhibited by microevaluation enthusiasts, on the one hand, and growth diagnosticians, on the other. The emerging "consensus" revolves not around a specific list of policies, but around how one *does* development policy. In fact, practitioners of this "new" development economics—whether of the "macro" type or "micro" type—tend to

I am grateful to Pranab Bardhan, Tim Besley, Jessica Cohen, Angus Deaton, Pascaline Dupas, Ricardo Hausmann, Asim Khwaja, Sendhil Mullainathan, Mead Over, Lant Pritchett, and Martin Ravallion for their comments on an earlier draft.

be suspicious of claims to ex ante knowledge about what works and what does not work. In their view, the answer lies neither in the Washington Consensus nor in any specific set of initiatives in health or education. Instead it should emerge from a recognition of the *contextual* nature of policy solutions. Relative ignorance calls for an approach that is explicitly *experimental*, and that is carried out using the tools of *diagnostics* and *evaluation*. Old dichotomies between states and markets play little role in this worldview, and *pragmatism* reigns. The proof of the pudding is in the eating: if something works, it is worth doing.

This convergence has remained largely hidden from view because the analytical and empirical tools used by economists at the macro and micro end of things—growth economists versus social policy economists—tend to be quite different. Nevertheless, such a convergence is clearly under way, it is a significant departure from the approaches that dominated thinking about development policy until a decade or so ago, and it represents a significant advance over the previous generation of research.

The bad news is the accentuation of the methodological divergence, which threatens to overshadow the convergence on policy. In particular, the randomized field trials revolution led by researchers in and around the MIT Poverty Action Lab, though greatly enriching the micro end of the field, has created bigger barriers between the two camps.[1] This is not just because randomization is rarely possible with the policies—such as trade, monetary, and fiscal—that macrodevelopment economists study. More important, it is because the stakes are higher with regard to what counts as "admissible" evidence in development. The "randomistas" (as Angus Deaton has called them) tend to think that credible evidence can be generated only with randomized field trials (or when nature cooperates by providing the opportunity of a "natural" experiment).[2] As Abhijit Banerjee puts it: "When we talk of hard evidence, we will therefore have in mind evidence from a randomized experiment, or, failing that, evidence from a true *natural experiment*, in which an accident of history creates a setting that mimics a randomized trial."[3] Randomized field experiments provide "hard" evidence, and by and large only such experiments do. Deprived of randomized (or natural) experiments, macrodevelopment economists would appear to be condemned to second-tier status as peddlers of soft evidence.

So randomizers tend to think real progress is possible only with their kind of evidence. For example, Esther Duflo attributes the periodic shifts in development

1. Banerjee (2007); Duflo (2006); Duflo, Glennerster, and Kremer (2006).

2. Deaton (2007).

3. Banerjee (2007, p. 12). This sentence is preceded by a paragraph that recognizes the weaknesses of inferences from such "hard evidence" (especially with respect to external validity and the feasibility of randomization), and that ends with a much more limited goal: "One would not want to spend a lot of money on an intervention without doing at least one successful randomized trial *if one is possible*."

policy paradigms and the fact that policy debates never seem to be resolved to the weakness of the evidentiary base to date. Randomization, she argues, provides the way out: "All too often development policy is based on fads, and randomized evaluations could allow it to be based on evidence."[4] Similarly, Banerjee argues that aid should be based on the hard evidence that randomized experiments provide, instead of the wishy-washy evidence from cross-country regressions or case studies.[5] When challenged that substantial progress in economic development has been typically due to economy-wide policy reforms (as in China or India recently), rather than the small-scale interventions in health or education that their experiments focus on, the randomizers respond: "That may well be true, but we have no credible evidence on which of these economy-wide policies work or how countries like China have in fact done it; so we might as well do something in areas we can learn something about."

Actually, it is misleading to think of evidence from randomized evaluations as distinctly "hard" in comparison with other kinds of evidence that development economists generate and rely on. This may seem an odd claim in light of the apparent superiority of evidence from randomized trials. As Banerjee puts it: "The beauty of randomized evaluations is that the results are what they are: we compare the outcome in the treatment with the outcome in the control group, see whether they are different, and if so by how much."[6] Case closed? Well, it depends on what the evidence is needed for and how it will be used. Economists might be interested in how responsive farmers are to price incentives or whether poor educational outcomes are driven in part by a lack of information about relative school performance. Policymakers may want to know what the impacts of a fertilizer subsidy or an informational campaign about school performance are likely to be. In each of these instances, a randomized evaluation can provide some guidance, but it will rarely be decisive. The typical evaluation will have been carried out in a specific locale on a specific group and under specific experimental conditions. Its generalizability to other settings—its "external validity"—is never assured—and it is certainly not established by the evaluation itself.[7]

Generalizability issues can be illustrated by a recent evaluation of an experiment in Western Kenya concerning the distribution of insecticide-treated bed nets to pregnant women.[8] Free distribution, Jessica Cohen and Pascaline Dupas find, was vastly more effective than charging a small fee for the bed nets. This would appear to debunk the commonly held view that the valuation and usage of bed nets must increase with price—at least in the specific setting in which the experiment was carried out. But do the results extend to other settings in Africa as well? One

4. Duflo (n.d., p. 2).
5. Banerjee (2007).
6. Banerjee (2007, pp. 115–16).
7. See also Basu (2005) for a very useful discussion of the limitations of randomized evaluations.
8. Cohen and Dupas (2007).

can certainly make the case that they do, but the arguments would perforce be informal ones and convincing to varying degrees. In fact, such arguments are not too different from those in defense of a set of instrumental variables (IVs) employed in a conventional econometrics study with weaker internal validity. Moreover, in the public discussion of the Cohen-Dupas evaluation, opponents of free distribution were able to offer a wealth of reasons as to why these results could not be generalized. The debate on free distribution versus cost sharing was hardly settled. Randomized evaluation did *not* yield hard evidence when it came to the actual policy questions of interest. This should not have been a surprise: the only truly hard evidence that randomized evaluations typically generate relates to questions that are so narrowly limited in scope and application that they are in themselves uninteresting. The "hard evidence" from the randomized evaluation has to be supplemented with lots of soft evidence before it becomes usable.

The real test of any piece of research is the Bayesian one: does the finding change our priors on the issue of interest? Randomized evaluations do pretty well when they are targeted closely at the policy change under consideration, but less so when they require considerable extrapolation.[9] In the latter case, evidence from randomized field experiments need not be more informative than other types of evidence that may have less airtight causal identification but are stronger on external validity (because of broader geographical or temporal coverage). In practice, internal validity—just like external validity—is not an either-or matter; some studies do better on this score than others and thus deserve more attention. But this preference has to be tempered with a consideration also of external validity. The bottom line is that randomized evaluations do not deserve monopoly rights—or even necessarily pride of place—in moving one's priors on most of the important questions in development economics.

But this discussion is not meant to be a critique of randomized evaluations, which have indeed greatly enriched the economist's empirical toolkit.[10] It is instead a plea for not letting prevailing methodological differences overshadow the larger convergence. My purpose is to get macrodevelopment economists and microdevelopment economists to see that they have much more in common than they realize. The former are increasingly adopting the policy mind-set of the latter, while the latter skate on thinner ice with their empirical work than is often

9. For example, the study by Bertrand and others (2007) of corruption in the driver's license system in Delhi, India, is of tremendous value to anyone who wants to understand and improve the regime of driver's license allocations in India. However, extrapolating from it to corruption in other types of service delivery or in other countries is extremely difficult and would require considerable care.

10. I do not deal here with the criticism that randomized evaluations typically entail very little theorizing, except insofar as this renders extrapolation to other settings more problematic. Even though this may be a legitimate complaint in practice, I do not think it is a fundamental issue. There is nothing in the nature of randomized trials that precludes either theory testing or more explicit use of theory. As I explain later, good use of experimentation in fact relies on explicit theoretical framing. For a broad discussion of the role of theory versus experimentation, see Kanbur (2005).

thought. I use a specific policy problem—whether insecticide-treated bed nets should be distributed for free or at some nominal fee—as a springboard for examining the different types of evidence, including randomized evaluations (in the vein of Cohen and Dupas), for what I believe is a new paradigm in the making.[11]

A Policy Problem: Should Bed Nets Be Given Out for Free?

It is well known that insecticide-treated bed nets (ITNs) are extremely effective in preventing exposure to malaria. It is also well recognized that ITNs should be subsidized rather than sold at cost: ITNs reduce the number of mosquitoes and the malaria parasites that can be passed on to others, so there are externalities involved on top of the direct income and health poverty impacts. The debate revolves around whether ITNs should be handed out for free or at a positive, if still below-cost, price.

One view, articulated forcefully by Jeffrey Sachs, is that ITNs should be free so as to achieve universal access and have the greatest possible impact on the disease. In this view, it is important to ensure ITNs are used by the community at large, rather than solely by those groups that are typically identified as being at greatest risk (mainly pregnant women and young children) and that are targeted by conventional public health campaigns.[12]

The other view is that free distribution is not cost-effective and sustainable, and that ITNs should be made available at a positive, if still nominal, price. There are several arguments in favor of this "cost sharing."[13] First, it may ensure better targeting insofar as only those who are likely to use the bed nets or those at greater risk will want to pay for them. Second, it may increase usage insofar as people are more likely to value something they have paid for (this is the so-called sunk-cost fallacy). Third, having to pay for a good or service is more likely to make users demand accountability on the part of health care providers. Fourth, cost sharing is more likely to sustain a private delivery mechanism over time (unlike free distribution, which relies on periodic public health campaigns). These are the arguments typically used by social marketing groups, which are particularly active in this area.

Obviously, one cannot choose between these two sets of views on the basis of theory or a priori reasoning. Both are plausible and are likely to be correct for a particular distribution of the underlying structural parameters that determine behavior. How does one gather evidence about the empirical validity of these contrasting viewpoints, which ultimately relates to effectiveness in eradicating malaria? Consider three strategies.

11. In case there is any doubt, I should clarify that I use the Cohen-Dupas study not because of any weaknesses in it, but, quite to the contrary, because it is a particularly well-done evaluation on a question of tremendous interest.

12. Sachs and others (2007).

13. See Over (2008).

Reduced-Form Econometrics

One research approach would be to look at the pattern of correlations across regions and over time between the type of policy or program employed and the malaria outcomes on the ground. So imagine the following regression for sub-Saharan Africa:

$$(2\text{-}1) \qquad Y_{it} = \alpha \, P_{it} + \Sigma_j \, \beta_j \, P_{it} X_{it}^j + \Sigma_j \, \gamma_j \, X_{it}^j + D_i + D_t + \epsilon_{it},$$

where Y_{it} stands for the malaria outcome of interest (rates of infection or incidence), P_{it} is an index that captures the nature of policy in place (in particular the extent to which the program relies on free distribution versus cost sharing), X_{it}^j is a set of conditioning variables (income level, population density, demography, other health indicators, and so forth), and D_i and D_t are region- and time-fixed effects. This specification allows policy to interact with background conditions, and it also controls for time trends and time-invariant regional differences.

Subject to the caveats mentioned in the next paragraph, this regression can indicate how effective different program types are, and also how effectiveness varies with the conditioning factors. So the expected impact of changing policy from P to P' in a country where the background conditions are given by X^j is simply $\hat{\alpha}(P' - P) + \Sigma_j \, \hat{\beta}_j X_{it}^j \, (P' - P)$, where $\hat{\alpha}$ and $\hat{\beta}_j$ are the estimated parameters from the foregoing regression.

The problems in this research design are many. First of all, it is difficult to specify and include all the background conditions that influence or may be correlated with policy effectiveness. That implies that the researcher may have to contend with various sources of omitted-variable bias. In addition, there may not be enough variation over time, so that equation 2-1 may need to be estimated as a pure cross section:

$$(2\text{-}2) \qquad Y_i = \alpha \, P_i + \Sigma_j \, \beta_j \, P_i X_i^j + \Sigma_j \, \gamma_j \, X_i^j + \epsilon_t.$$

Since one cannot control for time-invariant regional unobservables in this specification, any potential problem of omitted-variables bias becomes that much more severe.

A second problem is how to code and create a quantitative index for the type of policy in place in different regions or countries. Cost-sharing strategies come in many guises, and in any case, few programs will be of the pure free-distribution or cost-sharing types. In addition, one must take into account other aspects of the program as well: how extensive, how well administered, and how well funded it is, and so on.

Most important, any regression of this type will be open to the criticism that the right-hand-side variables, P in particular, are not exogenous, rendering identification of a truly causal effect problematic. Identification requires that P and the error term ϵ be uncorrelated, which is a demanding test. The most obvious source of bias in this connection is that the programs may have been selected *in response* to the type of malaria challenge being faced in each region. If a government knows or anticipates that free distribution will be more effective, it will use that type of program instead of the other. This is called the program placement effect in the microeconometric literature and wreaks havoc with all cross-sectional econometric work. More generally, interpretation of the coefficients α and β_j is always problematic in view of the fact that programs are not randomly assigned: they are selected for some reason. Any pattern of correlation desired can be generated by specifying those reasons and their cross-sectional variation appropriately.[14]

In practice, an empirical exercise of this sort is likely to generate a conversation and debate between those who find the results credible (the authors and their supporters) and those who have doubts. "You have measured policies very badly," the critics will say. "But here is an alternative measure with greater detail, and it makes little difference to the results," the authors will respond. "Policies are endogenous and respond to malaria outcomes," the critics will object. "But look, all these countries selected their programs for reasons that had little to do with what was going on the ground, and if you do not believe that, here is an instrumentation strategy that uses the identity of the main external donor as an instrument for the type of program," the authors will perhaps respond. The debate will go on and on, and some people will come to think that the results have some credibility, while others will remain unconvinced.

In theory, identification is an either/or thing. Either the causal effect is identified, or it is not. But in practice, identification can be more or less credible. If the study is done reasonably well and the authors have convincing answers to the criticisms leveled against it, one can (or should) imagine that one's priors on the policy question at hand would be moved by the results of the exercise. One would have to be a purist of the extreme kind to imagine that *nothing* could be learned from a regression of this type, regardless of the quality of the supporting argumentation.

Qualitative Evidence: Surveys

One drawback of the econometric strategy is that not many countries may yet have experimented with either cost-sharing or free distribution programs. So there may not be much variation in P of the type needed to identify the effects of concern.

A qualitative research strategy, based primarily on interviews, may be a substitute. Suppose a team of researchers travels around Africa to undertake in-depth interviews with health professionals and service providers. It would pose the following type of questions:

14. Rodrik (2005).

1. How important do you think cost is as an impediment to the use of bed nets in your region, compared with other obstacles (such as availability and knowledge about benefits)?

2. How likely do you think it is that people will value and use ITNs more if they actually pay for them?

3. Do you think private channels of supply are more likely to exist if ITNs are sold at a price?

4. What is the best way to get people who are less vulnerable (that is, adult males) to use ITNs?

One can imagine the response to these questions being coded for use in quantitative analysis. But the main purpose of the interviews would not be statistical analysis but taking stock of the state of "local knowledge"—what people closest to the problem think—about the key questions that determine the relative effectiveness of free distribution versus cost sharing. And open-ended questions such as the fourth one can help reveal new solutions that the outsider may not have thought about before.

Economists tend to be wary of qualitative research and of evidence that is based on interviews. But as Gary King, Robert Keohane, and Sidney Verba have argued, good qualitative studies use the same logic of inference as quantitative ones.[15] Needless to say, in this particular instance interviewees have limited knowledge, have their own preconceptions (which may or may not be idiosyncratic), have a stake in the outcome (which may affect the nature of their responses), and will be influenced by the environment in which they operate. But even with these limitations, their responses should shed some light on the effectiveness question. Indeed, it would be surprising if eliciting local information systematically in this manner did not serve to narrow the range of plausible outcomes. Experiential knowledge cannot be dismissed altogether.

Of course, conclusions from such research would naturally be contested. How representative were the interviewees, and can they really be expected to predict accurately the consequences of this or that program? But the relevant question here is not whether the interviews can provide a definitive answer; it is whether they can move the profession's priors. If the authors of the study have thought their methodology through, they will have answers for their critics that at least some will find convincing. Once again, only an extreme purist would deny that there is potential for learning from this kind of effort. The scientific method can be applied to qualitative as well as quantitative evidence.

Randomized Field Evaluation

Finally, consider a field experiment that randomizes across recipients as to whether they get ITNs for free or at a (subsidized) price. This provides a way to

---

15. King, Keohane, and Verba (1994).

look directly for any differential effects in uptake and usage and is exactly the method employed by Cohen and Dupas in Western Kenya.[16] Working with twenty prenatal clinics to offer ITNs at varying prices, they divided the clinics randomly into five groups of four, with four of the groups offering the ITNs at a (single) price ranging from $0 to $0.60 per ITN and the fifth serving as the control. They then measured the uptake of ITNs from the clinics and also spot-checked for usage (whether the nets were hanging on beds or not). In addition, they checked the hemoglobin levels (anemia rates) of women getting ITNs to see if cost sharing does a better job of selecting women at greater risk for malaria.

The results were for the most part unambiguous and quite striking. Cost sharing significantly reduced the number of ITNs that ended up in the hands of recipients without increasing actual usage among those who did receive the bed nets. Furthermore, there was no evidence of selection benefits from cost sharing: women who paid a positive price were no sicker than women in the control group. Under reasonable assumptions on private and social benefits, Cohen and Dupas show that free distribution is more cost-effective than cost sharing: the benefits of greater use more than offset additional budgetary costs.

My initial reaction to this study was that it settled the question once and for all. Free distribution is the way to go.[17] However, further reflection and reading on the topic made clear that I had overreached.[18] One can have genuine doubts as to the extent to which the Cohen-Dupas results can be generalized. As the advocates of cost sharing were quick to point out, the setting for this study was special in a number of respects.[19]

First, the area in Western Kenya where the experiment was carried out had been blanketed by social marketers for a number of years, with as many as half a million bed nets already distributed. There is reason to believe that the value of bed net use was already well understood. In other words, the experiment may have benefited from the earlier demand promotion activities of the social marketers.

Second, the experiment was narrowly targeted at pregnant women making visits to prenatal clinics. In other words, the recipients were a subgroup at high risk for malaria and had revealed themselves to be willing to engage with public health services. Moreover, these women were provided with information about malaria risks. The mass-distribution argument of Sachs, by contrast, is based on free distribution to the population at large.

Third, the experiment took care of supplying ITNs to the clinics, thus isolating the supply side from the demand side of the problem. Therefore the experi-

---

16. Cohen and Dupas (2007).

17. Hence the title of my blog entry summarizing the paper: "Jeff Sachs Vindicated." See http://rodrik.typepad.com/dani_rodriks_weblog/2008/01/jeff-sachs-vind.html.

18. Stimulated in part by comments on my blog post, mentioned in note 17.

19. See Mead Over, "Sachs Not Vindicated" (http://blogs.cgdev.org/globalhealth/2008/01/sachs_not_vindicated.php).

ment did not test the social marketers' claim that some degree of cost sharing is important to establish sustainable supply channels at the retail level.

Fourth, the difference between the subsidized price and zero was perhaps too small to trigger the "sunk-cost fallacy." Therefore, one should not necessarily rule it out in other settings.

The conclusion that cost-sharing advocates would like readers to draw is this: believe the results for Western Kenya at this particular juncture, but do not expect them to hold in other settings with other background conditions.

In terms of the regression framework discussed previously, what the randomized field experiment estimates is not the α and β_j separately, but the composite term $\alpha + \beta_j \Sigma_j X_{it}^j$, which also depends on the background conditions X_{it}^j. It identifies, quite accurately, the effect of policy P under one realization of X_i^j—but gives no way of parsing the manner in which those background conditions have affected the outcome and therefore does not allow one to extrapolate to other settings. That is why it is fair game to question the generalizability of the results.[20]

Now, I suspect that Cohen and Dupas (and Sachs) would have some good arguments as to why these objections to the generalizability of the field experiment results are overdrawn and why the results are likely to hold up in other settings as well.[21] And I suspect that the critics would stand their ground in turn. The key point, however, is that the randomized field evaluation cannot settle the larger policy question that motivated it. It is no different in that respect than the other two research strategies discussed earlier in the chapter. Despite the clean identification provided by the randomized field experiment, those who believe they have learned something general about free distribution have to resort to credibility-enhancing arguments that feel rather similar to those that practitioners of cross-section econometrics and qualitative studies have to resort to—although the effort will now be

---

20. Deaton (2007, pp. 60–61) puts it thus in his comments on Banerjee (2007): "Take Banerjee's example of flip charts. The effectiveness of flip charts clearly depends on many things, of which the skill of the teacher and the age, background, and previous training of the children are only the most obvious. So a trial from a group of Kenyan schools gives us the average effectiveness of flip charts in the experimental schools relative to the control schools for an area in western Kenya, at a specific time, for specific teachers, and for specific pupils. It is far from clear that this evidence is useful outside of that situation. This qualification also holds for the much more serious case of worms, where the rate of reinfection depends on whether children wear shoes and whether they have access to toilets. The results of one experiment in Kenya (in which there was in fact no randomization, only selection based on alphabetical order) hardly prove that deworming is always the cheapest way to get kids into school, as Banerjee suggests." Or as Mookherjee (2005) complains more generally about development microeconometrics: "A well-executed paper goes into a particular phenomenon in a particular location in considerable depth, data permitting. The research is consequently increasingly microscopic in character. We have very little sense of the value of what we have learned for any specific location to other locations." See also Ravallion (2008a) for a critique of randomized evaluations. Deaton's (2009) critique in his Keynes lectures appeared too late to be reflected in the present chapter.

21. For example, the argument that the results may have been contaminated by the prior presence of social marketing is irrelevant if one wants to extend free distribution to other areas of Kenya or Africa where social marketers have also been active.

directed at convincing critics about the generalizability of their results and not about identification or relevance. No, Western Kenya is not really that different from other settings. No, there was ample opportunity in the research design for sunk-cost effects to operate. No, prior exposure to social marketing could not have made a big difference. And so on. If these arguments are perceived as credible to outsiders like me with little stake in the outcome, it will (and should) move one's priors. But it will do no more than that.

Discussion

I have hardly scratched the surface of possible research strategies. One can add various other regression-based approaches such as structural econometrics or regression discontinuity. One can also think of additional qualitative strategies, such as the structured case-study approach. The point is not to be exhaustive but to illustrate that different styles have different strengths and weaknesses. Cross-sectional and panel regressions can have broad coverage and can control for at least some of the background conditions explicitly. Interviews and other qualitative approaches can be carried out in a more open-ended manner, allowing unanticipated new information to play a role. Randomized evaluations can nail down identification within the confines of the experiment.

In the technical jargon, the research strategies I have described have different degrees of internal and external validity. Internal validity relates to the quality of causal identification: Has the study credibly demonstrated a causal link between the policy or treatment in question and the outcome of interest? External validity has to do with generalizability: Are these results valid also for the broader population for which the policy or treatment is being considered? Sound inference requires *both*.

Randomized evaluations are strong on internal validity but produce results that can be contested on external validity grounds—as I illustrated with the malaria experiment. By contrast, the standard econometric and qualitative approaches are weaker on internal validity—but conditional on credible identification, they have fewer problems of external validity. (In the malaria illustration, they cover all or most of Africa as a whole, and they may also have a temporal dimension.)

Some advocates of randomized evaluations would argue that internal validity trumps all else, that there is no point in worrying about generalizability until a causal relationship is demonstrated clearly at least once.[22] Identification is an either/or matter: an effect is either clearly demonstrated or it is not. So nothing other than randomized trials (or perhaps some natural experiments) can possibly help reveal a truly causal effect. As for external validity, it can best be established through repeated replication of field experiments in different settings. In any case,

---

22. For the canonical statement of this position in social psychology, see Campbell and Stanley (1963).

one should proceed lexicographically: conduct randomized field experiments and fret about external validity later.

But does this make sense from a decision-theoretic standpoint? Suppose a policymaker needs to figure out which strategy to adopt—*now*. Or a journal editor has to decide whether a piece of research is sufficiently well done and interesting enough to merit publication. In both cases, the relevant point is whether the research *changes the priors on the question of interest*. This means the internal and external validity tests must be applied simultaneously. Identification alone is inadequate, unless there is strong enough reason to believe that the causal effects can be generalized to the broader population of interest. A study lacking internal validity is surely worthless; but a study lacking external validity is almost worthless too. After all, one is not interested in a result that solely applies to pregnant women visiting prenatal clinics in Western Kenya during a period of several months in 2007 and facing a particular schedule of fees. One is interested in whether the results say anything about the respective advantages of free distribution and cost sharing *in general, or in a specific setting that differs from that of the evaluation.*[23]

This is also in line with the revealed preference of the economics profession, which is to think of identification as gradations rather than as binary. Some identification strategies are viewed as more credible than others, and standards regarding what is credible change over time. In practice, internal validity is a matter of degree, just as external validity is. The implication is that the information content of these different kinds of studies cannot be rank-ordered on an a priori basis. The weights that should be put in the Bayesian updating process on (a) randomized evaluations and (b) other types of evidence must both lie strictly between 0 and 1, unless the nonrandomized evidence has no claim to internal validity at all. Moreover, the respective magnitude of these weights cannot be determined on the basis of a priori reasoning (except again in limiting cases). One may well be swayed more by a study that is less than airtight on internal validity but strong on external validity than by a study with strong internal validity but unclear external validity.

23. This is how Banerjee (2005) discusses a similar problem: "If our only really reliable evidence was from India but we were interested in what might happen in Kenya, it probably does make sense to look at the available (low quality) evidence from East Africa. Moreover, if the two types of evidence disagree, we might even decide to put a substantial amount of weight on the less reliable evidence, if it turns out that it fits better with our prior beliefs. Nevertheless, there remains an essential asymmetry between the two: The well-identified regression does give us the 'correct' estimate for at least one population, while the other may not be right for anyone. For this reason, even if we have many low quality regressions that say the same thing, there is no sense in which the high quality evidence becomes irrelevant—after all, the same source of bias could be afflicting all the low quality results. The evidence remains anchored by that one high quality result." I am not sure what the last sentence means, but I agree with the rest, which seems to grant the point that in general both types of evidence should receive positive weight. I am certainly not arguing that "the high-quality evidence" from the randomized evaluation should be treated as "irrelevant."

Of course, practitioners of randomized field evaluations do recognize problems of external validity. Duflo and her colleagues in particular provide an excellent and comprehensive discussion of external validity pitfalls in randomized trials.[24] As Duflo puts it: "Even if the choice of the comparison and treatment groups ensures the internal validity of estimates, any method of evaluation is subject to problems with external validity due to the specific circumstances of implementation. That is, the results may not be able to be generalized to other contexts."[25] What is less often recognized is that some methods of evaluation *may* have fewer problems of external validity because they allow greater coverage over time and space of the relevant population. Advocates of randomization easily slip into language that portrays experimental evidence as "hard," overlooking the fact that theirs is as "soft" as other types of evidence when it comes to the real questions at hand.

Consider Banerjee's complaint that the World Bank's sourcebook on empowerment and poverty reduction has only one recommendation based on a randomized trial (school vouchers, subjected to randomized evaluation in Colombia).[26] As for the recommendation on legal reform, he says "the available evidence, which comes from comparing the more law-abiding countries with the rest, is too tangled to warrant such a confident recommendation."[27] He faults the bank both for not showing more enthusiasm for programs like vouchers (for which there is a study with good internal validity) and for endorsing strategies like legal reform (for which there are many studies that do more poorly on internal validity). "What is striking about the list of strategies offered by the World Bank's sourcebook," Banerjee writes, "is the lack of distinction made between strategies based on the *hard* evidence provided by randomized trials or natural experiments and the rest."[28] But of course the experimental evidence from Colombia is equally problematic when it comes to *generalizability* to other countries. How would the results change if, as would be necessary, one altered the target population (children of secondary school age in Colombia's low-income neighborhoods)? Or the environment in which the experiment was conducted (for example, the availability and quality of nearby private educational facilities)? Or some details of the program (for example the share of private school costs covered by the voucher)?[29] No one knows. So it is not at all clear that the priors on the relevant policy question—what strategies are worth pursuing to empower the poor and reduce

24. Duflo and others (2006).
25. Duflo (n.d., p. 27).
26. Banerjee (2007).
27. Banerjee (2007, p. 14).
28. Banerjee (2007, p. 13), emphasis added.
29. The study in question is Angrist and others (2002). The authors conclude, cautiously: "Our findings suggest that demand-side programs like PACES can be a cost-effective way to increase education attainment and academic achievement, at least in countries like Colombia with a weak public school infrastructure and a well-developed private-education sector" (p. 1556).

poverty across the globe—should be moved more by the Colombia study than by the multitude of cross-national studies on legal institutions. The right way to present this would have been to recognize that both types of evidence have strengths and weaknesses when it comes to informing policymakers about the questions they care about.

The need to demonstrate credible identification is well understood in empirical economics today. When I was a young assistant professor, one could still publish econometric results in top journals with nary a word on the endogeneity of regressors. If one went so far as to instrument for patently endogenous variables, it was often enough to state that one was doing IV, with the list of instruments tacked into a footnote at the bottom of a table. No more. A large chunk of the typical empirical—but nonexperimental—article today is devoted to discussing issues having to do with endogeneity, omitted variables, and measurement error. The identification strategy is made explicit and is often at the core of the research. Robustness issues take a whole separate section. Possible objections are anticipated and counterarguments are advanced. In other words, considerable effort is devoted to convincing the reader of the internal validity of the study.

By contrast, the typical study based on a randomized field experiment says very little about external validity. If there are some speculations about the background conditions that may have influenced the outcomes and that do or do not exist elsewhere, they are offered in passing and are not central to the flow of the argument. Most important, the typical field experiment makes no claims about the generalizability of the results—even though without generalizability a field experiment is of little interest, as I have just argued. But little is said to warn the reader against generalizing, either.[30] And since the title, summary, motivation, and conclusions of the study typically revolve around the *general* policy question, careless readers may well walk away from the study thinking that they have learned more about the broader policy question of interest than they actually should have.

Interestingly, in medicine, where clinical trials have a long history, external validity is also a major concern, and it is often neglected. The question there is whether the findings of a randomized controlled trial, carried out on a particular set of patients under a specific set of conditions, can be generalized to the population at large. One recent study complains that published studies do a poor job of reporting on external validity, and that "researchers, funding agencies, ethics committees, the pharmaceutical industry, medical journals, and governmental regulators alike all neglect external validity, leaving clinicians to make judgments."[31] The long list of evidence adduced in support of this argument makes for

30. See the online draft version of Cohen-Dupas (2007), which contains stronger language in its introduction and conclusions warning against extrapolation to other settings (www.brookings.edu/~/media/Files/rc/papers/2007/12_malaria_cohen/12_malaria_cohen.pdf [May 19, 2008]).

31. Rothwell (2005, p. 82).

Box 2-1. *Neglect of Consideration of External Validity of Randomized Controlled Trials (RCTs) in Medicine*

Research into internal validity of RCTs and systematic reviews far outweighs research into how results should best be used in practice.

Rules governing the performance of trials, such as good clinical practice, do not cover issues of external validity.

Drug-licensing bodies, such as the U.S. Food and Drug Administration, do not require evidence that a drug has a clinically useful treatment effect or a trial population that is representative of routine clinical practice.

Guidance on the design and performance of RCTs from funding agencies, such as that from the U.K. Medical Research Council, makes virtually no mention of issues related to external validity.

Guidance from ethics committees, such as that from the U.K. Department of Health, indicates that clinical research should be internally valid and raises some issues that relate to external validity, but makes no explicit recommendations about the need for results to be generalizable.

Guidelines on the reporting of RCTs and systematic reviews focus mainly on internal validity and give very little space to external validity.

None of the many scores for judging the quality of RCTs address external validity adequately.

There are no accepted guidelines on how external validity of RCTs should be assessed.

Source: Reproduced from Rothwell (2005).

interesting reading in light of the parallels with current practice in economics (see box 2-1). Virtually all of these points have their counterpart in current experimental work in development economics.

One response to the external-validity critique is to say that the solution is to repeat the experiment in other settings, and to do it enough times so that the researcher feels confident in drawing general lessons. Repetition would surely help. But is it the magic bullet? Few randomized evaluations—if any—offer a structural model that describes how the proposed policy will work, if it does, and under what circumstances it will not, if it does not. Absent a full theory that is being put to a test, it is somewhat arbitrary to determine under what different conditions the experiment ought to be repeated. If one does not have a theory of which X_{it}^j's matter, one cannot know how to vary the background conditions. Moreover, everyone is free to come up with an alternative theory that would enlarge the set of conditioning variables. As Ravallion puts it: "The feasibility of doing a sufficient number of trials—sufficient to span the relevant domain of variation found in reality for a given program, as well as across the range of policy options—is far from clear. The scale of the randomized trials needed to test even one large national program could well be prohibitive."[32]

But the more practical objection to the repetition solution is that there is very little professional incentive to do so. It is hard to imagine that leading journals will be interested in publishing the results of an identical experiment that differs along one or two dimensions: perhaps it is a different locale, or perhaps the policy varies a bit, but in all other ways, the experiment remains the same. The conditions under which the repetition is most useful for purposes of external validity—repetition under virtually identical conditions, save for one or two differences—are precisely the conditions that will make it unappealing for purposes of professional advancement. It is possible that nongovernmental organizations and governments can step in to provide the replication needed. But these actors have their own interests and stakes in the outcome. Their efforts may be as problematic as those from clinical trials undertaken by the pharmaceutical industry.[33]

Perhaps ironically, other types of studies that have weaker internal validity generate much greater incentive for replication. Here the name of the game is improved identification, and there are ample professional benefits for researchers who come up with a new instrumental variable or a novel identification strategy.

Ultimately, the best way to render randomized field trials more useful is to make a careful consideration of external validity part and parcel of the exercise. It should be incumbent on the authors to convince the reader that the results are reasonably general and also to address circumstances under which they may not be. This is as important as justifying causal identification in other types of empirical work. A discussion of external validity will necessarily remain speculative along many dimensions. But that is its virtue: it will bring to the fore what is in many instances a hidden weakness. And the need to justify external validity ex post may also stimulate better experimental design ex ante. For instance, researchers may make a greater effort to target a population that is "representative," be more explicit about the theoretical foundations of the exercise, and incorporate (at least) some variation in the X's.[34]

The Good News: Convergence in Policy Mind-Sets

For Banerjee, "what is probably the best argument for the experimental approach [is that] it spurs innovation by making it easy to see what works."[35] The premise

32. Ravallion (2008a, p. 19).

33. Rothwell (2005).

34. An excellent example of a field experiment that uses theory to guide the exercise and inform issues of external validity is Jensen and Miller (2008). These authors were interested in the existence of a Giffen good, so they carried out the experiment in a setting that theory suggested is most conducive to locating it (very poor Chinese consumers facing variation in the price of their staple foods, rice or noodles). As a by-product, the analysis clarifies the circumstances under which their result would generalize.

35. Banerjee (2007, p. 122).

is that policy innovation is inherently useful—either because problems may need to be solved through unconventional ways or because different contexts require different solutions. This may be an uncontroversial premise in the domain of social policy, but until recently it ran counter to much thinking in the area of growth. Up until a decade or so ago, macrodevelopment economists thought they had a fairly good idea of what it would take to turn economic performance around in the closed, statist economies of Latin America, Africa, the Middle East, and South Asia. These economies needed to remove trade restrictions, free up prices, privatize state enterprises and parastatals, and run tighter fiscal policies. The list was clear-cut and in need of very little innovation or experimentation, save possibly for evading the political minefields associated with these reforms.

While it would be an exaggeration to say that the previous consensus has totally dissipated, today macrodevelopment economists operate in a very different intellectual environment. Gone is the confidence that they have the correct recipe, or that privatization, stabilization, and liberalization can be implemented in similar ways in different parts of the world.[36] Reform discussions focus on the need to get away from "one-size-fits-all" strategies and on context-specific solutions. The emphasis is on the need for humility, for policy diversity, for selective and modest reforms, and for experimentation. Gobind Nankani, the then vice president of the World Bank who oversaw the effort behind the bank's *Economic Growth in the 1990s: Learning from a Decade of Reform,* writes in the preface of the book: "The central message of this volume is that there is no unique universal set of rules. . . . [W]e need to get away from formulae and the search for elusive 'best practices.'"[37] The recent Spence report on growth encapsulates and reflects many of these changed views.[38]

My own work (with colleagues Ricardo Hausmann, Lant Pritchett, Charles Sabel, and Andrés Velasco) has focused on developing methodologies for designing country-specific growth strategies and on innovations in institutional arrangements for industrial policy.[39] We formulate the underlying problem as one of "growth diagnostics": how to discover the binding constraints on economic growth in a specific setting, and then how to come up with policy solutions that are cognizant of local second-best interactions and political constraints. The detective work consists of postulating a series of hypotheses about the nature of the economy and its underlying growth process (or lack thereof) and checking to see whether the evidence is consistent with the signals one would expect to

36. See World Bank (2005); Rodrik (2006).

37. World Bank (2005, p. xiii).

38. Commission on Growth and Development (2008).

39. On country-specific growth strategies, see Rodrik (2007); Hausmann, Pritchett, and Rodrik (2005); Hausmann, Rodrik, and Velasco (2008). On institutional arrangements for industrial policy, see Rodrik (2008); Hausmann, Rodrik, and Sabel (2007).

observe under those hypotheses. In other words, the approach follows the "scientific method" even though the answers it generates necessarily come with large margins of doubt. Policy design in turn relies less on "best practices" and more on a combination of experimentation and monitoring.

These ideas may have been new in the growth context, but in fact they run parallel to the thinking reflected in the work of microdevelopment economists focusing on randomized evaluations. For me, the epiphany occurred during an executive program we were offering at the Harvard Kennedy School, "New Thinking on Economic Growth and Development." I was sitting in on a discussion that Banerjee was conducting on the health crisis in Rajasthan and possible responses to it (which had been preceded by an excellent video produced by Banerjee and his colleagues). Over the course of the discussion, it became clear that the approach Banerjee was taking the class through was virtually identical to the Hausmann-Rodrik-Velasco (HRV) "diagnostic" approach—albeit in a very different setting. No basic presumption is made about having the answer (that poor health outcomes are due to inadequate public spending, say, or ignorance about the value of health). So the researcher conducts surveys and interviews and collects information.

The next step is to develop stories about what may account for the troubles. Are people not receiving good health care because there are no health clinics nearby? Because they do not think clinics are useful? Because there are "crack" doctors who provide apparently substitute services? Or because nurses and doctors are frequently absent? Each of these stories has implications for the patterns apparent in the surveys and the response people give in the interviews (they throw out different "diagnostic signals," in HRV terminology). If poor people spend a considerable share of their budget on health, for example, it is unlikely that they do not value it sufficiently. This kind of analysis helps narrow the list down to a smaller list of real problems ("binding constraints"). Then one gets creative and tries to come up with ways—often quite unconventional—in which to overcome these problems (lentils in exchange for inoculation, cameras in the classroom, and so on). Finally, the researcher subjects these ideas to rigorous evaluations through randomized experiments and amends them as required.

This thought process captures fairly well the spirit in which growth diagnostics exercises are supposed to be carried out as well. What my colleagues and I had begun to advocate for macrodevelopment economists was exactly the same kind of open-minded, open-ended, pragmatic, experimental, and contextual approach. If our ideas seemed (at the time, but perhaps no longer) unorthodox, it was largely because there was already a Washington Consensus to contend with. By contrast, the absence of an equally well-formed consensus for social policy left greater space for experimentalist approaches in that domain. The main difference, of course, is that our policy innovations cannot be subject to randomized evaluations (but as I have already argued, one can easily exaggerate the importance of this distinction where real policy learning is concerned).

When done well, both the macro- and microvariants of this "diagnostic" approach rely on explicit theorizing. Pragmatism does not imply absence of theory. The only meaningful way to sift through the evidence—or indeed to know what kind of evidence to look for—is through the prism provided by clearly articulated theoretical frames. Where pragmatism comes in is with the analyst's willingness to shift from one model of the world to another as the evidence accumulates, and with his or her proclivity to experiment with different potential policy solutions.

Perhaps the best way to bring this micro-macro convergence into sharper relief is to describe how it differs from other ways of thinking about reform. Here is a stylized, but (hopefully) not too misleading representation of the traditional policy frame that the new approach supplants:

—The traditional approach is *presumptive*, rather than *diagnostic*. That is, it starts with strong priors about the nature of the problem and the appropriate fixes. On the macro front, both import-substituting industrialization and the Washington Consensus, despite their huge differences, are examples of this frame. On the social policy front, the U.N. Millennium Project is a good example insofar as it comes with ready-made solutions—mainly an across-the-board ramping up of expenditures on public infrastructure and human capital—even though Jeffrey Sachs would presumably argue that the project's recommendations are based on highly context-specific diagnostic work.

—It is typically operationalized via a *long list of reforms* (the proverbial "laundry list"). This is true of all the strategies mentioned in the preceding paragraph. When reforms disappoint, the typical response is to increase the items on the list, rather than question whether the problem may have been with the initial list.

—It emphasizes the *complementarity* among reforms rather than their sequencing and prioritization. So trade liberalization, for example, needs to be pursued alongside tax reform, product-market deregulation, and labor-market flexibility. Investment in education has to be supported by investments in health and public infrastructure.

—There is a bias toward *universal recipes, best practices, and rules of thumb*. The tendency is to look for general recommendations and "model" institutional arrangements. Recommendations tend to be poorly contextualized.

The new policy mind-set has the following characteristics:

—It starts with *relative agnosticism* as to what works and what does not. It is explicitly *diagnostic* in its strategy to identify bottlenecks and constraints.

—It emphasizes *experimentation* as a strategy for discovery of what works. *Monitoring* and *evaluation* are essential in order to learn which experiments work and which fail.

—It tends to look for *selective, relatively narrowly targeted reforms*. Its maintained hypothesis is that lots of "slack" exists in poor countries. Simple changes can make a big difference. In other words, there are lots of $100 bills on the sidewalk.

—It is suspicious of best practices or universal remedies. It searches instead for *policy innovations* that provide a shortcut around local second-best or political complications.

Here is a litmus test to separate adherents to these two policy frames: "Do you believe there is an unconditional and unambiguous mapping from specific *policies* to economic outcomes?" If the answer is yes with little hesitation, then the individual is in the presumptive camp. If inclined to say no, one is a fellow traveler of the experimentalists.[40]

What, then, does it mean to be a macrodevelopment economist and an experimentalist at the same time? There is no contradiction here as long as "experimentalism" is interpreted broadly and not associated solely with randomized evaluations. Experimentalism in the macro context refers simply to a predisposition to find out what works through policy innovation. The evaluation of the experiment need be only as rigorous as the policy setting allows. Some of the most significant gains in economic development in history can in fact be attributed to precisely such an approach.

What I have in mind, of course, is China's experience with experimental gradualism. As Martin Ravallion recently noted: "Anyone who doubts the potential benefits to development practitioners from evaluation should study China's experience at economic reform."[41] The type of evaluation that Ravallion is referring to is not randomized field trials.

In 1978, the Communist Party's 11th Congress broke with its ideology-based approach to policy making, in favor of a more pragmatic approach, which Deng Xiaoping famously dubbed the process of "feeling our way across the river." At its core was the idea that public action should be based on evaluations of experiences with different policies: this is essentially what was described at the time as "the intellectual approach of seeking truth from facts." In looking for facts, a high weight was put on demonstrable success in actual policy experiments on the ground. The evidence from local experiments in alternatives to collectivized farming was eventually instrumental in persuading even the old guard of the Party's leadership that rural reforms could deliver higher food output. But the evidence had to be credible. A newly created research group did field work studying local experiments on

40. For a positive model of the choice that governments face between experimenting through policy innovation and emulating "best practices" from elsewhere, see Mukand and Rodrik (2005).

41. Ravallion (2008b).

the de-collectivization of farming using contracts with individual farmers. This helped to convince skeptical policy makers (many still imbued in Maoist ideology) of the merits of scaling up the local initiatives. The rural reforms that were then implemented nationally helped achieve probably the most dramatic reduction in the extent of poverty the world has yet seen.[42]

Not much is said about the nature of the fieldwork undertaken, but presumably it would not have satisfied the standards of the Poverty Action Lab. Nonetheless, Ravallion is undoubtedly correct in pointing to the Chinese example as perhaps the crowning achievement of the method of experimentation combined with evaluation. Some of the experiments that proved extremely successful were the household responsibility system, dual-track pricing, township-and-village enterprises, and special economic zones. "Seeing whether something worked" is hardly as rigorous as randomized evaluations. But it would be silly to claim that Chinese policymakers did not learn something from their experiments.

The experimentalist mind-set was deeply ingrained in China's approach to reform. As Sebastian Heilmann notes, "Though ambitious central state planning, grand technocratic modernization schemes, and megaprojects have never disappeared from the Chinese policy agenda, an entrenched process of experimentation that precedes the enactment of many national policies has served as a powerful correcting mechanism."[43] Heilmann documents that Chinese-style experimentation came in three distinct forms: (1) regulations identified explicitly as experimental (that is, provisional rules for trial implementation); (2) "experimental points" (that is, model demonstrations and pilot projects in specific policy areas); and (3) "experimental zones" (specially delineated local jurisdictions with broad discretionary powers to undertake experimentation). The second and third of these are relatively better known, thanks to such important examples as special economic zones. But what is striking is that no fewer than *half* of all national regulations in China in the early to mid-1980s had explicitly experimental status (see figure 2-1).[44]

The standard policy model presumes that analysis and recommendations precede the stage of policy formulation and implementation. The experimental approach implies instead "innovating through implementation first, and drafting universal laws and regulations later."[45] Interestingly, but predictably, the share of experimental regulations has declined precipitously in the aftermath of China's joining the World Trade Organization (figure 2-1).

42. Ravallion (2008b, p. 2, references not included).
43. Heilmann (2008, p. 3).
44. "Experimental" in this context refers to "ordinances, stipulations, and measures issued in the name of the State Council and ministerial organs of the central government that are marked in their title as provisional, experimental or as regulating experimental points/zones." See Heilmann (2008) for further details.
45. Heilmann (2008, p. 4).

Figure 2-1. *Indicators of Policy Experimentation in China, 1979–2006*

Percent

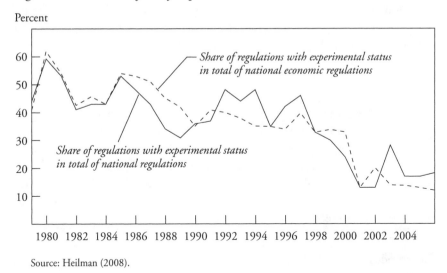

Source: Heilman (2008).

The China example is important because it illustrates, in a vastly significant real-world instance, how the experimental approach to policy reform need not remain limited in scope and *can* extend into the domain of national policies. China is, of course, a special case in many ways. The point is not that all countries can adopt the specific type of experimentation—what Heilmann calls "experimentation under hierarchy"—that China has used to such great effect. But the mind-set exhibited in China's reform process *is* general and transferable—and it differs greatly from the mind-set behind the presumptive strategies outlined in this chapter. It illustrates perfectly the potential convergence between the ideas of microdevelopment economists and macrodevelopment economists. One would hope that the response of microexperimentalists to China's experimentalism is not to say, "But this is worthless; none of the experiments were evaluated rigorously through randomization," but to say instead, "Great, here is how economists' ideas can make the world a better place, not just one school or health district at a time."

Concluding Remarks

The practice of development economics is at the cusp of a significant opportunity—not only for a reunification of the field, long divided between macro- and microdevelopment economists, but also for a progression from presumptive approaches with ready-made universal recipes to diagnostic, contextual approaches based on experimentation and policy innovation. If carried to fruition, this transformation would represent an important advance in how development policy is carried out.

Making the most of this opportunity will require some further work. Macro-development economists will have to recognize more explicitly the distinct advantages of the experimental approach, and a greater number among them will have to adopt the policy mind-set of the randomized evaluation enthusiasts. As the Chinese example illustrates, extending the experimental mind-set to the domain of economy-wide reforms is not just possible; it has already been practiced with resounding success in the most important development experience of the present generation. Microdevelopment economists, for their part, will have to recognize that one can learn from diverse types of evidence, and that while randomized evaluations are a tremendously useful addition to the empirical toolkit, the utility of the evidence they yield is restricted by the narrow and limited scope of their application. Above all, both camps have to show greater humility: macrodevelopment economists about what they already know, and microdevelopment economists about what they can learn.

References

Angrist, Joshua, and others. 2002. "Vouchers for Private Schooling in Colombia: Evidence from a Randomized Natural Experiment." *American Economic Review* 92 (December): 1535–58.

Banerjee, Abhijit V. 2005. "'New Development Economics' and the Challenge to Theory." In "New Directions in Development Economics: Theory or Empirics?" edited by Ravi Kanbur. *Economic and Political Weekly* symposium (August), typescript.

———. 2007. "Making Aid Work." In *Making Aid Work*, edited by Banerjee with others. MIT Press.

Basu, Kaushik. 2005. "The New Empirical Development Economics: Remarks on Its Philosophical Foundations." In "New Directions in Development Economics: Theory or Empirics?" edited by Ravi Kanbur. *Economic and Political Weekly* symposium (August), typescript.

Bertrand, Marianne, and others. 2007. "Obtaining a Driver's License in India: An Experimental Approach to Studying Corruption." *Quarterly Journal of Economics* 122 (November): 1639–76.

Campbell, D. T., and J. C. Stanley. 1963. *Experimental and Quasi-Experimental Designs for Research*. Chicago: Rand-McNally.

Cohen, Jessica, and Pascaline Dupas. 2007. "Free Distribution or Cost-Sharing? Evidence from a Randomized Malaria Prevention Experiment." Global Economy and Development Working Paper 11. Brookings (December).

Commission on Growth and Development. 2008. *Strategies for Sustained Growth and Inclusive Development*. Washington.

Deaton, Angus. 2007. "Evidence-Based Aid Must Not Become the Latest in a Long String of Development Fads." In *Making Aid Work*, edited by Abhijit V. Banerjee and others, pp. 60–61. MIT Press.

———. 2009. "Instruments of Development: Randomization in the Tropics, and the Search for the Elusive Keys to Economic Development" (Keynes Lecture, British Academy). Research Program in Development Studies, Princeton University (January).

Duflo, Esther. 2006. "Field Experiments in Development Economics." Prepared for the World Congress of the Econometric Society. Cambridge, Mass.: MIT Department of Economics and Abdul Latif Jameel Poverty Action Lab (January).

————. n.d. "Evaluating the Impact of Development Aid Program: The Role of Randomized Evaluations." Paper prepared for the AFD Conference, Paris, November 25.

Duflo, Esther, Rachel Glennerster, and Michael Kremer. 2006. "Using Randomization in Development Economics Research: A Toolkit" (December 12). Cambridge, Mass.: MIT Poverty Action Lab.

Hausmann, Ricardo, Lant Pritchett, and Dani Rodrik. 2005. "Growth Accelerations." *Journal of Economic Growth* 10: 303–29.

Hausmann, Ricardo, Dani Rodrik, and Charles F. Sabel. 2007. "Reconfiguring Industrial Policy: A Framework with Applications to South Africa." Harvard Kennedy School of Government (August).

Hausmann, Ricardo, Dani Rodrik, and Andrés Velasco. 2008. "Growth Diagnostics." In *The Washington Consensus Reconsidered: Towards a New Global Governance,* edited by Joseph Stiglitz and Narcis Serra. Oxford University Press.

Heilmann, Sebastian. 2008. "Policy Experimentation in China's Economic Rise." *Studies in Comparative International Development* 43 (Spring): 1–26.

Jensen, Robert, and Nolan Miller. 2008. "Giffen Behavior and Subsistence Consumption." *American Economic Review,* forthcoming.

Kanbur, Ravi, ed. 2005. "New Directions in Development Economics: Theory or Empirics?" *Economic and Political Weekly* symposium (August), typescript.

King, Gary, Robert O. Keohane, and Sidney Verba. 1994. *Designing Social Inquiry: Scientific Inference in Qualitative Research.* Princeton University Press.

Mookherjee, Dilip. 2005. "Is There Too Little Theory in Development Economics Today?" In "New Directions in Development Economics: Theory or Empirics?" edited by Ravi Kanbur. *Economic and Political Weekly* symposium (August), typescript.

Mukand, Sharun, and Dani Rodrik. 2005. "In Search of the Holy Grail: Policy Convergence, Experimentation, and Economic Performance." *American Economic Review* (March).

Over, Mead. 2008. "User Fees Can Sometimes Help the Poor." Washington: Center for Global Development (http://www.cgdev.org/doc/events/1.09.08/User_fees_can_sometimes_help_2008.pdf).

Ravallion, Martin. 2008a. "Should the Randomistas Rule?" Washington: World Bank, draft.

————. 2008b. "Evaluation in the Practice of Development." Policy Research Working Paper 4547. Washington: World Bank (March).

Rodrik, Dani. 2005. "Why We Learn Nothing from Regressing Economic Growth on Policies." Harvard University (March) (http://ksghome.harvard.edu/~drodrik/policy%20regressions.pdf).

————. 2006. "Goodbye Washington Consensus, Hello Washington Confusion?" *Journal of Economic Literature* 44 (December): 969–83.

————. 2007. *One Economics, Many Recipes: Globalization, Institutions, and Economic Growth.* Princeton University Press.

————. 2008. "Normalizing Industrial Policy." Working Paper 3. Washington: Commission on Growth and Development.

Rothwell, Peter M. 2005. "External Validity of Randomised Controlled Trials: To Whom Do the Results of This Trial Apply?" *Lancet* 365 (January): 82–93.

Sachs, Jeffrey D., Awash Teklehaimanot, and Chris Curtis 2007. "Malaria Control Calls for Mass Distribution of Insecticidal Bednets." *Lancet* 369 (June): 2143.

World Bank. 2005. *Economic Growth in the 1990s: Learning from a Decade of Reform.* Washington.

COMMENT BY SENDHIL MULLAINATHAN

So, what is new in the new development economics? Dani Rodrik looks at two kinds of newness: randomized evaluations and growth diagnostics. One of his key points (the softer point) is that "we can all get along," and he finds much similarity between the two approaches. Both are explicitly policy oriented. Both are "experimental." A caveat is in order here about terms. While some (Rodrik included) feel the growth diagnostics approach is experimental, others (the randomized evaluation proponents) would surely bristle at the use of that word. For Rodrik, "experimental" is about trying out new ideas and looking for policy innovations—that is, experimental in the one-armed bandit sense, not in the treatment-control sense. This is the positive side of the case. Proponents of the two approaches can agree on policy orientation and "experimentation." Development economics, Rodrik hopes, might finally be overcoming the long-standing split between micro- and macrodevelopment economists.

Unlike management consultants who recommend sandwiching negative feedback between two pieces of positive feedback, Rodrik appears to favor open-face sandwiches. The rest of his argument is a criticism of randomized evaluations. The up and coming view, according to Rodrik, is that learning can only come from microexperimental work, that randomized experiments are not just a "gold standard" but really the only currency that should remain in town. This view, Rodrik worries, makes macrodevelopment economists into second-class citizens, and he rejects it on two grounds.

The first is external validity. Randomized evaluations teach something about the contexts in which they are performed. But what does knowing the impact of microfinance provided by one lender in a particular district have to say about how it would work for other lenders in other places or times? External validity is not assured and often has to be argued using evidence of the "soft" type. This suggests that such evaluations are hard in the sense of internal validity but potentially soft in the sense of external validity. So looking at the broader question of "what has been learned," one has to say that randomized evaluations on net are no harder than other types of evidence.

Rodrik poses some important questions here. How do economists think about external validity? How do they use microevidence to think about macro questions? However, I felt his responses lacked analytical insight. Rodrik is not alone in this. Outside of a few technical studies in econometrics, there has been very little attempt to tackle these questions seriously. If economists are to move to a more scientific discussion (which, after all, is their comparative advantage), these questions need an analytical approach. Let me give some examples of what an analytical approach might entail. These examples are not fully worked out; they are mere fragments that underscore the desperate need for technical thinking on these questions.

First, empirical work clearly serves to reduce disagreement. The value of tests—in whatever form—is that they minimize the room for ex post disagreement. If I support theory A and someone else supports theory B, we can both look at the evidence and agree that it supported theory A or theory B. The challenge is that people who believe in theories (and I really do not want to malign either theory A or B) will defend their theories vigorously against the data. This raises two problems: empiricist bias and theorist bias. Empiricist bias arises because the choice of specification (very broadly construed) can be fiddled with to fit the facts. Theorist bias on the other hand arises because ex post criticism of empirical methods is far too easy. Omitted variable biases can go in any direction, so one can always pick a direction that favors one's pet theory. It is astonishing that economists who in every other domain espouse the need to protect against self-interest rely on econometric frameworks that do not account for phenomena like moral hazard. How does this relate to randomized evaluations? For a variety of reasons, randomized trials minimize this problem. Empiricists' hands are better (but not fully) bound. Theorists' biases must focus on external validity far more than internal validity.

Second, and this relates to the benefit of only having to think about external validity, *theories often provide information about external validity in powerful ways.* To take an example from behavioral finance, closed-end mutual funds are mutual funds that cannot simply be cashed out but have shares that must be sold. Theory makes a clear prediction here: the price of mutual fund shares should equal the price of the underlying shares the fund holds ("a rose by any other name . . ."). So if one believes in any form of efficient markets—not even a complicated one, but a really trivial form—those two prices should be the same, because there are two ways to buy apples: by the pound or by the kilo. It ought to produce the same thing. Empirical work quickly showed this was not the case. There was not only a discount (often) on the closed-end fund, but this discount predicted movements in other share classes. Could one raise the question of external validity here? Who cares if a small asset category violates the efficient-market hypothesis? No. Because the theory being tested is universal. Asset pricing did not say that no arbitrage condition holds—most of the time. I mean not always but most of the time. So external validity is not a vague intuitive construct but a specific one based on the theories being espoused. If one measures average wages in one district, some theories indicate what they will be in other districts (spatial arbitrage with low mobility costs), whereas some do not (immobility or wage rigidity).

Third, the external validity problem runs in both directions. Let me illustrate with wages. If I knew average wages in Kansas, I would have an external validity problem: I would need theory to help me (if possible) if I wanted to understand average wages in Oklahoma. But suppose I had an aggregate study, one that told me average wages in the United States. Would I be better off? Not much. I would still need theory to understand the average wages in Oklahoma. There seems to be some compositional fallacy here. If the world is so diverse that it is difficult to generalize from one context to another, very specific data from a different context are not helpful. On the other hand, aggregate data are of no help, either. It is just as hard to generalize up from one instance to another as it is to generalize from an aggregate to one instance. In other words, by all means, be concerned about external validity. But then be very concerned about aggregate growth regressions as well. Because they suffer from the *same problem*.

These examples illustrate the need for an analytical framework to think about these issues. In contrast to Rodrik, I think there is a massive divide in development economics right now, a divergence, not congruence. Those on one side make broad policy statements—about institutions or binding constraints. Those on the other side make guarded statements about specific interventions on specific issues. Each finds something to fault in the other: the other is too fast and loose with evidence; or the other is too focused on tiny questions, missing the forest for the trees. I think this divide matters a lot more than the technical divides (randomization versus mixed methods) that separate the microgroups. That seems to be largely inside baseball.

COMMENT BY MARTIN RAVALLION

Dani Rodrik deals with two important debates. The first is about a "policy rules" approach to policymaking (famously represented by the so-called Washington Consensus) versus a more pragmatic approach based on experimentation in specific contexts. The second is about experimental methods, particularly randomization.

Rodrik takes a pragmatic stance on both debates. He is against "one-size-fits-all" policy rules and favors experimentation, but he is skeptical of the experimental claims by the "randomistas." In short, he is a nonexperimental experimenter.

I do not have any serious disagreement with Rodrik's arguments regarding either debate. While one might quibble that every economist advising on policy will use some sort of "policy rule" in the face of limited information and limited resources, Rodrik's position seems to be that one should be ready to change those rules in the light of new information. It is hard to disagree with that view.

The second debate is more controversial, so I will focus on that. The main issue is not whether randomization should be on the menu of options for identifying causal impacts when feasible. To my knowledge, that has never been in contention, and evaluators have long recognized that randomization can sometimes be a useful tool. Rather, it is the claim that randomization is (pretty much) the *only thing* that should be on the menu—that nonexperimental evaluations are not "rigorous" or "credible." As Sendhil Mullainathan put it during the floor discussion of Rodrik's paper at the Brookings conference of May 2008, the randomistas see themselves as the guys with the lab coats—the scientists—while other types, the "policy analysts," worry about things like the external validity of randomized control trials.

The randomistas are having an impact. Journals are now less inclined to accept papers using nonexperimental methods. Doctoral students and young researchers have seen the signals and are searching for things to randomize. Some seasoned researchers are turning down opportunities to evaluate important public programs when randomization is not feasible. Philanthropic agencies are turning down nonexperimental evaluations. The World Bank is also responding, having been criticized for not doing enough randomized evaluations of its projects. For example, the largest donor trust fund yet for impact evaluations at the World Bank gave preference to randomized designs.

However, it is far from clear how much this new enthusiasm for social experiments in development will help fill the key knowledge gaps about development effectiveness. Indeed, there is a real risk of even further distorting the portfolio of things that get properly evaluated. The portfolio is already distorted; it is a decidedly nonrandom subsample of World Bank development projects and policies that get evaluated rigorously, raising obvious concerns about biases in knowledge. Add to this a new methodological filter: "thou shalt randomize," with no reason to suppose that it will compensate for the preexisting biases. The end result may well be lots of social experiments on a rather narrow subset of certain types of assigned interventions, for which the project staff and government officials are agreeable to randomization, with little clear strategic direction in terms of the real knowledge gaps.

Rodrik makes some good points about the external validity of randomized trials. While I agree with everything he says on this issue, I would go a bit further on the problems of both internal and external validity.

The classic randomized trial is not quite the "gold standard" for identifying the average impact of a program on those who receive it. As is well understood, selective compliance with the randomized assignment will bias the experimental findings. The standard solution is to use the randomized assignment as the instrumental variable (IV) for treatment. However, this also requires behavioral assumptions. A key assumption for the IV method to give an unbiased estimate of the average impact on those who receive a program is that there is no "essential heterogeneity," the term used by Jim Heckman and his colleagues. Essential heterogeneity means that there is some nonignorable factor unobserved by the evaluator, but observed by the participant, and that the latent factor influences the individual specific impact of the program in question; in other words, it is an error term that interacts with participation in influencing outcomes. The "nonignorability" comes into the picture through behavioral responses to the program, including the political economy of policymaking. Plausibly, people select into a program (including complying with the experimental assignment) on the basis of unobserved factors that influence their personal returns to participation. Then it can be shown that the IV method does *not* give the mean treatment effect on the treated even with the seemingly ideal IV of a randomized assignment.

Inferences for scaling up to a national program based on the results of a randomized trial can go horribly wrong under essential heterogeneity. The randomized trial randomly mixes low-impact people with high-impact people. The scaled-up program will tend to have higher representation from the high-impact types, who will naturally be attracted to the program. Given this purposive selection, the national program is fundamentally different from the randomized trial, and the latter may well contain rather little useful information about the former. One case in which the randomized trial gets it right for scaling up is when the program has the same impact on everyone (conditional on observables). But that would seem to be a very strong assumption indeed.

The existence of relevant factors unobserved by the evaluator also feeds into the debate on the ethics and political sensitivities of impact evaluations—issues that are downplayed by advocates of this "new development economics." The problem is a familiar one, namely that (by design) a social experiment denies the program to people who would benefit and gives the program to people who do not.

The usual defense by the randomistas is to randomize conditional on observables. But this is a lame response, once one realizes (again) that the set of "observables" to the evaluators is only a subset of what is observable on the ground. At the village level, people will see—on the basis of things that are observable in the village but are not in the data set used by the evaluator—that the program is being assigned to some people who do not need it and being withheld from some who do need it.

A further point concerns spillover effects. Recall that the topic of discussion is assigned programs, so it is meaningful to talk about a set of "nonparticipants." The further identifying assumption is that nonparticipants are not affected by the program. This is known to be implausible in many applications, especially when one is trying to assess impacts over more than a short time period. Randomization does not solve this problem either.

I have come to believe that spillover effects are pervasive in development applications. Take the example of probably the most common form of an aid-financed development project: a poor-area development project, which targets aid to poor countries or villages. Aid donors typically ignore the fact that their targeted poor areas exist within a government structure. There is a central government, of course, and this is the government the donor mainly deals with. But there are also local governments, which do things in *both* the targeted villages and the nonparticipants' villages. It is plausible that when the aid agency picks certain villages, the level of local government above the village will divert its own resources and efforts elsewhere; doing otherwise would be neither efficient nor fair. Where does at least some of the spillover go? Yes, it ends up in the comparison villages. The most likely outcome is that even with randomized assignment—though that is extremely unlikely to be ethically or politically acceptable in the case of poor-area development programs—one will underestimate the impact of the aid on the targeted villages.

Spillover effects also blur Rodrik's distinction between "macro" and "micro" approaches to development research. When these effects are pervasive, an assigned program becomes essentially an economy-wide program, and the sorts of tools more familiar to macroresearchers come to the fore.

The bottom line is that the process of learning from social experiments also requires behavioral assumptions, and they are no less questionable in principle than the assumptions the randomistas object to in nonexperimental evaluations.

That does not, of course, mean that the IV provided by the randomized assignment is useless; far from it. But there are real concerns about what can be learned from a research strategy that only admits social experiments as legitimate scientific tools.

Thankfully, the randomistas do not have a monopoly over the rigorous methods available for investigating what works and what does not in the fight against poverty. However, many challenges remain in using the full menu of tools available to address the gaps in knowledge about development effectiveness.[1]

1. I present a fuller discussion of the sources of current knowledge gaps and the strengths and weaknesses of the various tools available in "Evaluation in the Practice of Development," *World Bank Research Observer*, vol. 24, no. 1, February 2009, pp. 29–54.

3

Breaking Out of the Pocket:
Do Health Interventions Work?
Which Ones and in What Sense?

PETER BOONE AND SIMON JOHNSON

The only things that matter in this fallen world are transportation and sanitation.

—Rudyard Kipling, 1913

In the early 1960s, there was a great sense of progress and optimism among the world's epidemiologists and economists. Both had tied major breakthroughs in their respective fundamental sciences to pressing social problems. And both had created plausible policy "levers" that could be adjusted to improve people's lives and increase prosperity. Since then, much of this positive view has been further justified, especially in view of the advances in lowering the burden of infectious disease and in achieving sustained and unprecedented growth in a number of countries.

Public health has arguably progressed more as intended: new drugs, vaccines, and—most important—innovations in national and international delivery systems have had profound effects in increasing life expectancy and reducing ill health. By contrast, as Bill Easterly documents, economics has experienced more missteps, particularly in its policy recommendations or "interventions" funded for low-income countries.[1] Furthermore, Dani Rodrik rightly worries, the evi-

The views expressed here are those of the authors, not of any organization, governments, or other individuals.

1. Easterly (2001). Rosenstein-Rodan's (1961) forecasts of capital requirements and growth implications for "underdeveloped" countries might be seen as the high tide of incautious optimism about the preciseness of knowledge about economics.

dence on policies that work in any measurable cross-country sense is still uncomfortably weak.[2]

Yet seen in the bigger picture, modern economic thinking has contributed to the fall of communism and the closely associated intellectual defeat (or substantial retreat) of the idea that the state and its bureaucrats should run a large part of the economy.[3] Although the state and its controlling elite are far from finished as an economic actor, the idea that state-owned firms will predominate in the world is long gone.[4]

It is the consequent economic rise of both India and China that sets the stage for the next twenty years of growth worldwide, bumps included.[5] Their rise reflects a major transformation of the global division of labor started twenty years ago, with its profound effects only now being recognized.[6] The enabling factor, of course, was the revolution in "transportation," meaning the cost of moving goods and services, which began for goods with containerized shipping in the early 1960s and spread to services through the information technology innovations of the 1980s and 1990s. This transformation is as weighty and as irreversible as any other major wave of intertwined technological and social innovations.

The rapid growth of India and China, both in wealth and human capital, will pull along even the poorest regions. Their rise has already reversed a decades-long decline in commodity prices, opening up opportunities for major investment in Africa and poorer Asian countries. It will also change labor markets, encouraging the movement of low-value-added industries to countries with lower wages, and offering these poorer regions the opportunity to become low-value-added manufacturing *and* service bases in the future.[7]

2. For anyone feeling that there are easy answers or that outsiders can drop in with previously overlooked solutions, Rodrik's webpage and blog are appropriate antidotes: http://ksghome.harvard.edu/~drodrik/. His views are reminiscent of the mid-nineteenth-century pessimism about the effectiveness of medicine, known as "therapeutic nihilism" (Shorter [2006]). Of course, much of that pessimism, and its associated emphasis on the need for more careful study of the fundamentals, turned out to be justified.

3. The debate over the Washington Consensus and the apparent concern that this was in some sense inappropriate, was not applied, or did not work (see, for example, Spence and others [2008]) seems to miss the point. The consensus (and the underlying ideas that long predated it) prevailed in broad terms against the alternatives, and countries that figured out how to apply an appropriate version of it are now driving global growth (Johnson, Ostry, and Subramanian [2007]).

4. The rise of sovereign wealth funds suggests that the state may be "back" as a global creditor. More generally, of course, vast resources are controlled by elites in many countries. Whether they accept a label such as "state" for their activities is largely irrelevant. What matters is the nature, purpose, and operation of political connections.

5. In terms of direct economic consequences for the global economy, the fall of the Soviet bloc was a sideshow; the major issue, still unresolved, was how the fall would affect the provision of oil and gas to the world market. The countries of the former Soviet empire are in demographic decline and never had more than 300 million people even before the breakup. India and China have close to 3 billion people between them.

6. On the consequences of globalization, see International Monetary Fund (2007a, 2007b). On the difficulty of anticipating precise bumps in the road, see Berg, Ostry, and Zettelmeyer (2008).

7. The evidence strongly suggests that there are no insurmountable obstacles to Africa's development (Johnson and others [2007]). The key is to find ways to integrate with the global economy that can with-

Even so, this transformation and the prosperity it generates in what were, until recently, relatively remote and low-productivity parts of the world are undoubtedly leaving some people behind. It is therefore reasonable to expect that countries previously known as "poor" will be host to regions of high income (close to industrial country averages or higher), as well as to other, smaller pockets of extreme poverty.

What could make a substantial difference to people living in such pockets? The market is unlikely to reach down and lift them up anytime soon. In part, this is because they do not have access to high-quality public goods, particularly health care. "Interventions" that improve health could make a big difference, but only if (a) more is known about how to package health *and* education interventions, and (b) there are ways to also provide productivity-enhancing interventions. Point (a) is essential and also attainable. Point (b) may or may not be essential, and whether it is attainable remains unclear.

In the following pages we argue that health in these pockets can probably be improved dramatically and poverty reduced, but that new research strategies and evaluation methodologies are needed to get there. Since what works and does not work in interventions is a vast topic, we concentrate on a narrower one: how to reduce child deaths in pockets of poverty. Although some clinicians would argue that they already know how to dramatically reduce child deaths, closer scrutiny reveals a great deal of uncertainty. Departing somewhat from the current standard approach in development economics, we suggest that one way to make further progress is to build private services that for the most part bypass the public sector. However, improved child health may not necessarily raise per capita incomes and reduce poverty. While there may be some "end-runs" around this larger problem, such as migration, it cannot be adequately addressed without an integrated agenda to define, test, and implement packages that include direct measures to raise productivity and reduce poverty.

Pockets Defined

We define pockets of poverty as regions in extreme poverty, where the basic services needed to preserve and build human capital are poor or nonexistent, so that child mortality is high and literacy rates are low. Although no reliable, comprehensive surveys exist to calculate the population in such regions, their numbers would surely be in the hundreds of millions.[8] In the next twenty years, the pattern

---

stand internal and external shocks. Substantial progress has already been made in this regard, but the real test will be what happens when there is a large negative shock to these countries' terms of trade (International Monetary Fund [2008]).

8. According to World Bank estimates (2008a, 2008b), 2.7 billion people live on an income of less than $2 a day (in 2001). Most of them probably live in regions where health and education function poorly.

of poverty and poor health around the world is likely to change dramatically. The days of massive extreme poverty, such as that suffered in times of famine in Bangladesh and India, are certainly over.[9] The reality today is that pot-bellied, malnourished children are very rare, and in another two decades they should be almost unheard of.[10]

This change in the map of poverty has important ramifications for the design and use of development assistance, which now needs to shift more attention to the remaining pockets of poverty. The pattern in India is fairly representative of that in many poor nations.[11] Despite rapid growth and improvements in health and education, many regions in India approach levels in the poorest areas of sub-Saharan Africa. The mortality rate in the state of Bihar, for instance, is similar to that of Malawi, with 12 percent of its children dying before the age of five, whereas in urban Andhra Pradesh child mortality is one-third that level. And in villages three hours due west of wealthy Hyderabad neighborhoods, 6 percent of children die at birth, and schools and public health services hardly function. Statistics for lower-caste families in these communities and tribal areas are even worse.

The discrepancies in education are similar. Urban areas have public and private schools, and many of their students achieve standards equivalent to averages in wealthy nations. By contrast, schools in smaller towns and many villages hardly function. As a result, despite high official enrollment rates, overall 33 percent of children in grades 3–5 are unable to read at the level of a grade 1 student, and even more are unable to do simple subtraction.[12]

Although trickle-down will eventually make most pockets of extreme poverty better off, it may take many generations to remove them. This delay will have many costs. For some people, it will mean dying early in childhood, which otherwise might not have happened. For those that survive, education will be very poor, with adverse neurological and behavioral effects. According to recent studies, childhood is a critical period of development for human brains. Without early

9. We recognize that measured progress toward poverty reduction has been uneven (Chen and Ravallion 2007); in fact, this is part of our point. We are also aware that some countries may impose terrible burdens on their people, for example, by creating agricultural production disasters or refusing to allow outside support in the case of catastrophe. Amartya Sen's insight on the incompatibility of democracy and famine continues to hold.

10. The World Food Program, World Bank, and others are no doubt correct to emphasize the new food crisis of 2008, which may push back antipoverty progress by ten years. We believe a supply response will be forthcoming, as occurred after every past surge in commodity prices. We also see gains for many low-income countries coming from higher commodity prices. But it is true that changing terms of trade, if persistent, may deepen (and perhaps move the location of) pockets of poverty. It is certainly unlikely to eliminate the issue.

11. The pattern in China may be more similar than is commonly thought. But the data are poorer, so we confine ourselves to India as the plausible benchmark.

12. Pratham Resource Center (2007); Sathe (2005).

stimulation and education, children may suffer irreversible losses in their social and mental development.

These large pockets of poverty carry potential costs for rich countries, including the United States and European nations, as well as for local neighbors. Good monitoring systems and effective national programs are needed to limit the development and spread of Asian bird flu, AIDS, or other diseases likely to incubate in these generally "dysfunctional" areas. Many such pockets already maintain a human reservoir of infectious diseases such as malaria, making it necessary to develop new treatments as resistance builds and preventing any closely connected regions from permanently resolving disease.

This changing map also has important ramifications for how aid agencies with a moral agenda to reduce poverty should function. They need to recognize that inhabitants of these pockets will often be outcasts and have a weak voice in the political system. As long as that is the case, government funding and programs will probably fail to improve the lot of the poor. If these "outcast" regions cannot be turned into insiders, how can central governments truly use their resources to make these regions rise up to be more nearly equal to more privileged areas?

Why Do Pockets of Poverty Exist?

Information on the international pattern of child deaths (see figure 3-1, which plots child mortality against log per capita GDP) can shed some light on these outcast regions. As we discuss in the following paragraphs, child deaths are highly correlated with education, income, and the provision of public services, so they are probably good proxies for the general failure to promote human capital. But national statistics hide a very large variation within countries. Northern states of India, such as Bihar, have child mortality rates similar to those of western Africa; and India's rural rates average 30 to 50 percent higher than urban rates. Even in the better-off states, services to tribal populations and other "outsiders" are generally extremely poor.[13]

As already mentioned, India's pockets of poverty are widespread despite its rapidly growing wealth. Such pockets persist for many reasons and are likely to become the standard in poor African nations and other poor nations as they too become wealthier. One reason in any economic system is the interaction of family circumstances and geography. If children have illiterate parents who have not benefited from economic change, they will need to break with their parents' generation to undergo change themselves. Their ability and desire to do so will

---

13. In a baseline survey of 144,000 women ahead of a randomized controlled trial in tribal regions of Andhra Pradesh, not far from Hyderabad, we found 6 percent of children died before one month of age in 2007.

Figure 3-1. *Child Mortality and Income*

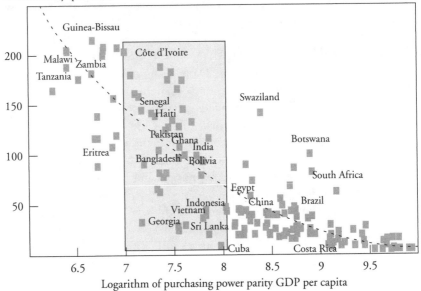

Child mortality (per 1,000)

Logarithm of purchasing power parity GDP per capita

depend on many factors, such as the extent of regional isolation or ethnic and religious constraints. Of course, some populations may be less quick to change by choice, but often this is not the case, especially for children.[14]

A second reason is the inherent nature of capitalist politics and interests. While rapid economic growth probably trickles down to everyone eventually, people with wealth concentrate in urban areas. They tend to control political power, and they demand good private or public services for themselves. This naturally leads to a concentration of the best services in wealthy areas.[15] Migration to urban areas may help eradicate the pockets, but if remote villages have not provided decent health and education to children, the migrants may not be well placed to succeed in urban areas, and this could slow the migration process.

Third, some groups exercise a tyranny over other groups. In the tribal regions of India, low-caste groups, Muslims, and others have historically faced prejudice from all levels of authority. It will take decades to truly change the ability of these peoples to fully benefit from rapid growth and to pull some communities out of their extreme poverty. If political power is based in part on oppression through

14. Sachs (2005) stresses the importance of geography. People living near water, rail links, and good roads will be better able to benefit from the coming growth than those in more remote regions with poor transport.

15. This is a version of "urban bias," but not exactly the versions in Lipton (1977) or Bates (1981).

the disregard of ill health, then there may be powerful opposition to sensible interventions by outsiders, especially if local notables feel that outsiders are organizing relatively poor people for political action.[16]

Fourth, there can be other obstacles to the regular provision of health and education services, even in the presence of demand, a primary one being civil conflict. Paul Collier and his colleagues calculate that in the past half century, nations in sub-Saharan Africa have experienced civil conflict once every six years on average.[17] This makes it difficult to maintain long-term investment and the regular supply of health, education, infrastructure, and private business. Friction between communities with different ethnic, religious, tribal, and other backgrounds living close together is a persistent problem that may keep those regions poor for a very long time.

It is difficult to quantify the relative importance of these various explanations within or across different locations. Practical experience, however, suggests that pockets of poverty exist primarily because they are neglected by the powerful elites and effective groups. It is neglect, rather than a sinister conspiracy of oppression, that prevents relatively isolated people from gaining access to decent health care or education. As a result, it is possible for outsiders to offer such services without fomenting adverse political reaction or some other means of oppression.

What Constitutes Good Evidence?

Needless to say, improved health and education alone will not eliminate poverty. The question is, how to determine what interventions are appropriate—in other words, how to assess the evidence in their favor. But the evidence considered acceptable to justify development policies and the evidence needed to gain regulatory approval for simple drugs, say, are strikingly different. The question then becomes, what constitutes good evidence?

The gold standard for evidence in the medical literature is a well-designed randomized controlled trial. Table 3-1 illustrates the phases of a drug's development and associated types of evidence necessary to get the drug approved by the U.S. Food and Drug Administration (FDA). Phases 1 and 2 are early stages in which initial evidence on safety and efficacy is gathered. The key necessary step for approval is phase 3. Here drug companies must prespecify the design and analysis in one or more randomized controlled trials, which are sufficient to demonstrate efficacy of the drug in a setting similar to public use post approval. The rules

16. The value to the elite of continued ill health and denial of health care to the poor is one element of "structural violence" emphasized by Paul Farmer (2004). No doubt this applies to many situations and thus may indeed suggest that "inequality" is bad for the poor, as Ravallion (2005) argues, but there is no compelling evidence (at least yet) that this implies a general first-order constraint on effective health interventions. Farmer's own medical work suggests these are possible even in the most difficult circumstances.

17. Collier and others (2003).

Table 3-1. *Phases of Drug Development and Evidence for Approval*

Development phase	Goals	Methods
1 and preclinical	Safety	Very small trials
2	Preliminary evidence of efficacy Dosing Optimal procedures for implementation Secondary analysis of well-designed randomized controlled trials	Survey data Small randomized controlled trials Randomized experiments Secondary analysis of well-designed randomized controlled trials
3	Substantial evidence of efficacy and safety	Several randomized controlled trials with registered protocols that: State prespecified primary and secondary endpoints Are powered appropriately Provide prespecified statistical analysis plan Have blinding and limited ability for investigators to learn results before the trial is completed

for the design of randomized trials have evolved over many decades, and they are structured to limit the scope for investigator and selection bias.

In general, medical science would classify the evidence appearing in the economics literature—as well as much of the public health literature—as phase 2 information. Creative secondary analysis of randomized experiments—such as the work of Edward Miguel and Michael Kremer—can, of course, provide valuable insights into optimal project design and add substantially to the understanding of the impact of interventions outside of the primary analysis.[18]

But in the view of medical science, retrospective analysis is subject to substantial investigator and selection bias, so would never satisfy the strict criteria required to demonstrate the efficacy of a drug. The medical community would also frown upon the randomized evaluations employed in economics, which may have greatly improved the quality of available evidence but fail to meet medicine's standards for randomized controlled trials. Most notably, they fail to prespecify primary and secondary endpoints or a statistical analysis plan, lack multiple endpoints, use nontestable hypotheses to analyze trial results, and

18. Miguel and Kremer (2004).

emphasize somewhat complicated regression analysis rather than simpler trial designs.[19]

The statistical importance of information quality can be readily seen from drug trial records. Approximately 70 percent of drugs that make it to human trials advance to phase 2 trials. Of those that succeed in phase 2, approximately 60 percent ultimately succeed during phase 3 trials; across therapeutic categories, this conditional success rate ranges from 39 percent to 83 percent. Hence approximately 40 percent of drugs that appear likely to be effective after phase 2 are rejected during phase 3.[20] These numbers probably understate the true failure rate of phase 2 information since many drugs that enter phase 3 are based on previously approved products (such as pain-relief ingredients) with different dosing regimes.

Unfortunately, evidence from well-designed randomized controlled trials (RCTs) that could aid in designing programs to reduce child deaths has thus far been limited. Such trials tend to focus on new or existing drugs in clinical settings or on specific interventions, such as hand-washing, introduced in community settings. Although these trials help identify which ingredients should be used in health packages to limit child deaths, they do not shed much light on the best means to ensure services are received by children that need them. Another flaw is that all-cause mortality is seldom a primary endpoint; instead, the trials target specific diseases or conditions. For example, although hand-washing may be shown to reduce diarrhea, its ultimate impact on mortality will remain uncertain without information on the exact relation between changes in diarrhea incidence and changes in child deaths.[21]

Another body of evidence that might be used in designing a program to reduce such deaths derives from household surveys. These are far less costly to implement

19. See, for example, the Consolidated Statement of Reporting Trials (CONSORT) regarding transparent reporting of trials and trial design (www.consort-statement.org); this has been endorsed by most leading medical journals. The rules are the product of an accrued consensus in medical science over the past several decades and reflect a long history of failures and successes in trial design. As they continue to evolve, the rules are becoming increasingly strict. Randomized evaluations in the economics literature typically fail two key tests: prespecification of the primary endpoint, and prespecification of the analysis plan. In medical trials, any secondary findings (all those that are not the prepecified primary analysis of the primary endpoint) are judged to be exploratory and must be confirmed by at least one further dedicated trial. This strict focus on prespecification reduces the risk of investigator bias, since investigators can otherwise pick and choose analysis strategies and endpoints to find significant results that in reality may be spurious. See Altman, Schulz, and others (2001).

20. Danzon, Nicholson, and Pereira (2005).

21. For example, Luby, Agboatwalla, and others (2005) found hand-washing with soap reduced diarrhea incidence in Karachi slums. However, there was no clear trend toward lower mortality in the intervention arm of the trial. The trial was not powered to measure mortality, and this was not a primary endpoint. In designing packages to reduce child deaths, not just child morbidity, one needs to assume that the reduced diarrhea will actually lead to lower deaths. However, there is no evidence that would permit one

than trials, and they can collect substantial information for analysis. Owing to their potential size, they can examine mortality outcomes with sufficient statistical power to capture important relationships. However, one can never be confident that these relationships are causal rather than spurious or biased, so the results need to be treated with caution.

Given the limited evidence base, as discussed in the next two sections, the impact of any potential package of measures will always be shrouded in uncertainty. Should one risk embarking on policies that have only phase 2 levels of evidence, and for which the assumed effectiveness might well have a 20–60 percent chance of being wrong? When the impact of alternative policies is uncertain, argues William Poole, the optimal response is to prefer policies offering the greatest certainty.[22] This argument suggests that wherever possible, active policy should focus on areas in which evidence from well-designed RCTs is available.

It would be dangerous, however, to assume an intervention can succeed without more experimentation and rigorous analysis. Well-designed trials that examine the impact of packages of health interventions in combination with creative secondary analysis based on techniques used in randomized experiments would be an important addition to the evidence base. In other words, not enough evidence is yet available to provide sufficient confidence regarding how to sharply reduce child deaths in pockets of poverty.

Clinical Evidence: Twenty-Three Measures That Could Dramatically Reduce Child Deaths

In 2003 the *Lancet* organized a team of leading medical experts known as the Bellagio Child Survival Group to assemble and judge current evidence regarding how to reduce the 10 million annual child deaths in low-income countries. One of the team's main findings (figure 3-2) was that 90 percent coverage of twenty-three simple measures could reduce child deaths by 63 percent, thereby saving 6 million lives a year.[23] The three largest measures (oral rehydration therapy, breastfeeding, and insecticide-treated bed nets) can all be conducted at home, with little or no cost, and they would prevent 35 percent of child deaths. The team recommended that a public outreach program be created, with frequent home visits by nurses, to ensure that children and pregnant mothers received the remaining interventions. At first glance, it would seem reasonable to simply

---

to define the relation between the lowered diarrhea incidence and mortality. The trials examining the impact of impregnated bed nets were more convincing since they were designed with all-cause mortality as the primary endpoint (Keiser, Singer, and others [2005]).

22. Poole (1970).

23. Bryce, el Arifeen, and others (2003); Bryce, Black, and others (2005); Darmstadt, Bhutta, and others (2005).

Figure 3-2. *Twenty-Three Interventions Tested by Bellagio Child Survival Group*[a]

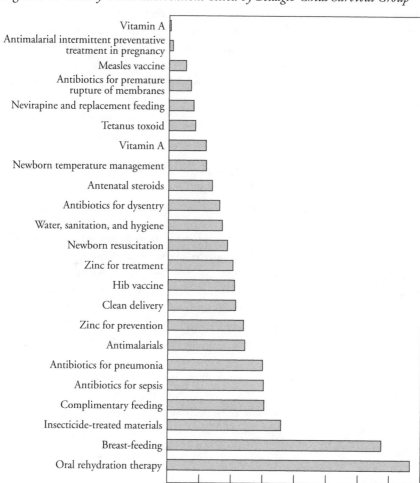

Percent

a. Interventions ranked by percent reduction in child mortality expected from each if implemented separately.

implement these measures in "pockets of poverty" to improve child health. However, several issues need to be considered beforehand.

First, the clinical evidence derives from experiments with single interventions whereas a package of interventions is needed to bring down child deaths. Furthermore trials with single interventions cannot indicate how an intervention would work in a package. In the case of bed nets and antimalarials in figure 3-2, there is very good evidence that the use of insecticide-treated bed nets reduces child mortality from all causes in regions of Africa with moderate and high incidence of malaria.[24] There is also good evidence that timely use of artemisinin-based therapies could resolve virtually all malaria in Africa, and that with second-line treatments nearly all malaria deaths could be prevented.[25] Therefore bed nets and drug therapy are potential substitutes, so if the population could be covered with good clinical services and malaria recognized early, bed nets might have little additional impact.[26] And if the population were treated quickly and fully, the reservoir of malaria would decline, and eventually malaria would disappear altogether.

Since few well-designed trials have examined the impact of a package of measures for their interactions, the Bellagio team had to rely on guesswork and personal experience to assess the relative importance of bed nets and antimalarials. They also had to do this for many other interventions that could be complements or substitutes.

A second issue ahead of practical implementation is cost-effectiveness. The Bellagio group did not explicitly consider cost-effectiveness but concentrated on major interventions for which there was evidence that a substantial number of lives could be saved.[27] With an estimate of costs and the interactions between different interventions, one could theoretically determine the best package of measures, subject to a budget constraint. Possible measures might then go beyond those discussed by the Bellagio group so that instead of substitutes, for example, one might aim for greater coverage of complements.

In practice, the cost-effectiveness of these interventions is a relatively minor issue. Each is fairly inexpensive on its own, while the bulk of any health budget will consist of quasi-fixed costs of items such as personnel and transportation for outreach and general implementation.[28] In the Bellagio estimate, the only expen-

---

24. There is also a strong case for distributing bed nets free of charge (see, for example, Cohen and Dupas [2007]).

25. See, for example, Mutabingwa and others (2005).

26. The issue is far more complicated, of course. The World Health Organization recommends that all cases of fever be treated as presumptive malaria. This may increase resistance and can be costly in regions where nonmalarial fevers are common. The use of impregnated bed nets could reduce the frequency and cost of treatments but might also reduce the development of resistance if the reduced incidence of disease slows resistance. Some of these complications could be better understood or modeled if one ran trials with packages of interventions and compared outcomes of alternative packages that excluded specific ingredients.

27. According to Bryce and others (2005), the cost of implementing the twenty-three recommended measures universally in the forty-two countries responsible for 90 percent of deaths would be $5.1 billion a year, in 2002 dollars.

28. For example, a package of oral rehydration salts cost $0.10 in the spring of 2008, a course of the antibacterial co-trimoxazole cost $0.50 per child, and a child's course of the antimalarial coartem $0.90. If chloroquine can be used instead of coartem, the cost falls to $0.20. These are the three main treatments that children would need from the age of one month to five years. They are likely to have three to four bouts of symptoms of each disease over a year. However, the need for treatment will depend on the course of the disease. If an individual has two treatments for each disease a year, the cost of providing drugs to all children in the low-income countries studied by the Bellagio group would be just $0.6 billion a year.

sive intervention would be water and sanitation infrastructure, which would reduce child deaths by just 3 percent and yet cost 16 percent of the overall budget for the program.[29] In aid of cost-effectiveness, water and sanitation infrastructure might be removed in order to increase spending on areas related to hygiene and behavior change, which could be cheaper and just as effective.[30]

Yet another issue, of perhaps the greatest concern, is the Bellagio recommendation that 90 percent coverage of these interventions be achieved through public outreach programs in communities. The team called for $5.1 billion from national governments to hire nurses, provide them with transportation, and arrange frequent community visits to households with children. This is surprising because outreach programs have been tried in many regions of the world, including many extremely poor regions, and very often have failed. This recommendation not only had no backing from well-designed studies but failed to acknowledge the constraints that today prevent such programs from being successful.

Survey Evidence on How to Reduce Child Deaths

The measures listed in figure 3-2 are neither breakthrough science nor a hard-and-fast recipe. Many poor nations and communities have managed to substantially reduce child mortality long in advance of the Bellagio study and its clinical tests.[31] Moreover, the Bellagio team confirms there are no "missing drugs" and child mortality can be greatly reduced at low cost with existing technologies. The question is, how to ensure that populations get these interventions in the sustained manner (over a decade or more) necessary to dramatically reduce child deaths. More specifically, what mechanism can ensure that children get the needed treatments, and should it favor either the public or private sector? Furthermore, what stages of disease need to be targeted to reduce the probability of death?

Figure 3-3 outlines the general stages of mortal disease for children. The first stage consists of exposure to a risk such as a virus or bacterial infection, or possibly an unsafe practice during birth. If the risk manifests itself in disease, people close to the child, usually the parents, will take some action, perhaps administer a medicine or take the child to a clinic, or perhaps do nothing at all. If in a clinic, the child may be treated either effectively or ineffectively. A child death can therefore be thought of as being conditional on the probability of passing through each stage without resolving the disease, which means interventions could target each stage.

29. Bryce and others (2005).
30. Luby and others (2005); Curtis and Cairncross (2003).
31. The former Soviet Union, Cuba, the Indian state of Kerala, Costa Rica, Vietnam, and China all demonstrate good child health despite relatively low incomes (and pockets of poverty). Some small communities also appear to have achieved impressive results (see Arole and Arole [1994]) despite extreme poverty, although no well-designed studies have verified this achievement.

Figure 3-3. *Steps to Child Mortality and Possible Interventions*

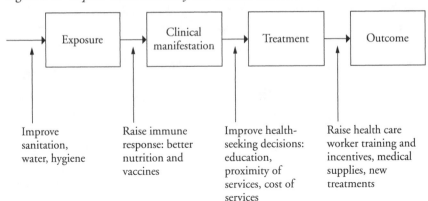

The relative importance of different interventions, household characteristics, and other factors that have an impact on child deaths has been widely studied through survey data. One of the richest data sources, the Demographic Health Survey database (DHS), contains information ranging from answers to question-naires by women of fertile age, household heads, and village leaders to birth records and child-survival histories, education levels, wealth measures, and other household and village indicators. The DHS also documents recent disease symp-toms of children that match World Health Organization (WHO) criteria for suspected malaria, pneumonia, and diarrhea. These are the three main causes of postneonatal child deaths. The combined survey data cover 278,000 child-survival records and 20,000 clusters.

One recent study examined the impact of alternative interventions on all-cause child mortality in the forty-five countries for which DHS data are available.[32] To this end, Peter Boone and Zhaoguo Zhan constructed indexes to proxy for treatment-seeking behavior, morbidity levels, wealth, education, distance to clin-ics, and access to safe water and sanitation. They constructed the "treatment-seeking" indicator using principal component analysis across a range of measures that demonstrate whether a mother tended to seek modern treatments for her child's health but that were not directly correlated with survival of the child. These measures included the mother's antenatal and delivery care and child vac-cinations near birth that protect against diseases from which there is very little or no child mortality. Household and community-level logistic regression equations were then formulated to examine if postneonatal child deaths could be predicted by this treatment indicator and other right-hand-side variables.

32. Boone and Zhan (2006).

Figurre 3-4. *Impact of Four Packages of Measures for Reducing Child Mortality Calculated from Global Data*

Percent

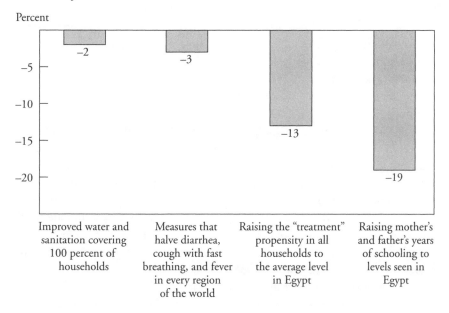

| Improved water and sanitation covering 100 percent of households | Measures that halve diarrhea, cough with fast breathing, and fever in every region of the world | Raising the "treatment" propensity in all households to the average level in Egypt | Raising mother's and father's years of schooling to levels seen in Egypt |

One of the main conclusions of this survey (see figure 3-4) was that if all households had access to improved sanitation and water, child mortality would fall by 2 percent. This small predicted decline reflects the fact that approximately half the households in the survey already had improved water and sanitation, and that this variable was insignificant, with a small coefficient in the estimated regression equations. In the remaining exercises of this study, the objective was to (a) raise the estimated treatment indicator in each household to the average level in Egypt (Egypt had the median level of the forty-five countries in the sample), (b) raise schooling to the average level in Egypt (eight years for boys and six years for girls), and (c) reduce by half the morbidity levels in each survey cluster of roughly fifty households.

As opposed to results from well-designed randomized controlled trials, these results cannot be assumed to reflect causality. Furthermore, confounding factors that were not adequately controlled for, measurement error, and other potential biases could affect the results. Even so, the data support potentially informative correlations, and the DHS has the advantage of covering a large number of households across most of the countries and regions in which one would be likely to implement policies to reduce extreme poverty.

Interestingly, the study's findings are similar to those of the Bellagio group and other surveys. Most notably, the impact of improved water and sanitation appears to be empirically small. A recent analysis of the impact of water and sanitation trials found evidence for a reduction of disease, but not of all-cause mortality.[33] Others would counter that the advent of public water and sanitation services in the United States can explain a large reduction in population death rates of about 100 years ago.[34] It seems plausible that with the much wider coverage of water and sanitation today and the introduction of vaccines and treatments for the main causes of death from infectious disease, further water and sanitation improvements may no longer be necessary to eliminate remaining deaths.

There was a very weak correlation between reported morbidity and child mortality. On average, children in pockets of poverty suffer one to four bouts each of diarrhea, fever, and cough with rapid breathing annually.[35] If a large difference in morbidity rates did explain the differences in mortality across countries, then these morbidity indicators could play a more important role in explaining cross-country differences in deaths. This weak correlation suggests appropriate treatment for sick children is more important than preventing children from becoming ill in low-income countries. However, since the data on morbidity may be biased owing to a mother's recall, and since the prevalence of disease reflects only the previous two weeks from the day of the survey rather than the history of the mother's child-survival data, measurement error and other sources of bias could be driving this relationship.[36]

Also noteworthy, the "treatment" indicator used by Boone and Zhan (see figure 3-4) proved highly significant, implying that children living in households where mothers sought out antenatal care and early childhood vaccines were far less likely to die in the postneonatal stage, despite the fact that these factors have little direct impact on postneonatal survival odds. This finding is not surprising—it is consistent with the Bellagio study since both imply that increased coverage of modern treatments will substantially reduce child deaths.[37]

However, there is one major difference between the Boone and Zhan survey findings and those of the Bellagio study. Their results are similar to a common finding of survey studies, namely that parental education appears to be an impor-

33. Clasen and others (2007).

34. Cutler and Miller (2005).

35. These three sets of symptoms are considered sufficient for presumptive treatment for diarrhea (using ORS), malaria (with coartem or other antimalarial substances), and pneumonia (using cotrimoxazole). See World Health Organization (2006), especially its guidelines on the integrated management of childhood illness.

36. For example, the strong role of parent education may reflect parents' ability to reduce disease prevalence, so the impact of lower morbidity may be better captured in the regressions through their education. On mother recall, see Manesh and others (2008).

37. The treatment indicator was calculated using the first principal component from indicators of antenatal care, place of delivery, and BCG vaccinations. None of these should directly affect whether a child survives if it survived to one month of age. The dependent variable in these regressions is survival from one month to five years of age.

tant predictor for child survival. In Boone and Zhan, combined maternal and paternal years of schooling were a highly significant and empirically important predictor for survival outcomes. Since they controlled for wealth in their regressions, this probably reflects the greater health knowledge of educated parents. More educated parents are probably better able to treat disease at home and more likely to seek out care in clinics and hospitals as needed.

The Bellagio group made no explicit mention of improving parents' education or their health knowledge as an important intervention. At the time, the group had no credible evidence that this factor affected child survival. Moreover, health professionals generally prefer to separate delivery from interventions, with the implicit or explicit assumption that public health services will find means to provide interventions. This is reasonable in certain cases, but often the delivery method is closely bundled with the type of treatment or intervention. For example, in the choice between a one-time vaccine and treatment for an infectious disease, there are good reasons to think far more success could be achieved with vaccines. Vaccination campaigns have been carried out regularly in regions that otherwise receive virtually no health care. Medical trials cannot indicate whether an implementation method is feasible unless they are conducted with that purpose in mind in the relevant regions.

The risk taken by not including parents' education in a package of measures may actually be very large. Recent neurological studies have confirmed the intuitive understanding that a love for one's child is probably a highly potent mechanism for ensuring child survival. In a functional MRI scanning study, mothers shown pictures of their own children demonstrated greater neurological activity in reward zones of the brain compared with mothers shown pictures of children that they knew but were not their own.[38] This natural biological link arguably makes parents the single best agent to ensure their child survives during its first few risky years of life. Since parents make the crucial first decisions regarding antenatal care, location and type of delivery, recognition of symptoms of disease, and the choice of treatment, they are potentially a major agent for change, or a factor that can prevent change, when child mortality reduction is targeted. Indeed, a program that neglects to sufficiently work with parents to change behavior may not succeed even if it makes available all twenty-three interventions highlighted in the Bellagio study.

Nevertheless, surprisingly few randomized controlled trials have measured the potential for better educating parents to limit child deaths. The potential may be quite large, according to a recent study of the impact of organizing women's participatory discussion groups in rural regions of Nepal.[39] The groups discussed safe delivery, pregnancy, and care of the neonate. Compared with control regions in

38. Bartels and Zeki (2004).
39. Manandhar and others (2004).

which no discussion groups had been introduced, these intervention regions had 28 percent lower neonatal deaths after two years.

There is good evidence that parents in low-income regions know little about health. Maternal knowledge regarding the use of fluids to prevent diarrhea is a case in point. Children suffering from diarrhea can quickly die from dehydration, so it is important to provide additional fluids in order to prevent death. Yet approximately one-third of Indian mothers believe fluids should be withdrawn from a child with diarrhea. This indicator is highly correlated with actual child mortality rates in each of India's states.[40]

Parental knowledge is also poor throughout Africa, although it varies by disease. Of 600 parents we interviewed in rural Guinea-Bissau, for example, only 16 percent had ever heard of pneumonia, although it is probably responsible for one-third of postneonatal child deaths in the region. By contrast, 61 percent of women attending a clinic in Nigeria knew that difficulty breathing is a symptom of pneumonia.[41] Perhaps parental education could be both necessary and sufficient to dramatically reduce child deaths. Note that approximately 35 percent of the gains in figure 3-2 are due to factors that can be implemented at home, such as breastfeeding, using impregnated bed nets, and treating diarrhea with oral rehydration salts (ORS). Such measures impose no financial burden on the public sector and require no clinics or pharmacies. Behavior change alone should permit these gains.

The remaining interventions can be divided into those that can be implemented with simple drugs in the community or at home and those that necessitate a visit to a clinic or a health professional. In reality, only a small fraction of cases require a clinic in order to save lives, and these clinics need not be in the public sector. The question is whether evidence favors public or private clinics for improving health in pockets of poverty.

Public versus Private Delivery of Health Services

In general, the health profession tends to promote public care over private systems in low-income countries. According to the WHO's Commission on Macroeconomics and Health, a large public build-out is needed because the private sector cannot be relied on to provide sufficiently equitable and affordable services to reduce mortality. However, the commission has not presented empirical evidence to justify this argument.[42]

---

40. Boone and Zhan (2007).

41. Uwaezuoke, Emodi, and Ibi (2002).

42. World Health Organization (2001). The Bellagio Child Survival Study Group was less decisive, although its general assumption was that the public sector would be responsible for most services, and that the private sector "should be involved whenever possible, especially in monitoring and ensuring quality and equity" (Bryce and others [2003]).

Figure 3-5. *Postneonatal Child Mortality and Share of Child Health Services in the Private Sector in Forty-Five Low-Income Countries*

Child deaths 7+ per 1,000 children born

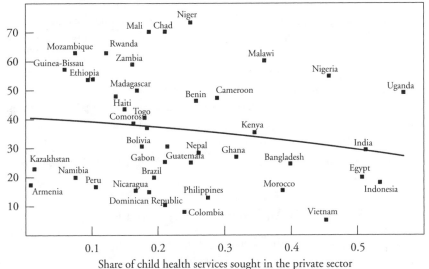

Share of child health services sought in the private sector

In extremely poor regions, the public sector today invariably provides inadequate services, may suffer from corruption, and appears to serve wealthier political elites better than the poor. Whether it can perform better than the private sector in helping pockets of poverty is clearly an empirical question and depends upon local circumstances. As a result, there may be no right solution for any region.[43]

Using the ample data on the private sector from the forty-five countries covered by the DHS, we have plotted postneonatal child mortality rates against the share of child health services in the private sector (figure 3-5).[44] These plots show no clear relationship between public/non-public management of the health system and mortality outcomes for these children.[45] Rather, both public and private systems appear consistent with very low child mortality. This is borne out in the Indian state of Kerala, Egypt, Indonesia, and Vietnam, for example, where most

43. Bustreo, Harding, and others (2003).

44. DHS reports in which mothers sought out care when their child was most recently sick with symptoms of diarrhea, fever, or cough with rapid breathing. We have used these reports to calculate the percentage of visits only to clinics in either the public or private sector. Many parents in low-income countries seek advice at pharmacies, usually in the private sector. If we included pharmacies in the calculations, the share of the private sector would rise substantially for each country, although the qualitative relationship between mortality and size of the public sector would not change.

45. Boone and Zhan (2007) use similar data to show that inequality of health care services is unrelated to the public or nonpublic management of care.

child care is sought in the private sector, as well as in Cuba, many states of the former Soviet Union, and regions in Latin America that generally rely on the public sector. China, too, has achieved low child mortality, but there parents pay a user fee equal to 75 percent of total costs.

These findings suggest there are multiple systemic routes to low child deaths. Regions with stable governments and political elites that are willing to spend on the poor may find it makes sense to channel interventions through the public sector. Others may prefer to develop a private supply and hope that parental education and experience will boost the demand for health services. To reduce the risk of supply disruptions, regions could buttress both public and private services. Public sector contracting of services can be a highly successful means to deliver services to children while avoiding the pitfalls of public implementation— although such programs do require public sector willingness and ability to provide financing.[46]

The Macroeconomic Consequences of Improved Health

There is good reason to believe that child deaths could be sharply reduced in pockets of poverty through an appropriate package of measures. The measures in figure 3-1 could be introduced rapidly enough to lower deaths by more than 50 percent over a period of five years. In our view, this result is attainable even in the poorest parts of Asia or Africa.

However, if the purpose of the package is to reduce extreme poverty, or at least make sure poverty is not exacerbated, then one needs to consider the implications of rapid improvements in health for poverty. Here the evidence is mixed. A considerable amount of microeconomic evidence suggests that better health leads to better economic outcomes for individuals—for example, in the form of higher wages.[47] So improving health for people born into pockets of poverty would undoubtedly make them better off than those not in pockets in the same country.[48] Health improvements across regions of Brazil between 1970 and 2000, for instance, had a welfare value equal to roughly one-third of that of the growth in income per capita and contributed about a quarter of the improvement in welfare.

Cross-country correlations strongly support a number of claims for the effects of health on income.[49] Reducing ill health appears to have a positive effect on pro-

---

46. Loevinsohn and Harding (2005).

47. Strauss and Thomas (1998) survey the research through the late 1990s. Important recent studies include Behrman and Rosenzweig (2004); Bleakley (2003, 2007); Miguel and Kremer (2004); and Schultz (2002).

48. In addition, health improvements should be valued for their own sake, of course, and this may outweigh any income considerations (Becker, Philipson, and Soares [2005]).

49. See, for example, Bloom and Canning (2005); Bloom and Sachs (1998); World Health Organization (2001); and Lorentzon, McMillan, and Wacziarg (2008).

ductivity directly, as well as indirectly through increased education and savings.[50] When the microeconomic evidence is aggregated, health appears to explain about 25 percent of the variation in the cross-sectional log income per worker across countries (about the same as education and more than physical capital).[51]

None of this speaks to causation, of course, and it is hard to find well-identified experiments with plausibly exogenous increases in collective health (of the appropriate kind and scale to improve health in pockets of poverty). Never-theless, some insight may be drawn from the post–World War II "international epidemiological transition," in which new drugs, chemicals, and delivery mecha-nisms spread quickly from a few industrial countries to other regions around the world, providing quick and positive effects on life expectancy and health.[52] But the effects on GDP per capita or per working-age population were much slower to emerge—taking at least forty years and, in some cases, even longer. The prox-imate cause of this delayed effect was the population increase, or fertility transi-tion, that followed the health improvements but occurred over time. This phe-nomenon is reflected in the considerable convergence in life expectancy among the countries that were poor, middle income, and rich around 1940, in contrast to the far smaller convergence in income per capita (see figures 3-6 and 3-7).[53]

The effects of health improvements in this major postwar episode can arguably be identified by measuring (a) the initial burden of disease in terms of deaths from specific infectious diseases and (b) changes in "predicted mortality," that is, the extent to which mortality should have fallen if the new medical technologies were adopted.[54] Between 1940 and 1980 there was a strong negative correlation between changes in predicted mortality and changes in log life expectancy (fig-ure 3-8); that is, countries having a larger initial burden of infectious disease also had a larger increase in life expectancy. A similar negative relationship emerged between predicted mortality and log population (figure 3-9); here, places with more to gain (and presumably more gains) from the reduction in infectious dis-eases experienced larger increases in population. In the case of GDP, the change

50. Case and Paxson (2008) find that height is associated with cognitive ability. This suggests, although it does not prove, that health improvements that increase height could have direct effects on cognition, and therefore presumably on productivity.

51. Weil (2007).

52. Acemoglu and Johnson (2007). Because of data limitations, a clear picture of what happened to health in Africa during this period has not yet emerged.

53. As Deaton (2004) points out, the convergence in life expectancy in broad terms suggests there are more gains to be had if globalization can bring better health care to the world's least healthy.

54. Acemoglu and Johnson (2007) provide data on fifteen diseases, but most of the action comes from reductions in deaths from tuberculosis, pneumonia, and (for some countries) malaria. The increase in life expectancy for many countries, from around age forty to around sixty, is similar to what could be achieved in pockets of poverty today. However, the pattern of disease burden in today's developing countries is some-what different, with child mortality higher than adult mortality than was the general case in 1940. We would also stress that the effect of reducing HIV-AIDS in particular may have quite different (and more positive) consequences for income per capita.

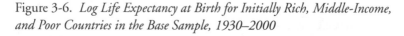

Figure 3-6. *Log Life Expectancy at Birth for Initially Rich, Middle-Income, and Poor Countries in the Base Sample, 1930–2000*

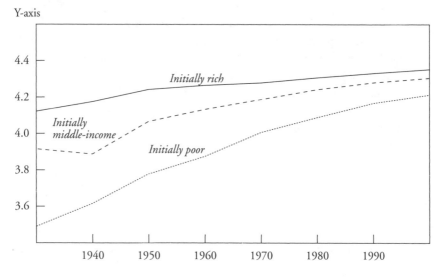

over this period was also higher for countries experiencing bigger declines in predicted mortality (figure 3-10), but the effect was not large enough to make up for the increase in population. In short, there is no evidence that these dramatic and rapid improvements in health led to higher income per capita (or even per worker).

These empirical findings are consistent with neoclassical theory if there is an important fixed factor of production, such as land. A recent analysis of exogenous

Figure 3-7. *Log GDP per Capita for Initially Rich, Middle-Income, and Poor Countries in the Base Sample, 1930–2000*

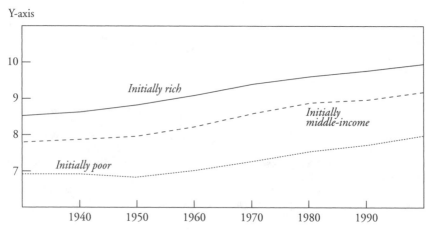

Figure 3-8. *Change in Log Life Expectancy and Change in Predicted Mortality in the Base Sample, 1940–80*

Change in log life expectancy

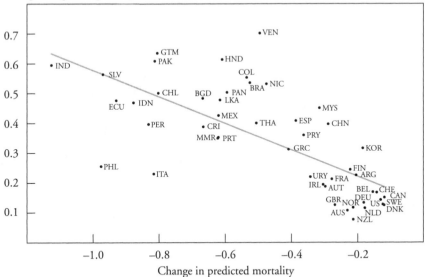

Change in predicted mortality

Figure 3-9. *Change in Log of Population and Change in Predicted Mortality in the Base Sample, 1940–80*

Change in log population

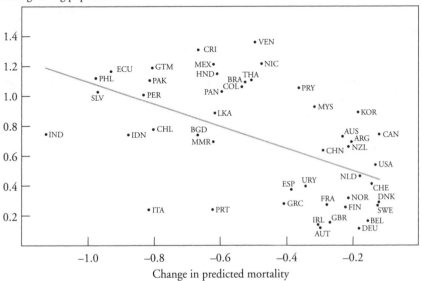

Change in predicted mortality

Figure 3-10. *Change in Log of Total GDP and Change in Predicted Mortality,*
1940–80

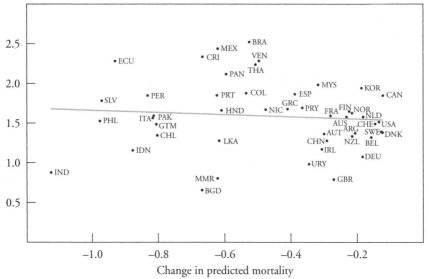

health improvements in relation to income and the available evidence on key
parameters suggest health improvements are likely to produce a population increase
that can substantially delay the positive effects on income at the macro level.[55]

None of this recent work suggests that health improvements should not be
pursued. They are surely important enough in their own right, irrespective of
their effect on income. The question of interest here is whether health (and education) interventions will, by themselves, lift people out of poverty, and what
other plausible interventions could address this issue. Could the availability of
(micro) finance have an impact, or the availability of subsidized fertilizer? The dissemination of new and (hopefully) "appropriate" technologies (perhaps cell
phones)? Or the development of roads? All of these, and more, have their proponents. Not only is this an open issue, but social science seems to be some distance
from even designing interventions that would provide meaningful tests and guidance on how to move forward.[56]

55. Ashraf, Lester, and Weil (2008). Still, their calibration of the fertility effect is less than what Acemoglu and Johnson find. Either something is missing in the theory, or the postwar experience in developing countries had some features that are not in the model. Acemoglu, Fergusson, and Johnson (2008) suggest that part of the "missing link" may be that population increases led to more social conflict and violence
as there was greater competition for resources. In turn, this is linked to who gets access to health care services in general and in the face of shocks (such as the arrival of HIV-AIDS).

56. One approach would be to encourage birth control, that is, to try to accelerate the fertility transition. There is obviously a great deal of activity in this area (see, for example, www.hewlett.org/Programs/

In a sense, the broad "Millennium Villages" package advocated by Jeff Sachs is a sensible approach.[57] This is an integrated set of interventions aimed directly at health, education, agricultural productivity, and other factors connected to poverty. But the design of this project gives little hint of the most effective components, except to suggest that (presumably) large inflows of foreign money and attention will have a positive impact on recipients, at least while the flows continue. Still, a broadly based approach along these lines within an "experimental" framework could have considerable appeal.

Designing Programs to End Pockets of Poverty

The Millennium Villages Project has one important flaw: the design provides no means of confidently assessing success down the line. The project could have been modeled on a drug trial, with villages randomly selected for support and the outcomes of those villages compared with circumstances in nonselected villages in a prespecified analysis plan. Such rigorous analysis would be an extremely valuable tool in determining how well the project works and how to improve its outcomes. By combining the best aspects of medical trial design discussed earlier in the chapter with creative techniques for secondary analysis, one could learn a lot about how best to reduce poverty in rural African villages.[58]

We are currently moving along this path through Effective Intervention (www.effint.org/), a U.K.-based charity, and its large trials aimed at improving health and education in extremely poor regions. To this end, we have partnered with medical statisticians at the London School of Hygiene and Tropical Medicine along with local health professionals to design and implement projects to reduce child mortality in rural regions of Africa and India. Although these are aid projects, they are designed as randomized controlled trials identical to a drug approval trial and are testing whether a comprehensive package of interventions, including intensive provision of community health education and contracted-out clinical services, will be sufficient to rapidly reduce child deaths.[59] The trials are being implemented in 600 villages and cover a total population of 500,000. It will take three years to accumulate sufficient events (child deaths) to credibly determine the impact on overall child mortality for each trial. At the end of each trial, we expect to learn whether the system we have put in place is truly capable of rapidly reducing deaths within three years and its costs.

Population/). But relatively little is yet known about how to make this effective in pockets of poverty, other than by improving female education. Proposing a different approach, Lant Pritchett (2006) would let labor move more freely across borders. International migration would then remove the fixed (local) factors of production problem. But it remains to be seen if this is politically feasible.

57. See www.unmillenniumproject.org/, and associated press coverage.

58. On secondary analysis, see Miguel and Kremer (2004).

59. The details of the study protocol are described in Boone and others (2007).

We have also begun planning a project that will combine improved child survival with education in pockets of poverty. One objective of the trial will be to determine the percentage of children at age ten who are literate and numerate at a level consistent with middle-income countries, and then to track these children and compare them with controls for at least ten years after the trial. This procedure should indicate whether children in remote impoverished regions who become literate and numerate by age ten gain benefits from this additional education. We also expect to learn how to implement such projects and what can be achieved in these communities at modest cost.

Our ultimate aim is to build a rigorously evaluated and validated package of measures that can help lift current and future generations of children out of pockets of poverty. However, much more knowledge is needed to judge how to achieve this.

Conclusion

Enough evidence is now available to indicate that it is possible to rapidly reduce child deaths in pockets of poverty. Success will depend on whether an appropriate package of measures is designed and can be sustainably delivered to children and pregnant mothers who need them. This is both a feasible and compelling objective, quite aside from any economic considerations.

A dramatic improvement in health conditions has the potential to reduce poverty. But it may also lower per capita income by raising total births or fertility, or both, particularly if fixed factors of production prompt additional population to create negative "crowding" effects. Although investments in human capital can help reduce poverty, education and health improvements alone are not sufficient to eradicate it.

Despite the close links between health, education, and poverty established in surveys, a much broader package of measures is needed to eliminate pockets of poverty. What could be achieved on this "grander" scale remains to be determined. The standard approach of medical research, which is to test single interventions in trials, may not be ideal here. Rather, *packages of measures* should be tested, preferably in randomized controlled trials with clearly defined endpoints and prespecified goals. Such tests would provide much stronger evidence regarding what works and what can be achieved.

References

Acemoglu, Daron, Leopoldo Fergusson, and Simon Johnson. 2008. "Population and Social Conflict." Manuscript under preparation, MIT, Department of Economics.

Acemoglu, Daron, and Simon Johnson. 2007. "Disease and Development: The Effect of Life Expectancy on Economic Growth." *Journal of Political Economy* 115 (December): 925–85.

Altman, Douglas G., Kenneth F. Schulz, and others. 2001. "The Revised CONSORT State-ment for Reporting Randomized Trials: Explanation and Elaboration." *Annals of Internal Medicine* 134 (April): 663–94.

Arole, Mabelle, and Raj Arole. 1994. *Jamkhed: A Comprehensive Rural Health Project.* London: Macmillan Education.

Ashraf, Quamrul, Ashley Lester, and David Weil. 2008. "When Does Improving Health Raise GDP?" Paper prepared for Twenty-Third Annual Conference on Macroeconomics. National Bureau of Economic Research (www.nber.org/~confer/2008/Macro08/weil.pdf).

Bartels, Andreas, and Semir Zeki. 2004. "The Neural Correlates of Maternal and Romantic Love." *NeuroImage* 21, no. 3: 1155–66.

Bates, Robert. 1981. *Markets and States in Tropical Africa.* University of California Press.

Becker, Gary S., Tomas Philipson, and Rodrigo Soares. 2005. "The Quantity and Quality of Life and the Evolution of World Inequality." *American Economic Review* 95 (March): 277–91.

Behrman, Jere R., and Mark R. Rosenzweig. 2004. "The Returns to Birthweight." *Review of Economics and Statistics* 86 (May): 586–601.

Berg, Andy, Jonathan D. Ostry, and Jeromin Zettelmeyer. 2008. "What Makes Growth Sus-tained?" Working Paper WP/08/59. Washington: International Monetary Fund (March).

Bleakley, Hoyt. 2003. "Disease and Development: Evidence from the American South." *Jour-nal of the European Economic Association* 1 (April–May): 376–86

———. 2007. "Disease and Development: Evidence from Hookworm Eradication in the American South." *Quarterly Journal of Economics* 122 (February): 73–117.

Bloom, David E., and David Canning. 2005. "Health and Economic Growth: Reconciling the Micro and Macro Evidence." Working Paper 42. Stanford Institute on International Stud-ies, Center on Democracy, Development, and the Rule of Law (February).

Bloom, David E., and Jeffrey D. Sachs. 1998. "Geography, Demography, and Economic Growth in Africa." *Brookings Papers on Economic Activity,* vol. 2, pp. 207–95.

Boone, Peter, and Zhaoguo Zhan. 2006. "Lowering Child Mortality in Poor Countries, The Power of Knowledgeable Parents." Discussion Paper 751. London School of Economics, Centre for Economic Performance.

Boone, Peter, and others. 2007. "Community Health and Medical Provision: Impact on Neonates (the CHAMPION Trial)." *BMC Pediatrics* 7 (July) (http://www.biomedcentral.com/1471-2431/7/26).

Bryce, Jennifer, Shams el Arifeen, and others. 2003. "Reducing Child Mortality: Can Public Health Deliver?" *Lancet* 362, no. 9378: 159–64.

Bryce, Jennifer, R. E. Black, and others. 2005. "Can the World Afford to Save the Lives of 6 Million Children Each Year?" *Lancet* 365, no. 9478: 2193–200.

Bustreo, Flavia, April Harding, and others. 2003. "Can Developing Countries Achieve Ade-quate Improvements in Child Health Outcomes without Engaging the Private Sector?" *Bul-letin of the World Health Organization* 81, no. 12: 886–94.

Case, Anne, and Christina Paxson. 2008. "Stature and Status: Height, Ability and Labor Mar-ket Outcomes." *Journal of Political Economy* 116, no. 3: 499–532.

Chen, Shaohua, and Martin Ravallion. 2007. "Absolute Poverty Measures for the Developing World, 1981–2004." Policy Research Working Paper WPS 4211. Washington: World Bank (June).

Clasen, Thomas, and others. 2007. "Interventions to Improve Water Quality for Preventing Diarrhoea: Systematic Review and Meta-Analysis." *British Medical Journal* 334 (April 14): 782.

Cohen, Jessica, and Pascaline Dupas. 2007. "Free Distribution or Cost-Sharing? Evidence from a Randomized Malaria Prevention Experiment." Global Economy and Development Working Paper 11. Brookings (December).

Collier, Paul, and others. 2003. *Breaking the Conflict Trap: Civil War and Development Policy.* Oxford University Press.

Curtis, Valerie, and Sandy Cairncross. 2003. "Effect of Washing Hands with Soap on Diarrhoea Risk in the Community: A Systematic Review." *Lancet Infectious Diseases* 3, no. 5: 275–81.

Cutler, David, and Grant Miller. 2005. "The Role of Public Health Improvements in Health Advances: The Twentieth-Century United States." *Demography* 42, no. 1: 1–22.

Danzon, Patricia, Sean Nicholson, and Nuno Sousa Pereira. 2005. "Productivity in Pharmaceutical-Biotechnology R&D: The Role of Experience and Alliances." *Journal of Health Economics* 24 (March): 317–39.

Darmstadt, G. L., Z. A. Bhutta, and others. 2005. "Evidence-Based, Cost-Effective Interventions: How Many Newborn Babies Can We Save?" *Lancet* 365, no. 9463: 977–88.

Deaton, Angus. 2004. "Health in an Age of Globalization." In *Brookings Trade Forum*, edited by Susan Collins and Carol Graham. Brookings.

Easterly, William. 2001. *The Elusive Quest for Growth.* MIT Press.

Farmer, Paul. 2004. *Pathologies of Power: Health, Human Rights, and the New War on the Poor.* University of California Press.

International Monetary Fund. 2007a. "Globalization and Inequality." In *World Economic Outlook* (October), chap. 4 (www.imf.org/external/pubs/ft/weo/2007/02/index.htm).

———. 2007b. "The Globalization of Labor." In *World Economic Outlook* (April), chap. 5 (www.imf.org/external/pubs/ft/weo/2007/01/index.htm).

———. 2008. "Globalization, Commodity Prices, and Developing Countries." In *World Economic Outlook,* chap. 5 (April) (www.imf.org/external/pubs/ft/weo/2008/01/index.htm).

Johnson, Simon, Jonathan Ostry, and Arvind Subramanian. 2007. "The Prospects for Sustained Growth in Africa: Benchmarking the Constraints." Working Paper 13120. Cambridge, Mass.: National Bureau of Economic Research (May).

Keiser, Jennifer, Burt H. Singer, and others. 2005. "Reducing the Burden of Malaria in Different Eco-Epidemiological Settings with Environmental Management: A Systematic Review." *Lancet Infectious Diseases* 5, no. 11: 695–708.

Lipton, Michael. 1977. *Why Poor People Stay Poor: A Study of Urban Bias in World Development.* London: Temple Smith.

Loevinsohn, Benjamin, and April Harding. 2005. "Buying Results? Contracting for Health Service Delivery in Developing Countries." *Lancet* 366, no. 9486: 676–81.

Lorentzon, Peter, John McMillan, and Romain Wacziarg. 2008. "Death and Development." *Journal of Economic Growth* 13 (June): 81–124.

Luby, Stephen P., Mubina Agboatwalla, and others. 2004. "Effect of Intensive Handwashing Promotion on Childhood Diarrhea in High-Risk Communities in Pakistan: A Randomized Controlled Trial." *Journal of the American Medical Association* 291, no. 21: 2547–54.

———. 2005. "Effect of Handwashing on Child Health: A Randomised Controlled Trial." *Lancet* 366, no. 9481: 225–33.

Manandhar, D. S., and others. 2004. "Effect of a Participatory Intervention with Women's Groups on Birth Outcomes in Nepal: Cluster-Randomised Controlled Trial." *Lancet* 364 (September 11–17): 970–79.

Manesh, A. O., and others. 2008. "Accuracy of Child Morbidity Data in Demographic and Health Surveys." *International Journal of Epidemiology* 37 (February): 194–200.

Miguel, Edward, and Michael Kremer. 2004. "Worms: Identifying Impacts on Education and Health in the Presence of Treatment Externalities." *Econometrica* 72 (January): 159–217.

Mutabingwa, Theonest, and others. 2005. "Amodiaquine Alone, Amodiaquine + Sulfadoxine-Pyrimethamine, Amodiaquine + Artesunate, and Artemether-Lumefantrine for Outpatient Treatment of Malaria in Tanzanian Children: A Four-Arm Randomised Effectiveness Trial." *Lancet* 365, no. 9469: 1474–80.

Poole, William. 1970. "Optimal Choice of Monetary Policy Instruments in a Simple Stochastic Macro Model." *Quarterly Journal of Economics* 84 (May): 197–216.

Pratham Resource Center. 2007. *ASER: Annual Status of Education Report*. New Delhi (www.pratham.org).

Pritchett, Lant. 2006. *Let Their People Come: Breaking the Policy Gridlock on International Labor Migration*. Brookings.

Ravallion, Martin. 2005. "Inequality *Is* Bad for the Poor." Policy Research Working Paper 3677. Washington: World Bank (August).

Rosenstein-Rodan, P. N. 1961. "International Aid for Underdeveloped Countries." *Review of Economics and Statistics* 43 (February): 107–38.

Sachs, Jeffrey D. 2005. *The End of Poverty: Economic Possibilities for Our Time*. Penguin Press.

Sathe, Dhanmanjiri. 2005. "Interventions and Learning Abilities: 'Read India' Project in Maharastra." *Economic and Political Weekly* 1 (January 8).

Schultz, T. Paul. 2002. "Wage Gains Associated with Height as a Form of Health Human Capital." *American Economic Review* 92 (May): 349–53.

Shorter, Edward. 2006. "Primary Care." In *The Cambridge History of Medicine*, edited by Roy Porter, chap. 4. Cambridge University Press.

Soares, Rodrigo. 2007. "Health and the Evolution of Welfare across Brazilian Municipalities." *Journal of Development Economics* 84 (November): 590–608.

Spence, Michael, and others. 2008. *The Growth Report: Strategies for Sustained Growth and Inclusive Development*. Washington: World Bank, Commission on Growth and Development (www.growthcommission.org/index.php?option=com_content&task=view&id=96&Itemid=169).

Strauss, John, and Duncan Thomas. 1998. "Health, Nutrition, and Economic Development." *Journal of Economic Literature* 36 (June): 766–817.

Uwaezuoke, S. N., I. J. Emodi, and B. C. Ibe. 2002. "Maternal Perception of Pneumonia in Children: A Health Facility Survey in Enugu, Eastern Nigeria." *Annals of Tropical Paediatrics: International Child Health* 22 (September): 281–85.

Weil, David N. 2007. "Accounting for the Effect of Health on Growth." *Quarterly Journal of Economics* 122 (August): 1265–1306.

World Bank. 2008a. "Achieving Better Results in Human Development." In *Global Monitoring Report 2008: MDG's and the Environment*, chap. 2. Washington.

———. 2008b. Understanding and Measuring Poverty. PovertyNet (http://web.worldbank.org/WBSITE/EXTERNAL/TOPICS/EXTPOVERTY/0,,contentMDK:20153855~menuPK:373757~pagePK:148956~piPK:216618~theSitePK:336992,00.html#measuring [May 23, 2008]).

World Health Organization, Commission on Macroeconomics and Health. 2001. *Macroeconomics and Health: Investing in Health for Economic Development* (www.who.int/macrohealth/en/).

———. Division of Child Health and Development. 2006. *Integrated Management of Childhood Illness Chart Booklet*. New York.

COMMENT BY ANNE CASE

It would be hard to exaggerate the importance of early-life health. Reducing child mortality improves the health of children at very young ages, which improves both their physical and cognitive development. These benefits spill over to educational attainment, and all subsequently cascade into labor market opportunities, marriage prospects, fertility, and then the health of the next generation. So the health channel is important to improving life chances and reducing the intergenerational transmission of poverty. It is also a channel in which real progress is possible.

For Peter Boone and Simon Johnson, the critical question is what is going to be necessary to establish robust, sustainable delivery mechanisms for health services in a world with pockets of poverty. There is a good deal to comment on in their discussion, but I want to draw attention to three threads of their argument.

The first thread—which gives rise to their clever title, "Out of the Pocket"—pertains to a *change in the map of poverty*: "It is reasonable to expect that countries previously known as 'poor' will be host to regions of high income . . . as well as to other, smaller pockets of extreme poverty." That is an interesting idea, and if true is it really something new? Some of the mechanisms that give rise to pockets of poverty have probably been in place for a very long time. Migration patterns, for example, have caused some places to thrive for centuries and other areas to be left behind. Oppression by a dominant group might be another long-lasting channel of poverty in some areas. Also, are these pockets necessarily *smaller* than the regions of higher income?

On closer examination, one wonders whether the focus on pockets in this chapter was perhaps misplaced. I do not see anything in the discussion that depends on there being pockets of poverty within a country, rather than just poverty. High child mortality and low rates of literacy would seemingly be enough. If the "pockets" are important to the authors' story, then they should say more about why that is the case—why a pocket is something important to keep an eye on.

A second thread of the argument is that, of all the reasons that pockets of poverty might exist, it is neglect rather than a "sinister conspiracy of oppression" that prevents relatively isolated people from having access to decent health care or education. And here comes the punch line: "As a result, it is possible for outsiders to offer such services without fomenting adverse political reaction or some other means of oppression," which I take to mean that aid in the form of health care service delivery will be well received.

There are many reasons to wonder whether that is going to be the case. A "sinister conspiracy of oppression" is only one reason that outside intervention may not be effective. The evidence for the effectiveness of aid, even with an optimist's eyes, is mixed at best and requires considerably more discussion.

The third thread has to do with public versus private delivery of service. Boone and Johnson could have gone into the relative merits of the two channels in greater depth, in order to buttress comments such as "the public sector today provides inadequate services, suffers from corruption, and better serves wealthier political elites than the poor." That reminds me of a story of two old ladies waiting in line for a bus just after transportation had been privatized in Britain. After waiting and waiting and waiting, one of the old ladies turns to the other and says, "Well, what do you expect? It's the private sector."

The authors use postneonatal child mortality rates against the share of the private sector (see figure 3-5) to make the case that there are multiple routes to low child death. However, their case seems weak without information on (among other things) the size of the health care sector in relation to the population it is trying to serve.

A growing body of evidence suggests that where the public sector does poorly in providing health care, the private sector does poorly as well. More "qualitative-quantitative data" would aid in assessing these channels. Some information along these lines has already been gathered by Jishnu Das and Jeff Hammer in their study of what providers *know*, to try to better understand competence, and what providers *do,* to evaluate their practice.[1]

Das and Hammer's team visited 300 families in seven neighborhoods of Delhi every week for eighteen months, collecting an anthropological-economic mix of information on health problems and treatment choices, together with a complete list of health care providers visited by any members of those families. It also took a census of all health care providers within fifteen minutes of the neighborhood and from these two lists drew a stratified sample of more than 200 public and private providers to interview. It gave all of the public and private health care providers in the sample vignettes to see what they actually knew. Then the team sat and watched what these health care providers actually did.

The team found systematic differences in private and public health care delivery. Public doctors were more often guilty of what Das and Hammer call "errors of omission," in exerting less energy. They know what they are supposed to do but

1. Das and Hammer (2004a, 2004b).

do not do it. And the private doctors? They were more often guilty of "errors of commission." They know what the mother wants and give it to her because otherwise "she'll go to the doctor next door." From this study at least, it seems that in those places where the public services cannot be provided well, private services often cannot be relied upon to step in and get things right.

A big question for me in health care delivery is whether there is a way around this catch-22: that if the public sector cannot provide it effectively, it cannot provide the oversight necessary for the private sector to deliver it well. Qualitative-quantitative data of the sort collected by Das and Hammer are essential to understanding what works and why it works—and if it does not work, why not.

Although Boone and Johnson are optimistic that more testing and experimentation with packages will uncover the best routes to eliminating pockets of poverty, I am a little less sanguine. These pockets, if they do exist, probably exist for a whole host of reasons that vary greatly in different places and thus make it necessary to examine these cases one at a time. Place-specific qualitative-quantitative research may therefore be a more effective research tool, or at least a tool that needs to be included in the mix.

References

Das, Jishnu, and Jeff Hammer. 2004a. "Strained Mercy: The Quality of Medical Care in Delhi." Policy Research Working Paper 3228. Washington: World Bank.
———. 2004b. "Which Doctor? Combining Vignettes and Item Response to Measure Clinical Competence." Policy Research Working Paper 3301. Washington: World Bank.

Comment by Jessica Cohen

Peter Boone and Simon Johnson make two important points about improving the value and relevance of randomized trials in child health. Although they focus specifically on child survival, these issues apply to the design of randomized evaluations in health more generally. First, they see a need, especially in the social sciences, for more randomized evaluations that have mortality as an outcome. Second, they feel randomized evaluations should focus on packages of interventions rather than on single interventions such as deworming and bed net distribution.

The first question is, should randomized evaluations have broader outcome measures? Most economists would agree that it would be useful to measure as many outcomes as possible, but there are trade-offs. If a field trial is to evaluate a program designed by a nongovernmental organization (NGO), it probably makes sense to focus on a narrower goal like hand-washing or bed-net use. Since such a program typically targets a specific outcome, information on how successfully the program achieves that objective will be most useful to the program implementers and most valuable to its beneficiaries. This does not mean that the evaluation needs to be narrow in scope—whether or not the program is successful usually depends on complex behavioral responses, selection effects, and so on—but it does mean that one cannot know whether this NGO program that focuses on hand-washing, for example, is ultimately reducing child mortality.

Economists have traditionally cared about "welfare," but this loose concept is impossible to measure in a randomized trial. Nonetheless, measuring outcomes such as mortality and income might bring these studies closer to welfare than bed-net usage and hand-washing. One appealing aspect of randomized trials with broader outcome measures is that they may feed more readily into macrodevelopment studies. Focusing on a common outcome measure such as mortality would also make it easier for development practitioners to compare the effectiveness of different health interventions.

Despite the obvious appeal of capturing the impact of a health intervention on mortality, there are two important reasons why it is typically left out in randomized evaluations. The first, of course, is that to measure mortality the researcher needs a huge sample size. Since the number of observations is one of the biggest determinants of cost in a randomized evaluation, being able to measure mortal-ity probably means cutting back on other things.

One possibility is to disregard intermediate outcomes and focus only on mor-tality. For example, one could implement a wide-scale intervention—such as bed-net distribution to 100,000 households—and collect only mortality estimates, bypassing intermediate outcomes such as illness episodes, health care spending, and so on. Another possibility is to design programs with more breadth, which tackle mortality through multiple interventions. So, in addition to distributing bed nets, one could design a broader child survival program that included vacci-nations, oral rehydration therapy, and subsidies for antimalarials and pneumonia treatment, for instance. Since the expected mortality impact is greater with a pro-gram such as this, the sample size requirements to measure mortality would be less prohibitive. Either way, measuring mortality will be expensive.

Another reason mortality has rarely been measured up to now is that there is considerable existing research on the link between the use of a health tool and mortality. Bed nets are again a good example. The impact of bed nets on child mortality is extremely well established through medical and epidemiological tri-als, and many policies and programs seek to increase bed-net uptake and usage (for example, through subsidies, social marketing, and supply chain manage-ment). Should randomized trials evaluating these programs measure primarily mortality instead of just "intermediate outcomes" like uptake and usage? On the one hand, as mentioned earlier, if all evaluations measure the impact of the par-ticular policy on mortality, it will be much simpler for governments and donors to decide which approach is best. On the other hand, if a fixed budget requires trade-offs and there are already good estimates of the impact of the health tool on mortality, why not focus on measuring the less-understood relationships between the policy and intermediate outcomes?

There are at least two reasons why stopping at intermediate outcomes and then imputing the mortality impact of the policy might not quite make it. One is that the policy may have some important unmeasured selection effect on the relation-ship between the health tool and mortality. In joint work with Pascaline Dupas, I find that demand for bed nets among pregnant women is highly sensitive to price, but that usage rates are basically flat across prices. Since the number of preg-nant women sleeping under a net is highest when bed nets are free, it can be assumed that the mortality impact of a 100 percent subsidy policy would be larger than that of partial subsidization. However, we also find that pregnant women who receive free bed nets are somewhat healthier in terms of measured anemia (an indicator of vulnerability and exposure to malaria) than women who pay small user fees. The demand effect still far outweighs this selection effect, with the most anemic women receiving a net when it is free, but there could be many other unmeasured selection effects influencing the relationship between bed-net use and mortality. The epidemiologists who measured the mortality impact of bed-net use did not estimate how this impact varies with the characteristics of the user. If heterogeneous treatment effects are important, then one cannot infer the mortality impact of an intervention on the basis of intermediate outcomes only.

A second reason to measure mortality or other broad outcomes rather than just intermediate ones is behavioral spillover effects. A subsidy policy that encourages bed-net use or water purification could cause people to slack on other methods to avoid mosquitoes or to stop washing their hands. So if heterogeneous treatment effects and behavioral spillovers are considered important for a particular health program, Boone and Johnson's advice to include mortality as an outcome measure seems warranted.

While including broad outcome measures in more randomized trials could perhaps facilitate better comparisons across evaluations and help to unify micro and macro approaches to development, it would likely put even more strain on external validity claims. Since measuring mortality is expensive, it will most likely be done at the expense of a more detailed analysis of intermediate outcomes, but less will be known about each of the links in the chain from policy to mortality, and thus less can be said about replicability. It is arguably easier to judge the cross-country replicability of price sensitivity to bed nets than the reduced-form effect of bed-net prices on mortality.

As for Boone and Johnson's second major point, about the need for a more comprehensive approach to child survival, they would like to see randomized evaluations focus on packages of interventions rather than just on attacking child malaria, say, or teaching mothers about the importance of breastfeeding. Again, this will require bigger budgets for randomized trials, not to mention a shift in development finance away from prioritizing vertical programs. The drawbacks of such programs are becoming evident. For example, "home management of malaria" programs, based on the necessity for prompt treatment of children under the age of five, emphasize presumptive treatment of fever with antimalarials by mothers and community medicine distributors. While some of these programs have had great success, there is increasing evidence that fever alone is a poor predictor of malaria infection and that many of these children may be suffering from some other type of illness, principally pneumonia and other respiratory infections. Antimalaria programs that emphasize presumptive treatment of fever with antimalarials could in many cases be delaying proper treatment. Interventions such as the community health worker programs that Boone and Johnson are conducting, which emphasize comprehensive approaches to child survival including improved diagnostics, are a priority for increasing the effectiveness of foreign aid for child health.

Most of the intervention packages discussed in chapter 3 are demand-side packages. Equally important for child survival are packages that address the demand and supply side of such issues simultaneously. This is challenging for randomized trials since researchers often have to carefully control supply in order to analyze demand, and vice versa. However, an evaluation that bundles incentives for some sort of desirable behavior—like prompt antimalarial treatment—with incentives to clinics and pharmacies to have the drugs stocked, have regular hours, not overprescribe, and so on, would be immensely useful to policymakers trying to understand how to operationalize the recommendations coming from these evaluations. When randomized trials look at ways to encourage bed-net or water-purification use but control the supply of such products perfectly, governments and NGOs interested in bringing the intervention to scale are often uninformed and uncertain about how to make the program happen from the supply side. This is a particular problem for the community health worker (CHW) programs that Boone and Johnson discuss. Training CHWs to treat common childhood illness and educate mothers about preventive health behaviors is a promising approach to child survival, but evaluations of these types of programs generally control the supply of drugs completely. An unstable drug supply is a common impediment to successful CHW programs, which have been attempted for decades. To a government facing a dysfunctional supply chain, adding treatment variation in supplier incentives to the experimental design could facilitate the implementation of such programs at scale.

Boone and Johnson stress that one benefit of evaluating packages of interventions is that various health tools could be substitutable or complementary, a major element of cost-effectiveness that would be missed with analyses of single interventions. The potential substitutes they cite are bed nets to prevent malaria and artemisinin combination therapies (ACTs) to treat it. One could extend this argument to packages combining supply- and demand-side interventions as well, say, in maternal mortality programs. It is still fairly uncommon in Africa for women to give birth in a health facility, even though maternal mortality rates remain high (they exceed half a million a year in sub-Saharan Africa) and the great majority of complications in delivery can be handled by nurses or even less-trained birth attendants at a clinic. While a package of demand-side interventions encouraging delivery at a health facility is sensible, this is a case in which simultaneous demand and supply interventions could be highly effective. Since poor-quality care, drug stockouts, and overall miserable environments lead most women to prefer delivering at home, one could imagine that demand-side programs such as vouchers for clinic costs and supply-side programs such as improving clinic quality are substitutable to some extent.

To conclude, chapter 3 offers many good ideas about how to use randomized evaluations and other qualitative methods to decrease child mortality. Broadening outcome measures and exploring intervention packages could increase the impact of randomized evaluations. But both of these steps will require much bigger budgets for randomized trials, which means that donors, development agencies, and governments will first need to be convinced of the value of expanding the scope of evaluations.

4

Pricing and Access: Lessons from Randomized Evaluations in Education and Health

MICHAEL KREMER AND ALAKA HOLLA

O ver the past ten to fifteen years, randomized evaluations have gone from being a rarity to a standard part of the toolkit of academic development economics. Research is now at a point where, at least for some issues, it is possible to stand back and look beyond the results of a single evaluation to see whether certain common lessons emerge and what the implications may be for models of human capital investment.

In this chapter, we review the evidence from randomized evaluations on one issue that has been the subject of extensive and often contentious policy debate: the impact of pricing on take-up of education and health services and products.[1] The idea that development projects should aim at financial sustainability has become the driving force behind much development thinking and practice. According to advocates of charging, the poor can (and do) pay at least some fee for important services and products, such fees are vital to sustainability and to motivating providers, charging may screen out those who place low value on the product or service (thus concentrating take-up on those who value it most), and there is a psychological effect known as the sunk-cost fallacy, whereby paying a

We thank Rachel Glennerster, Paul Romer, David Weil, and participants in the Brookings conference "What Works in Development: Thinking Big and Thinking Small" for many useful comments and suggestions.

1. See Easterly (2006); and Christopher Shea, "A Handout, Not a Hand Up," *Boston Globe*, November 11, 2007.

higher price can make someone feel committed to a product and thus use it more.[2] Population Services International (PSI), a leading social marketing non-profit organization with activities in more than sixty countries, has argued that "when products are given away free, the recipient often does not value them or even use them."[3] Hence its approach to condom, mosquito net, and water disinfectant promotion relies primarily on charging rather than free distribution. For many aid organizations, charging at least something is a matter of principle.

Yet the idea of charging for education and health products and services in developing countries has come under great criticism as well.[4] The World Bank has started shifting away from this position under pressure from activists, and the World Health Organization (WHO) recently, and controversially, endorsed free distribution of mosquito nets.[5] PSI is also shifting to free distribution of mosquito nets for pregnant women in Kenya.

In chapter 2, Dani Rodrik argues that it is hard to derive general lessons from randomized evaluations, illustrating his case with a discussion of a randomized evaluation of the impact of pricing on access to mosquito nets in Kenya.[6] That study found that charging for mosquito nets at antenatal clinics greatly reduced take-up, did not serve to target those most in need, and did not induce greater use. Rodrik concludes that one cannot generalize too much from these results because they are likely to be context dependent.

Of course, any attempt to generalize from randomized evaluations or indeed from any particular piece of evidence requires an underlying theory of what is likely to be important and what is not. Take the case of the PROGRESA program in Mexico, which provided cash transfers conditional on children's school attendance. Randomized evaluations show the transfers increased school enrollment. Was this effect dependent on there being less than universal enrollment to begin with? Presumably yes. Was the impact of the program dependent on the local currency's being called the peso? Presumably not.

If our theories are not very good and the impact of treatment depends on context in a way that is complicated, subtle, and difficult to predict, results from one setting are unlikely to generalize in other settings that may look similar to reasonable people. If indeed it is so difficult to generalize, then this raises questions not simply about randomized evaluations but more generally about the extent to

2. On the screening-out, see Oster (1995); on the psychological effect, see Thaler (1980).

3. PSI (2006).

4. Morduch (1999) argues that the pursuit of sustainability by microfinance organizations has led them to move away from serving the poor. Meuwissen (2002) argues that a health cost-recovery program in Niger led to unexpectedly large drops in health care utilization.

5. Sachs (2005); WHO, "WHO Releases New Guidance on Insecticide-Treted Mosquito Nets," news release, August 16, 2007; "Science at WHO and UNICEF: The Corrosion of Trust," *Lancet* Editorial, vol. 370 (2007), p. 1007.

6. Cohen and Dupas (2007).

which one can learn from social science. For example, if treatment effects vary across countries, then cross-country estimates of the impact of different policies or institutions will typically yield biased estimates.[7]

On the other hand, if our theories about the world are sufficiently accurate, then randomized evaluations would not be necessary. If one could be confident that decisions on school attendance were made to maximize lifetime income, for example, and that the correlation between wages and level of education reflected the causal impact of education on earnings (rather than confounding this with a selection effect in which richer, higher-ability, or more hard-working children stay at school longer and have higher earnings), then it would be possible to build a general model that could simulate the impact of arbitrary changes in school fees on education decisions, wages, and welfare. Or if one were confident that households, schools, and clinics were distributed randomly and knew how much people valued their time, one could estimate a travel-cost model based on differences in take-up of education and health services in relation to distance from schools and clinics and could use the model to predict how changes in price would affect access.

Current evidence on how price affects take-up suggests that an intermediate position is warranted, at least in this case. A range of studies on price and take-up of health and education services—including Mexico's experience with PRO-GRESA, early randomized evaluations in Kenya, and recent studies in Zambia—find remarkably similar results in very different contexts. Imposing even small costs consistently leads to dramatic reductions in take-up, both for well-known technologies like mosquito nets and for less familiar technologies like deworming medication. However, the standard model of human capital investment may need to be expanded to incorporate time-inconsistent preferences and peer effects if it is to fit the data. The evidence from randomized evaluations may help point the way toward better modeling of human behavior in these areas, but it seems unlikely that existing models fit well enough to put a high degree of faith in the results of structural estimation of simple models of human capital investment.

Before turning to our review of the evidence, we should note that the relationship between prices and welfare depends not only on the relationship between prices and take-up but also on the relationship between take-up and welfare and on how prices affect the supply side of service delivery. First, there are positive externalities from some products, such as mosquito nets and deworming medication. Second, credit constraints may cause human capital investment to be suboptimal. Third, time-consistency problems may cause underinvestment. Fourth, for new technologies there may be information externalities. Finally, many of the investments are on behalf of children, and there may be a divergence between

7. See Pande and Udry (2005).

investment levels preferred by parents and those that society prefers. Finally, as further discussed in the conclusion, charging for health and education may also affect provider incentives, and one could imagine a case for charging on these grounds, but that is beyond the scope of this discussion.

User Fees

To examine the impact of price on take-up in health and education, we search the current evidence not only for the extent to which higher prices reduce take-up but also for any positive impact of higher prices, as reflected in increases in take-up among those who most value or most need the product. In addition, we look for signs of whether prices induce a psychological commitment to use the product more due to a sunk-cost effect.

Deworming Drugs

Intestinal worms are among the most widespread health problems in the developing world, with 2 billion people infected and many suffering from anemia and listlessness as a result.[8] School-aged children are particularly at risk and a locus for spreading them. A randomized evaluation in rural Kenyan schools found that treating school-aged children for worms has strong externalities.[9] These externalities provide an economic rationale for subsidies. To avoid costly individual parasitological screening, the WHO recommends yearly treatment for all children in schools where more than half the children are believed to be infected with soil-transmitted helminths (roundworm, hookworm, and whipworm) or where more than 30 percent of children have schistosomiasis. This type of mass treatment program, however, is most cost-effective when take-up is high.

In the initial evaluation of the program, deworming reduced the baseline school absence rate of 30 percent by 7 percentage points (or one-quarter), a gain in attendance that reflects both the direct effect of deworming and any within-school externalities. Including the cross-school externalities, deworming increased schooling by 0.14 years per pupil treated. Overall, it proved to be among the most cost-effective ways to boost school enrollment, requiring only $3.50 per additional year of school participation.

The nongovernmental organization (NGO) administering this program, ICS-Africa, typically requires communities to contribute to the costs of its projects—as is common among development NGOs. Three years into the deworming program, it introduced cost sharing in a randomly chosen subset of schools. Parents were charged for the use of the deworming drugs, and as was often the case in Kenyan schools, fees were charged on a per family rather than a per child basis.

8. WHO (2005).
9. Miguel and Kremer (2004).

The average price charged per child was \$0.30, which amounted to roughly one-fifth of the per child cost of the program if it had been delivered to all children.[10]

When a school-based NGO deworming program in western Kenya introduced cost sharing, the take-up of deworming medication fell sharply and revenue failed to outpace administrative costs, despite the health and education benefits of the program.[11] User fees did not help target treatment to the sickest students. As deworming pills are delivered directly into children's mouths, there was no gap between take-up and usage, so pricing had no potential psychological impact on use through sunk costs.

After the introduction of cost sharing, the take-up rate in the cost-sharing schools was only 19 percent, compared with 75 percent in the free-treatment schools. There is no evidence that this dramatic difference resulted from the fact that people were initially receiving the medication for free and somehow anchored on the price of zero or felt a sense of entitlement since cost sharing triggered a similar decline in schools exposed to free treatment for different lengths of time.[12]

There is no evidence that charging a higher price helped target the drugs to those who most needed them. Students with helminth infections did not appear any more likely to pay for the drugs in the cost-sharing schools.

Although take-up was highly sensitive to having a positive price, there is less evidence that it was sensitive to variation within the positive price range. Since user fees were implemented in the form of a per family fee, the deworming price per child varied with the number of primary school children in a household. However, take-up was not sensitive to these variations in the exact (positive) price level.[13] Given the dramatic reduction in take-up at any positive price level, it may be particularly counterproductive to charge small positive prices for the treatment of infectious diseases.

As mentioned earlier, fees amounted to about 20 percent of program cost and raised little revenue over administrative costs. At the same time, charging for the medication sharply increased the administrative costs per pupil because the fixed costs of visiting the school to deliver drugs were amortized over many fewer pupils, so charging would allow only about a 5 percent increase in the number of children given a fixed budget.

In addition to sensitivity to any non-zero price, take-up of the deworming medicine also exhibited social network effects. The randomization of the program across schools created random variation in people's social links to treatment

---

10. The \$1.50 per child cost for this program was relatively high because it was delivered as a small-scale pilot program with an evaluation built in and NGO workers went to each school to provide the medication each time. The cost of a large-scale program is less than \$0.50 per child.

11. Kremer and Miguel (2007).

12. Kremer and Miguel (2007).

13. Kremer and Miguel (2007).

schools, conditional on their total number of social links.[14] Unlike what the non-experimental correlations in the data would have suggested, social networks depressed take-up: having more social links to parents of students in treatment schools reduced the probability that children took deworming medication by 3.1 percentage points and increased the likelihood that parents said that deworming drugs were "not effective" by 1.7 percentage points. These negative peer effects, combined with the sensitivity of take-up to any positive price, suggest that temporary subsidies intended to spur imitation are unlikely to lead to a sustainable increase in this kind of technology adoption and that ongoing subsidies might be necessary. This may be attributable to social learning about the technology, for in other settings in which technologies proved to be more attractive than people originally believed, such social learning would likely lead to positive spillovers in adoption.[15]

Mosquito Nets

Mosquito nets have long been used to combat malaria, a disease responsible for about a quarter of all young child deaths in Africa and for more than 1 million African deaths a year, according to WHO 2002 estimates. Pregnant women are particularly vulnerable since pregnancy reduces a woman's immunity to malaria. Maternal malaria can also have effects in utero since it increases the risk of spontaneous abortion, stillbirth, premature delivery, and low birth weight. Nets can create positive externalities by reducing transmission of disease. Insecticide-treated nets have a better record than untreated nets but until recently had to be re-treated frequently, and since many people failed to re-treat their nets, their usefulness was limited. Newer, long-lasting insecticide-treated nets, however, do not have this problem.

Nonetheless, a study in rural Kenya found that charging even a small fraction of the full cost of nets dramatically reduces take-up, and that charging has no positive effect on the probability that a net is hung in the home, either through a screening mechanism or through a psychological impact.[16] Another study in rural Uganda indicates free nets are as likely to be used as those that are paid for, and free ones are more likely to be used by those who need them most—children under five.[17]

In western Kenya, net usage was quite low in 2003 despite the preventive benefits of nets. The 2003 Demographic Health Survey estimated that 19.8 percent of households had at least one mosquito net, only 6.7 percent had an insecticide-treated net, and only 4.8 percent of children under the age of five and 3 percent

14. Kremer and Miguel (2007).
15. See Kremer and Miguel (2007).
16. Cohen and Dupas (2007).
17. Hoffman (2008).

of pregnant women slept under an insecticide-treated net.[18] PSI distributed nets in Kenya for a price that corresponded to an 87.5 percent subsidy. However, it did not go to entirely free distribution.

Since children and pregnant women are most vulnerable to malaria, antenatal clinics are a logical place to distribute nets. Researchers in Kenya incorporated a two-stage randomization design to separate out the two potential routes through which pricing can affect use.[19] In the first stage, patients in antenatal clinics were offered a menu of subsidized prices for insecticide-treated nets. Women who agreed to this price then received a randomly chosen discount, generating random variation in both the initial price of the net *and* the final transaction price. The initial randomization occurred at the level of the health clinic, so every woman going to a particular clinic faced the same initially offered price, whereas discounts were randomly chosen from an envelope once a patient agreed to purchase a net. With this design, the effect of the initial price indicates how prices can change the composition of buyers, and the effect of the final transaction price (the initial price minus the amount of the discount) indicates whether a higher price increases the likelihood that a given buyer will use the net.

In the clinics that offered free nets, take-up was 99 percent. By comparison, take-up in clinics that charged for the nets declined at an increasing rate as prices moved from Ksh 10 to Ksh 20 to Ksh 40 (or US$0.15 to $0.30 to $0.60) by 7.3, 17.2, and 60.5 percentage points, respectively, according clinic-based surveys conducted throughout the first six weeks of the program.[20] The linear estimates of the effect of price on take-up imply that take-up drops by 75 percent when the price of a net increases from zero to $0.75, the cost-sharing price at which insecticide-treated nets were sold to pregnant women in Kenya at the time of the intervention.[21] Although there was no discontinuity at a price of zero, since the highest price examined already represents a 90 percent subsidy relative to the cost of nets and take-up is very low at that level, it does appear that charging any substantial amount will radically cut take-up and that the revenues generated by any price that would induce a large fraction of mothers to take up the intervention might well be modest when compared with the administrative costs of charging for nets.

There was no evidence of screening or psychological sunk-cost effects in this study in western Kenya. The results are not consistent with the role that prices might play in targeting nets to individuals who need them the most: in terms of

18. Cohen and Dupas (2007).

19. Cohen and Dupas (2007).

20. Cohen and Dupas (2007).

21. This reduction in take-up drops to 55 percentage points, however, when Cohen and Dupas (2007) restrict their sample to women experiencing first pregnancies in order to avoid contaminating their results with another campaign that had distributed free insecticide-treated nets to families with children nine months before the intervention.

measured anemia, an important indicator of malaria, those who paid higher prices appeared no sicker than the prenatal clients in the comparison group. This could be due to credit constraints: the sickest women may be least able to pay. According to enumerators making house visits, women who received the free insecticide-treated nets were not less likely to have hung their net above a bed than those who paid positive subsidized prices.

A related field experiment in Uganda suggests that relative to free distribution, charging for a net changes the distribution of net usage within the household.[22] Participants in this intervention were randomly assigned to receive either cash or insecticide-treated nets with the opportunity to trade the nets for cash or the cash for nets, with the amount of cash being sufficient to purchase nets to cover every household member under current sleeping arrangements. They were also read a statement about malaria and the particular vulnerability of young children and pregnant women to the disease. Of those offered the nets for free with the opportunity to trade them for cash, 99 percent took home at least one net, and the average number of nets obtained per household member was 0.42; of those who were given cash with the opportunity to trade it for nets, 85 percent took home at least one net, and the average number of nets obtained per household member was only 0.33. Conditional on a household's buying at least one net, however, the average number of nets obtained per member was statistically the same in households with free nets and those with purchased ones.

As in Kenya, nighttime checks roughly three weeks later showed that usage was as high for free nets as for purchased ones. Households in both cases had statistically indistinguishable numbers of unused nets, as well as propensities to leave at least one net unused. In fact, conditional on the number of nets per household member, the probability that an individual household member was using a net was higher for households receiving free nets, although insignificantly so.

Who was using the net did vary with price. In households with free nets, the proportion of children younger than five sleeping under a net, conditional on the number of nets acquired, was 12.2 to 14.3 percentage points higher than in households offered cash, where 56 percent of children under the age of five were sleeping under a net.[23] For households with purchased nets, those most likely to use the nets were members perceived to experience at least one malaria episode a year, adults in this case, while young children were no more likely to be sleeping under a net than other household members. These results suggest separate mental accounts for free and purchased goods, which is consistent with a growing literature in behavioral economics and psychology that finds separate mental accounts linked to different needs and different sources of income.[24]

22. Hoffman (2008).
23. Hoffman (2008) instruments the number of nets acquired with treatment status.
24. Thaler (1990); Duflo and Udry (2004).

Water Disinfectant

Two-stage pricing randomization has also been used to test the two potential routes by which pricing could affect use in a door-to-door marketing campaign for water disinfectant on the outskirts of Lusaka, Zambia.[25] As with deworming and nets, pricing led to a rapid drop-off in take–up, with no evidence of increased targeting to the most vulnerable. Pricing had no statistically significant psychological effect on use. The authors of the study argue that there was some screening effect since those who were more willing to pay for the disinfectant were more likely to have chlorine in their water at later random checks than those who received it for free. But since usage was measured two to six weeks after the intervention, it is not clear that pricing screened out substantial numbers of people who would have *never* used the product. Moreover, as discussed next, unless people repeatedly, and over the long term, would accept a product they did not intend to use, any wastage from non-usage due to free distribution would be a small fraction of the amount distributed in the long run.

In the Lusaka experiment, water disinfectant was offered to households at a randomly chosen price. Households that agreed to this price then received a randomly chosen discount, generating random variation in both the initial price of the disinfectant and the final transaction price. Two follow-up surveys two and six weeks later measured use of the water disinfectant both from household self-reports and from tests of the chemical composition of water stored in the house.

The results showed a strong relationship between the initially offered price and the share of households that agreed to purchase the disinfectant at the initial offer price: a price increase of ZMK 100 ($0.03) triggered a 7 percentage point reduction in the probability of purchase, which corresponds to a price elasticity of nearly -0.6 when evaluated at the mean offer price and purchase probability.[26] When offered an initial price of ZMK 300 (ZMK 200 less than the prevailing price at health clinics and ZMK 500–700 less than at retail outlets), 80 percent of respondents purchased the disinfectant, whereas only 50 percent purchased it at ZMK 800.

There was no statistically significant evidence that the discounts altered the likelihood that a household used the disinfectant once it had already made its purchase decision. When the final transaction prices increased by ZMK 100, household reports of disinfectant usage increased, but only by a statistically insignificant 0.9 percentage point. More reliable specifications that use measured chlorination rather than self-reports show an insignificant negative effect of 0.7 percentage point.

25. Ashraf, Berry, and Shapiro (2007).
26. Ashraf and others (2007).

The Zambian study also looked for a discontinuity at zero in this sunk-cost effect, to see whether just the act of paying any non-zero price influences use. Here the authors found positive point estimates of 5.7 percentage points for self-reported use and 3.2 percentage points for measured chlorine, but again these estimates are not statistically significant.[27]

The initially offered price also did not help target the disinfectant to households that could benefit from it the most. Families with young children, who are more prone to water-borne diseases, or pregnant women were not more likely to purchase the disinfectant.

However, the authors argue that higher prices did screen out some buyers who were not planning to use the product.[28] For a given transaction price, a 10 percent increase in the initial offer price led to purchase by a set of buyers who were 3 to 4 percentage points more likely to be using the product two weeks later—in other words, raising the price somewhat disproportionately screened out those who would not have used the product within two weeks, although it also screened out many who would have used the product during that time. This result, however, should be interpreted with considerable caution and is subject to two concerns. First, households offered a product at a discount after a household visit may be more likely to purchase the product than under more realistic conditions. Second, chlorine disinfectant is a durable good. Since the follow-up surveys that measured disinfectant use occurred only two to six weeks after the marketing intervention, this cannot be considered evidence that the observed non-users would never use the disinfectant. Some of the households may have been saving the product for later use.

In our view, charging a 10 percent higher price would be unlikely to reduce non-use of the product by 3.6 percent on an ongoing basis: although some households might buy a single bottle of disinfectant, try it, and ultimately not use it, they are unlikely to indefinitely accumulate bottles of disinfectant they do not intend to use. Therefore the longer-term screening effect is likely to be much smaller than the short-run effect.

The most likely danger posed by ongoing programs of free distribution is not that people would accumulate large stocks of water disinfectant or mosquito nets that they do not plan to use, but rather that there would be diversion through secondary markets to alternative uses that were not efficient. For example, people

27. When they divide their sample into households that displayed a sunk-cost effect when responding to a hypothetical scenario posed to them by surveyors and those that did not, they find coefficients of much larger magnitude for the hypothetical-sunk-cost households, although these remain insignificant and cannot be statistically distinguished from the estimated effects for households that did not display this hypothetical-sunk-cost effect. Ashraf and others (2007) identify hypothetical-sunk-cost households from their answers to the following question posed during the follow-up survey: "Suppose you bought a bottle of juice for KMZ 1,000. When you start to drink it, you realize you don't really like the taste. Would you finish drinking it?"

28. Ashraf and others (2007).

might use the chlorine solution intended to disinfect water for washing clothes, or they might use mosquito nets for other purposes. The likelihood of this happening and the extent to which it could be controlled administratively (for example, by limiting the number of free units distributed per person) merit further investigation. It is worth noting, however, that evidence from Kenya showed no widespread diversion among households that had not hung up their nets three weeks after distribution, even though these nets had quite a high resale value (94 percent of non-users still had the nets in their houses).

School Uniforms

In many countries where primary school is meant to be free, the costs of attending are still substantial, with a large fraction taken up by school uniforms. Kenyan students, traditionally required to wear uniforms, now cannot officially be turned away for not doing so, but the social pressure in favor of uniforms continues to be strong. In 2002 a primary school uniform in Kenya cost nearly $6—a considerable expense in a country with an annual per capita GDP of $340.[29] Three studies of reductions in the cost of schooling through the provision of free uniforms in Kenya show a high responsiveness to price at different ages.

The first intervention targeted pupils in early primary school, where uniforms were distributed to students by lottery. Student presence was then recorded from multiple unannounced visits to each school. The students randomly chosen to receive a free uniform were 6 percentage points more likely to be attending school (from a base attendance rate of 82 percent) than students who did not receive a uniform through the lottery.[30] Students who did not own a uniform before the program were 13 percentage points more likely to be attending school, which represents a 64 percent decrease in absence.

A similar intervention in the same area that targeted pupils in grade 6 yields further evidence that uniforms serve as a financial barrier to school attendance.[31] Children randomly chosen to receive free uniforms dropped out of primary school 13.5 percent less often than their counterparts in comparison schools. This program also led to a 1.5 percentage point decline in teenage childbearing (from a baseline rate of 15 percent), most likely because girls who become pregnant typically leave school, and the provision of uniforms made being in school more attractive than the alternative of getting pregnant and leaving school. In fact, providing uniforms proved to be more successful in reducing teenage pregnancy than training teachers to teach the national HIV/AIDS curriculum.

These results are consistent with an earlier randomized evaluation in 1995, in which randomly selected schools in rural Kenya received the Child Sponsorship

---

29. Evans, Kremer, and Ngatia (2008).
30. Evans and others (2005).
31. Duflo and others (2006).

Program—a package of assistance that included free uniforms, textbooks, and classroom construction. Students in treatment schools remained enrolled an average of 0.5 years longer after 5 years and advanced an average of 0.3 grades further than their counterparts in comparison schools. The program not only led to greater retention of existing students, but it also attracted many students from neighboring schools. The average treatment class had about 8.9 more students than it would have had in the absence of the intervention.[32]

Although the intervention was implemented as a package, the financial benefit of free uniforms was probably the main reason program schools retained pupils and attracted transfers. A program that provided textbooks alone did not reduce dropout rates.[33] While the new classrooms may also have had an impact, the first ones were not built until the second year of the program, whereas dropout rates fell dramatically after the first year, before any new classrooms were constructed. Although this could have been due to anticipation of later classroom construction, dropout rates in upper grades also fell during the first year of the program, casting doubt on this hypothesis, since students in upper grades often already had good classrooms, and the new classrooms would not have been completed in time for older students to benefit.

Incentives for Participation

As the evidence just reviewed shows, moving from a small positive price to free distribution can have large effects on take-up. The following studies suggest there is a similar nonlinearity for negative prices or incentives—that is, small incentives can have a disproportionate impact on take-up; they also can create strong peer spillovers. Furthermore, the timing of payments can be as important as their level—a result found in other randomized evaluations in very different contexts.

Conditional Cash Transfer Programs

In 1998 Mexico launched Programa de Educacion, Salud y Alimentacion (PROGRESA), a program of incentives for school attendance and take-up of health care services in rural Central and South Mexico. It provided up to three years of cash grants for poor mothers whose children attended school 85 percent of the time. Subsidy amounts increased with grade level to offset the increasing opportunity cost of going to school for older children and provided premiums for girls enrolled in junior secondary school. The monthly grant for a ninth-grade girl, for example, corresponded to about 44 percent of the typical male day-laborer's wage in 1998, or roughly two-thirds of what a child that age could earn if she worked full-time. The program also disbursed cash transfers if households

---

32. Kremer, Moulin, and Namunyu (2003).
33. Glewwe, Kremer, and Moulin (2007).

participated in certain health- and nutrition-related activities such as prenatal care, immunization, nutrition monitoring and supplementation, and educational programs about health and nutrition.

The program phase-in was structured to allow for a rigorous evaluation. Using administrative and census data, the designers of the program identified approximately 500 of the country's poorest rural areas and those least likely to experience economic growth and then randomly allocated the program to two-thirds of these areas for the first two years. The remaining third were phased into the program by the third year.

School enrolment as reported in household surveys increased an average 3.4 to 3.6 percentage points across all students in grades 1 through 8.[34] However, this masks important heterogeneity: the program had little scope for affecting enrollment rates in the lower grades since enrollment rates there were already very high. The largest enrollment increase—11.1 percentage points from a baseline rate of 58 percent—occurred for children who had already completed grade 6 and were transitioning to junior secondary school. Girls' enrollment among these older children increased by 14.8 percentage points, significantly more than the 6.5 percentage point gain for boys. PROGRESA is estimated to have increased total schooling attainment by 0.66 years (from a baseline of 6.8 years) and to have generated an internal rate of return of 8 percent under certain assumptions about the effect of education on earnings.[35]

PROGRESA also led to changes in health-seeking behavior and improved child health outcomes. Public health clinics in treatment areas received 2.09 more visits per day (or an 18.2 percent increase).[36] PROGRESA beneficiaries accounted for only about one-third of the number of families in a clinic's service area, so if all of this increase can be attributed to beneficiaries, visits in the treatment group increased by 60 percent.

Children under the age of three who received the conditional cash transfers were 22.3 percent less likely to be reported as ill in the previous four weeks than the children in the comparison group. Children young enough to be exposed to the program for twenty-four months were 39.5 percent less likely to be reported ill, which suggests that the program generated cumulative health benefits. They were also about 1 centimeter taller and 25.5 percent less likely to display hemoglobin levels indicative of anemia.[37]

In addition, PROGRESA generated spillovers that increased enrollment of other children. In a comparison of enrollment rates of ineligible (wealthier) children in treatment and comparison villages, those in the treatment villages were 5 percentage points more likely to attend secondary school (from a base of 68 percent) than

34. Schultz (2004).
35. Schultz (2004).
36. Gertler and Boyce (2001).
37. Gertler (2004).

those in the comparison villages, with most of this increase concentrated among the poorest of the ineligible households.[38] Furthermore, primary school attendance among ineligibles in treatment villages increased by 2.1 percentage points (from a base of 76 percent) compared with the ineligibles in comparison villages.[39] It is not entirely clear whether these spillovers arose from peer effects, increases in school quality in the treatment villages, or an increased expectation of future treatment among ineligibles in treatment villages, but they do suggest that targeted conditional cash transfer programs may have a social multiplier effect. In the case of deworming, the spillovers were possibly due to information transmission and social learning, but in this case, since education is a well-known service, that channel is less plausible. There may be a social norm effect, or perhaps children want to be with their friends, and if their friends are in school they want to be there as well. Note, too, that in this case the spillovers were positive rather than negative.

Partly on the clear evidence of a program impact from the randomized evaluation, the Mexican government expanded the program to cover poor rural and urban households in the rest of country.[40] By 2006, 5 million families, or one-quarter of Mexico's population, were participating in the program, now called Oportunidades.[41] Similar conditional cash transfer programs are now under way in nearly thirty other countries, including Brazil (Bolsa Escola, now Bolsa Familia), Ecuador (Bono de Desarrollo Humano, BDH), Honduras (Programa de Asignacion Familiar, PRAF), and Nicaragua (Red de Proteccion Social, RPS). Randomized evaluations of a number of these programs have found similar effects.[42]

Where both short-term liquidity constraints and savings constraints limit human capital investment, these kinds of conditional cash transfer programs might be made more effective by altering the timing of cash disbursements. In a program employing this approach in Bogotá, Colombia (Conditional Subsidies for School Attendance Program, Subsidios Condicionados a la Asistencia Escolar), the timing of payments was as important as the level of payments. This not only provides some insight into pricing's strong effect on take-up but also shows how these types of programs can be designed to have a bigger impact on participation for a given budgetary cost.

Like PROGRESA, one variant of the Colombian program provided families with a cash grant ($15 a month) conditional on school attendance. A second variant, a savings treatment, reduced the monthly grants by one-third; this third of the grant was saved each month and only made available to students' families dur-

---

38. Bobonis and Finan (2008).

39. Lalive and Cattaneo (2006).

40. See Levy (2006).

41. WHO (2006). For an evaluation of the urban Oportunidades program, see Parker, Todd, and Wolpin (2006).

42. See Maluccio and Flores (2005); Schady and Araujo (2006); and Glewwe and Olinto (2004).

ing the period in which students enroll and prepare for the next school year. The third variant, a graduation/matriculation treatment, was similar to the savings treatment, but in addition it offered students who graduated from secondary school and enrolled in a tertiary institution a transfer of $300, equivalent to 73 percent of the average cost of the first year in a vocational school.

While all variants of the program increased contemporaneous secondary school attendance, the savings and graduation/matriculation treatments also affected enrollment in the subsequent year.[43] According to attendance data collected directly from random classroom visits, students in grades 6 through 11 receiving the basic or savings treatments attended school 2.8 to 3.3 percentage points (or 4 percent) more often than their counterparts in a comparison group. Placing the conditionality on graduation from secondary school and subsequent enrollment in a tertiary institution also increased contemporaneous school attendance by 5 percentage points (or 6 percent).

Changing the timing of the transfer with the savings incentive, however, also increased subsequent enrollment in secondary and tertiary institutions by 3.6 and 8.8 percentage points (5 and 39 percent), respectively. These gains were significantly different from those experienced by both the comparison group and the group assigned to the basic PROGRESA-like treatment. The graduation/matriculation treatment variant generated gains of similar magnitude in secondary school while raising enrollment in a tertiary institution by a staggering 50 percentage points (or 258 percent). Despite its effect on attendance, however, the basic treatment did not significantly affect enrollment rates.

Thus despite the lower monthly transfers, daily attendance rates under the savings and graduation/matriculation treatments did not suffer relative to both no treatment and the basic treatment, while enrollment in the subsequent year significantly improved when payments were delayed until the period immediately before enrollment for the subsequent school year or when funding for further education was guaranteed upon graduation.

These findings suggest that in this setting longer-term saving constraints may represent more important barriers to academic participation than more short-term liquidity constraints.[44] (If the problem had been short-term liquidity constraints, then the promise of funds in the future should have exerted a less powerful incentive effect, whereas if time-consistency problems make savings difficult, people may well have found the commitment device valuable.) This is consistent with evidence from Kenya on the take-up of fertilizer and from the Philippines on demand for commitment savings products.[45]

43. Barrera-Osorio and others (2007).

44. Barrera-Osorio and others (2007).

45. On fertilizer, see Duflo, Kremer, and Robinson (2009); on the demand for commitment savings products, see Ashraf, Karlan, and Yin (2006).

The baseline survey in Colombia also contained detailed data on friendship networks and allowed the authors to estimate the extent of any peer effects generated by the program.[46] Since program participation was assigned by lottery and randomization was at the level of the student, it is possible to estimate any peer effects associated with the program because the fraction of a student's friends who were treated, conditional on their registering for the initial lottery, should also be randomly assigned. For the average participant (the participant with the average number of treated registered friends), the estimated magnitude of the effect of one treated friend on attendance equals the direct impact of treatment. Any additional treated friends, however, do not imply similar gains in attendance.

Children who were registered but not selected for treatment in the lottery appear to have suffered from negative spillovers within the household as their families may have redistributed resources within the household to facilitate the education of treated children. When untreated siblings in households that registered two children but only received one treatment were compared with untreated children in households that registered two children but received no treatment, the untreated in the treated households attended school 2.9 percentage points less often in one locality and worked 1.2 hours less per week in another.[47] Thus spillovers to children in other families were positive, whereas spillovers from the program to other children within the family were negative.

School Meals

School meals are a common, though controversial, incentive to attend school. The Indian Supreme Court, for example, has made them mandatory. One potential advantage of school meals is that they provide automatic targeting and would not be subject to teachers' discretion in documenting attendance in programs that give families rewards based on attendance.[48] In a randomized evaluation of a school feeding program in preschools in Busia and Teso districts of Kenya, attendance rates were generally lower than in regular schools.[49] The average class enrollment in community-run preschools (for children aged four to six) was eighty-five according to enrollment rosters, but only thirty-five students showed up on a typical day. School meals, however, had very strong attendance effects.

Preschools were randomly selected to receive fortified flour and money to hire a cook to make porridge for breakfast every day. In order to assess the impact of this program on the attendance rates of children currently in school and those who had never even enrolled in school before the program, baseline statistics were collected for children aged four to six who at the time were either in school them-

---

46. Barrera-Osorio and others (2007).
47. Barrera-Osorio and others (2007).
48. For evidence of this kind of manipulation, see Shastry and Linden (2007).
49. Kremer and Vermeersch (2004).

selves or had siblings in the treatment or in comparison schools—either in preschool or in the attached primary schools. With attendance measured by direct observation during an average of six annual surprise visits, the results suggest that after one year, the average attendance of children in treatment schools increased by 8.5 percentage points compared with the attendance of children in comparison schools, who were attending school an average of 27 percent of the time. For children not attending school before the intervention, this increase was 4.6 percentage points; for children who were enrolled before the school feeding program, it was 11 percentage points.

Attendance gains in the second year of the program were smaller. However, the introduction to the program in treatment schools seems to have induced competitive effects in the comparison schools. After the start of the program, treatment schools increased school fee collection by 57 percent, while many nearby comparison schools decreased fee collection and started feeding programs of their own. Thus these estimated differences in school participation between treatment and control schools may in fact represent a lower bound for the effect of school meals on attendance since the higher school fees in treatment schools could have deterred some children from attending, and since these price hikes might not have arisen if all schools had simultaneously offered the same amenity.

This program also increased scores on curriculum tests for students enrolled at baseline in treatment school classrooms with experienced teachers. Anthropometric measurements and cognitive tests suggest that these gains do not derive from increased nutrition or cognitive ability. Rather, they appear to be due to the improvement in school attendance.

The Girls' Scholarship Program

Yet another example of the incentive effect can be seen in a randomized evaluation of the Girls' Scholarship Program in primary schools in western Kenya, where merit scholarships helped increase attendance rates before receipt of the awards.[50] Grade 6 girls in program schools who scored in the top 15 percent in the annual district exam were to receive a two-year award consisting of a yearly grant to cover school fees that was paid directly to the school for grades 7 and 8 (the remaining two years of primary school), a yearly grant for school supplies paid to the recipient's family, and public recognition at an awards assembly held for students, parents, teachers, and local government officials.

The first cohort of eligible grade 6 girls scored 0.18 standard deviations higher than their counterparts in comparison schools, and the gains accruing to the second cohort were statistically indistinguishable from this. Overall teacher attendance also improved in treatment schools, increasing by 4.8 percentage points, or 6 percent.

50. Kremer, Miguel, and Thornton (2008).

The results for these and other outcomes such as student attendance or effects for boys, however, point to the possibility of heterogeneous program effects across geographic areas. ICS-Africa, the NGO administering the program, chose program schools in both Busia and Teso districts. Only schools in Busia district showed any gains in school participation, with a 3.2 percentage point increase in school attendance relative to comparison schools. Similarly, all of the increase in teacher attendance and all of the test score gains were concentrated in Busia. In this successful district, the program also appears to have had spillover effects on boys (who were ineligible for the scholarships), whose test scores increased by 0.15 standard deviations in the first cohort affected by the program. There also seem to have been peer effects on girls with low pre-scores, who were unlikely to receive scholarships under the program. Researchers here could not reject the hypothesis that treatment effects were equal for all quartiles of the baseline test score distribution, so girls with little or no chance of winning the awards also benefited from the program.[51]

Retrieving HIV Results

Knowledge of HIV status is said to be crucial to fighting HIV/AIDS, yet many people seem reluctant to learn their status, supposedly because of the stigma surrounding the disease or their fear of obtaining positive results. An evaluation of an HIV testing program in Malawi, however, found that small incentives and deadlines can be sufficient to induce people to pick up their test results at designated testing centers. Distance to the center was also a key determinant of attendance there. This suggests that procrastination and the inconvenience of travel, rather than deep-rooted stigma, can explain much of the failure to pick up HIV test results.

In a field experiment in Malawi, nurses visited households and administered free HIV tests, randomizing the amount of vouchers (from $0 to $3) offered to participants, which were redeemable upon learning their HIV results in a voluntary counseling and testing center (VCT) open for one week two to four months later. Before the intervention, only 18 percent of people had been tested before, and only half of those had learned their results. After the intervention, those receiving any voucher amount were twice as likely to visit a testing center as those receiving nothing, who went to learn their results 39 percent of the time.[52] The probability of attendance increased by 9.1 percentage points for every additional dollar offered; even those assigned a voucher equivalent to one-tenth of a day's wage displayed sizable attendance gains.

There is also evidence of particularly large effects around a price of zero. A change in the voucher amount from $0 to $0.10 generated an increase in the likelihood of attendance by more than 20 percentage points, which is larger than the changes associated with any other $0.10 increase between $0.10 and $3.

51. Kremer, Miguel, and Thornton (2008).
52. Thornton (2008).

Since vouchers were redeemable for only a week after VCT assignment, the results are consistent with the hypothesis that deadline effects are important and that procrastination plays a role in explaining the low rates of retrieving HIV results before the intervention. It may be a mistake to assume the relevant choice is between learning one's status and not learning it. The trade-off may be between learning the status today and learning it tomorrow, with people continuously postponing the learning of it.

The distance between a household and its assigned VCT center was another randomized component of the program. The average straight-line distance to a center was 2.1 kilometers, and the average time it took to reach the center was forty-two minutes. Individuals assigned to a VCT center more than 1.5 kilometers away were 4 percentage points (or 6 percent) less likely to go to the center to learn their results than those assigned to a closer location. No one visited VCT centers that were 9 kilometers away from sample households.

Conclusion

The interventions reviewed in this chapter (see table 4-1) show that some generalization seems possible in the case of prices and their impact on the take-up of education and health services: increases in prices decrease take-up across a wide range of contexts. This is consistent with standard theories of human capital investment. A more detailed examination of the data suggests, however, that our models of take-up of education and health services must also incorporate peer effects and insights from behavioral economics.

Peer effects have been widely documented for both the take-up of new health technologies and for primary education.[53] Although peer effects were negative for the take-up of deworming medication in Kenya, they seem more generally positive for school participation rates. As is well understood, peer effects of this type have implications for generalizing from randomized evaluations: they suggest that the aggregate response to price changes may actually exceed the responses found in randomized evaluations not designed to check for the possibility of such effects.[54] Indeed, when a number of African countries recently abolished school fees or charges in clinics, reported usage went up dramatically: Malawi's reported primary school enrollment increased by 51 percent from approximately 1.9 million pupils in 1993–94 to 3 million in 1994–95; Uganda saw its reported enrollment skyrocket from 3.1 million to 5.3 million in 1996.[55] Similar influxes in reported enrollment occurred in Cameroon in 1999, Tanzania in 2001, and Kenya in 2003. When Uganda's president banned user fees in government health

53. On new technologies, see Kremer and Miguel (2007); Kremer and others (2008). On primary education, see Bobonis and Finan (2008); Kremer, Miguel, and Thornton (2008).

54. See, for example, Miguel and Kremer (2004).

55. Kattan and Burnett (2004).

Table 4-1. *Price Effects on Access according to Randomized Evaluations*

Intervention	Setting	Estimated effect	Author
User fee			
Average $0.30/child for deworming medicine	Rural Kenya	Compared with free treatment, charging causes take-up to drop by 62 percentage points (82 percent). Take-up drops for any non-zero price and not sensitive to the exact positive price level. No evidence that prices target medicine to sickest.	Kremer and Miguel (2007)
Varying offer price and final transaction price of a water disinfectant at or below market price of $0.25 in a door-to-door marketing campaign	Peri-urban Zambia	Estimated price elasticity of −0.6. Offer price increase of 10 percent leads to purchase by people who are 3.6 percent more likely to use product. No significant effects of final transaction price on use. Insignificant increase in use for non-zero price. No evidence that prices target the product to the most vulnerable.	Ashraf, Berry, and Shapiro (2007)
Varying offer price and final transaction price of insecticide-treated mosquito nets in antenatal clinics from $0 to $0.75	Rural Kenya	Compared with free-nets condition, charging prevailing cost-sharing price reduces take-up by 75 percent. No evidence that final transaction price increases use. No evidence that prices target nets to sickest women.	Cohen and Dupas (2007)
Free mosquito nets or cash to purchase nets	Rural Uganda	Probability of acquiring at least one net is 99 percent in free-nets group, 85 percent in purchased-nets group. Conditional on acquiring at least one net, total acquired nets per household member is the same. Net usage is statistically indistinguishable in free-nets and purchased-nets households. In free-nets group, proportion of children under age five sleeping under a net is 12.2 to 14.3 percentage points higher than in the purchased-nets group, where the proportion is 56 percent.	Hoffman (2008)

Incentive

PROGRESA			
Paying for textbooks, school construction, and uniforms	Rural Kenya	After five years, class size increased by 8.9 from base of 29 students via increased attendance of prior students and transfers of new students.	Kremer, Moulin, and Namunyu (2003)
		After five years, years of enrollment increased by 0.5 (13 percent) and grade advancement increased by 0.3 (16 percent).	
Free uniforms, average price $5.82	Rural Kenya	For younger pupils, 6 percentage point increase (7 percent) in school attendance and a 13 percentage point (15 percent) increase for students without a uniform before program.	Evans, Kremer, and Ngatia (2008) and Duflo and others (2006)
		For older pupils, 13.5 percent decline in absence and 10 percent decline in teenage childbearing.	
PROGRESA	Rural Mexico	*Education*	
Cash transfers conditional on school attendance and take-up of health services		Attendance increased 3.4–3.6 percentage points for all children in grades 1 to 8.	Schultz (2004)
Education grants reduce private cost of going to school by 50–75 percent		Attendance increased 11.1 percentage points (19 percent) for students who have completed sixth grade and 14.5 percentage points for girls who have completed sixth grade.	Bobonis and Finan (2008)
Health grants equivalent to 20 percent of household income		Spillovers to ineligibles in treatment villages amounted to 5 percentage points (7 percent) in secondary enrollment.	Lalive and Cattaneo (2006)
		Spillovers to ineligibles in treatment villages amounted to 2.1 percentage points (3 percent).	Gertler and Boyce (2001)
		Health	Gertler (2004)
		Health clinics in treatment areas receive two (18 percent) more visits per day.	
		Children under three years of age in treatment areas are 22.3 percent less likely to be reported ill in past month.	
		Treatment children 1 cm taller.	
		Treatment children 25.5 percent less likely to display hemoglobin levels indicative of anemia.	

(continued)

Table 4-1. *Price Effects on Access according to Randomized Evaluations (continued)*

Intervention	Setting	Estimated effect	Author
Three variants of conditional cash transfers based on attendance: a. PROGRESA variant ($15/month) b. Savings treatment: one-third of each monthly transfer delayed until enrollment part of school year c. Graduation/matriculation treatment, like variant b, plus large transfer ($300) upon secondary school graduation and matriculation in tertiary institution	Bogotá, Colombia	The three variants improved attendance by 2.8–5 percentage points (4–6 percent). Basic treatment had no effect on enrollment in subsequent year. Enrollment in secondary institutions increased by 3.6 percentage points (5 percent) under both saving and tertiary treatments. Enrollment in tertiary institutions increased by 8.8 percentage points (39 percent) under savings treatment and by 50 percentage points (258 percent) under tertiary treatment.	Barerra-Osorio and others (2007)

Intervention	Location	Findings	Source
Free school meals in preschools	Rural Kenya	School attendance increased by 8.5 percentage points (31 percent) in treatment schools. Attendance gains both for current students and students who had never attended before. In response, comparison also introduced by second year of program and treatment schools increase fees by 57 percent.	Kremer and Vermeersch (2004)
Merit scholarships of $19.20 for school fees and school supplies for sixth-grade girls	Rural Kenya	0.18 standard deviation (SD) increase in girls' test scores. Heterogeneous treatment effects across districts. In successful district, 5 percentage point increase in student attendance and 0.18 SD increase in boys' test scores.	Kremer, Miguel, and Thornton (2008)
Varying vouchers from $0 to $3 and the distance to go to a testing center to learn results of a free HIV test administered at home	Rural Malawi	Vouchers double likelihood of attendance from a base of 39 percent. Likelihood of attendance increases 9.1 percentage points with every $1 increase in voucher. Large discontinuity when raising voucher from $0 to $0.10. An increase in testing center distance of 1.5 km leads to a 4 percentage point (6 percent) decline in likelihood of attendance.	Thornton (2008)

clinics in 2001, new outpatient attendance grew a reported 83 percent.[56] (These figures should be taken with a grain of salt, however, since local officials may have incentives to understate usage when fees are required and overstate it when fees are replaced with central government subsidies.)

In standard models of human capital investment, people weigh the opportunity costs of time against the discounted value of returns.[57] Small fees should not make much difference unless people happen to be right at the margin of going to school. In fact, relatively small short-run costs (for example, the cost of uniforms) and subsidies (a $0.10 voucher to go to a HIV testing center) generate sizable movements in take-up, consistent with models of time-inconsistent preferences.[58] The finding that people are much more likely to learn their HIV status when faced with a deadline for receiving a small reward is also consistent with models of procrastination driven by time-inconsistent preferences.[59] Also consistent with such models is evidence that people show a preference for committing themselves to save.[60] Finally, there is some evidence that take-up behavior is particularly sensitive to price at prices close to zero.[61] It should be emphasized, though, that these behavioral effects are not unique to developing countries. Default rules in tax-deferred-account retirement plans, like 401(k) plans in the United States, have a large impact on employee participation and their choice of portfolio.[62] There is also evidence of peer effects in the decision to enroll in such plans.[63] Mandatory education laws are in one sense a response to these sorts of behavioral effects.

Although this discussion has focused on positive rather than normative issues, some of the findings on the role of behavioral factors in take-up imply that the steep decline in take-up of education and health products and services with price could have serious consequences for welfare. Under a standard model of human capital investment, the welfare consequences of eliminating small fees are likely to be small or even negative, since the people whose behavior is affected by these price changes will be those with low returns from the services. To the extent that these services were subsidized initially and that their associated externalities were internalized, people may have been overconsuming them, and further subsidies might have a negative welfare impact. Under some behavioral models, on the other hand, many people may be underconsuming the products and services (such as deworming medicine), and price elimination could substantially increase welfare. Although economists have not yet even agreed on a conceptual framework for thinking about welfare in such settings and are far from being able to

56. World Bank, Poverty & Social Impact Analysis Sourcebook.

57. See Becker (1993); Ben-Porath (1967); and Rosen (1977).

58. Laibson (1997).

59. Thornton's (2008) finding is consistent with O'Donoghue and Rabin (1999).

60. Barerra-Osorio and others (2007); Duflo and others (2009); Ashraf and others (2006).

61. For example, Kremer and Miguel (2007); Thornton (2008).

62. See, for example, Madrian and Shea (2001).

63. Duflo and Saez (2003).

estimate the welfare consequences of price changes in these cases, considerable evidence does seem to indicate that charging for health services does not target services to those with the most medical need.

Of course, the take-up of education and health products is a means to an end: namely, learning and health. For some products (for example, mosquito nets), simply increasing their use can be assumed to lead to these ultimate goals because their impact on health has been solidly documented. In other cases, such as learning one's HIV status, the evidence on whether take-up has positive effects remains inadequate. In some cases, such as school participation, the benefits depend strongly on the quality of services participants receive and their subsequent behavior.[64] Longer-term follow-up of participants in programs such as PROGRESA could shed light on whether those attracted to education by lower fees have a low or high return to education.

Credit constraints and externalities from consumption provide two other potential rationales for subsidies in some cases. Eliminating prices for deworming medicine and mosquito nets is likely to be welfare-maximizing because of these externalities, and the same may well be true of water disinfectant. Reducing costs of education for students who do well academically may generate positive externalities within the classroom.

An important caveat is that how consumer behavior varies with price is not dispositive for policy debates regarding cost sharing. Other rationales for cost sharing could be advanced. In particular, we have not discussed how charging consumers affects provider incentives or the utility of cost-sharing requirements in overcoming asymmetric information problems for donors. Given the weakness of provider incentives in the developing world and the asymmetric information problems between donors and aid organizations, one could probably build a stronger theoretical case for user fees on the basis of their role in incentivizing providers and screening out aid organizations providing useless services rather than on their role in motivating consumers to value products.[65] Yet if these are the problems that user fees are designed to address, it seems worth considering alternatives, such as motivating providers through voucher programs or screening out projects by requiring randomized evaluations before introducing large-scale funding.

Another caveat is that the randomized trials discussed here do not test the role of people's background understanding of the value of the product or the role of the marketing surrounding products such as mosquito nets and water disinfectant. People may well be responding in part to the idea that they have been offered a particularly good opportunity. Marketing campaigns may be effective, and it is conceivable that a marketing campaign for a free product is harder to design or that free distribution over long periods changes people's perceptions of the

64. See Hanushek (2008).
65. Kremer is working with Sendhil Mullainathan on a model along these lines. On provider incentives in the developing world, see Chaudhury and others (2006).

value of a product. Still, this should invite exploration of whether this is in fact the case—indeed, several ongoing and planned randomized evaluations are addressing some of these issues. It may well be possible to advertise products effectively while providing them free through certain channels (for example, mosquito nets through antenatal clinics).

This review has focused on the impact of price on access, but evidence is also accumulating on the potential role of information in increasing access[66] and on the more difficult problem of improving the *quality* of social service delivery through channels such as school inputs (extra teachers and textbooks);[67] provider incentives;[68] remedial education;[69] citizens' report cards, the hiring of contract teachers, or increased oversight of local school committees;[70] school choice programs;[71] and contracting out the provision of basic health care services.[72] More experimentation in these areas would aid in fully capitalizing on gains in access and in generalizing about the most effective ways to deliver social services.

References

Angrist, Joshua, Eric Bettinger, and Michael Kremer. 2006. "Long-Term Consequences of Secondary School Vouchers: Evidence from Administrative Records in Colombia." *American Economic Review* 96, no. 3: 847–62.

Angrist, Joshua, and others. 2002. "Vouchers for Private Schooling in Colombia: Evidence from a Randomized Natural Experiment." *American Economic Review* 92, no. 5: 1535–58.

Ashraf, Nava, James Berry, and Jesse M. Shapiro. 2007. "Can Higher Prices Stimulate Product Use? Evidence from a Field Experiment in Zambia." Working Paper W13247. Cambridge, Mass.: National Bureau of Economic Research.

Ashraf, Nava, Dean Karlan, and Wesley Yin. 2006. "Tying Odysseus to the Mast: Evidence from a Commitment Savings Product in the Philippines." *Quarterly Journal of Economics* 121, no. 2: 673–97.

Banerjee, Abhijit, Suraj Jacob, and Michael Kremer with others. 2005. "Promoting School Participation in Rural Rajasthan: Results from Some Prospective Trials." Working Paper. Cambridge, Mass.: MIT.

Banerjee, Abhijit, and others. 2007. "Remedying Education: Evidence from Two Randomized Experiments in India." *Quarterly Journal of Economics*, 122, no. 3: 1235–64.

Barrera-Osorio, Felipe, and others. 2007. "Using Conditional Transfers in Education to Investigate Intra-Family Decisions: Evidence from a Randomized Experiment" (www.cid.harvard.edu/neudc07_s1_p06_barrera-osorio.pdf).

---

66. Jensen (2007); Dupas (2009); Pandey and others (2007).

67. Banerjee, Jacob, and Kremer, with others (2005); Duflo, Dupas, and Kremer (2007); Glewwe and others (2007).

68. Glewwe, Ilais, and Kremer (2003); Muralidharan and Sundararaman (2007).

69. Banerjee and others (2007); Duflo and others (2007); He, Linden, and MacLeod (2007).

70. Bjorkman and Svensson (2007); Duflo and others (2007).

71. Angrist and others (2002); Angrist, Bettinger, and Kremer (2006); Bettinger, Kremer, and Saavedra (2007).

72. Bloom and others (2006).

Becker, Gary. 1993. *Human Capital.* 3rd ed. University of Chicago Press.

Ben-Porath, Yoram. 1967. "The Production of Human Capital and the Life Cycle of Earnings." *Journal of Political Economy* 75, no. 4: 352–65.

Bettinger, Eric, Michael Kremer, and Juan Saavedra. 2007. "Are Educational Vouchers Only Redistributive?" Working Paper 08-08. Harvard University Program for Education Policy and Governance (www.harvard.edu/pepg/PDF/Papers/Bettinger_Kremer_Saavedra.PEPG 08-08).

Bjorkman, Martina, and Jakob Svensson. 2007. "Power to the People: Evidence from a Randomized Experiment of a Community-Based Monitoring Project in Uganda." Discussion Paper 6344. London: Centre for Economic Policy Research.

Bloom, Erik, and others. 2006. "Contracting for Health: Evidence from Cambodia." Brookings (www.brookings.edu/views/papers/kremer/20060720cambodia.pdf).

Bobonis, Gustavo, and Frederico Finan. 2008. "Neighborhood Peer Effects in Secondary School Enrollment Decisions." *Review of Economics and Statistics.* Forthcoming.

Chaudhury, Nazmul, and others. 2006. "Missing in Action: Teacher and Health Worker Absence in Developing Countries." *Journal of Economic Perspectives* 20, no. 1: 91–116.

Cohen, Jessica, and Pascaline Dupas. 2007. "Free Distribution vs. Cost-Sharing: Evidence from a Malaria-Prevention Field Experiment in Kenya." Global Economy and Development Working Paper. Brookings.

Duflo, Esther, Pascaline Dupas, and Michael Kremer. 2007. "Peer Effects, Pupil-Teacher Ratios, and Teacher Incentives: Evidence from a Randomized Evaluation in Kenya" (www.cid.harvard.edu/neudc07/docs/neudc07_s6_p03_duflo.pdf).

Duflo, Esther, Michael Kremer, and Jonathan Robinson. 2009. "Nudging Farmers to Use Fertilizer: Evidence from Kenya" (http://people.uscs.edu/~jmrtwo/fertilizer_behavioral.pdf).

Duflo, Esther, and others. 2006. "Education and HIV/AIDS Prevention: Evidence from a Randomized Evaluation in Western Kenya." Policy Research Working Paper 4024. Washington: World Bank (http://ssrn.com/abstract=935173).

Duflo, Esther, and Emmanuel Saez. 2003. "The Role of Information and Social Interactions in Retirement Decisions: Evidence from a Randomized Experiment." *Quarterly Journal of Economics* 118, no. 3: 815–42.

Duflo, Esther, and Christopher Udry. 2004. "Intrahousehold Resource Allocation in Côte d'Ivoire: Social Norms, Separate Accounts, and Consumption Choices." Working Paper 10498. Cambridge, Mass.: National Bureau of Economic Research.

Dupas, Pascaline. 2009. "Do Teenagers Respond to HIV Risk Information? Evidence from a Field Experiment in Kenya." Working Paper 14707. Cambridge, Mass.: National Bureau of Economic Research.

Easterly, William. 2006. *The White Man's Burden: Why the West's Efforts to Aid the Rest Have Done So Much Ill and So Little Good.* New York: Penguin Press.

Evans, David, Michael Kremer, and Muthoni Ngatia. 2008. "The Impact of Distributing School Uniforms on Children's Education in Kenya." Washington: World Bank (http://site resources.worldbank.org/ETIMPEVA/Resources/evans_kenya_uniforms.pdf).

Gertler, Paul. 2004. "Do Conditional Cash Transfers Improve Child Health? Evidence from PROGRESA's Control Randomized Experiment." *American Economic Review Papers and Proceedings* 94, no. 2: 336–41.

Gertler, Paul, and Simone Boyce. 2001. "An Experiment in Incentive-Based Welfare: The Impact of PROGRESA on Health in Mexico." University of California, Berkeley (http://faculty.haas.berkeley.edu/gertler/working_papers/PROGRESA%204-06.pdf).

Glewwe, Paul, Nauman Ilais, and Michael Kremer. 2003. "Teacher Incentives." Working Paper 9671. Cambridge, Mass.: National Bureau of Economics.

Glewwe, Paul, Michael Kremer, and Sylvie Moulin. 2007. "Many Children Left Behind? Textbooks and Test Scores in Kenya." *American Economic Journal: Applied Economics.* Forthcoming.

Glewwe, Paul, and Pedro Olinto. 2004. "Evaluating the Impact of Conditional Cash Transfers on Schooling: An Experimental Analysis of Honduras PRAF Program." Final Report for USAID. Washington: International Food Policy Research Institute.

Hanushek, Eric A. 2008. "Incentives for Efficiency and Equity in the School System." *Perspektiven der Wirtschaftspolitik* 9 (Special Issue): 5–27.

He, Fang, Leigh Linden, and Margaret MacLeod. 2007. "Helping Teach What Teachers Don't Know: An Assessment of the Pratham English Language Program" (http://cid.harvard.edu. neudc07/docs/neudc07_s6_p02_he.pdf).

Hoffman, Vivian. 2008. "Psychology, Gender, and the Intrahousehold Allocation of Free and Purchased Mosquito Nets" (www.people.cornell.edu/pages/veh4/intra_hh.pdf).

Jensen, Robert. 2007. "The Perceived Returns to Education and the Demand for Schooling" (www.princeton.edu/rpds/seminar/spring-2008/jensen_Perceived_Returns_Schooling.pdf).

Kattan, Raja Bentaouet, and Nicholas Burnett. 2004. "User Fees in Primary Education." Human Development Network Paper. Washington: World Bank.

Kremer, Michael, and Edward Miguel. 2007. "The Illusion of Sustainability." *Quarterly Journal of Economics* 112, no. 3: 1007–65.

Kremer, Michael, Edward Miguel, and Rebecca Thornton. 2008. "Incentives to Learn." *Review of Economics and Statistics.* Forthcoming.

Kremer, Michael, Sylvie Moulin, and Robert Namunyu. 2003. "Decentralization: A Cautionary Tale." Paper 10. Cambridge, Mass.: MIT, Poverty Action Lab (April).

Kremer, Michael, and others. 2008. "Trickle Down: Diffusion of Chlorine for Drinking Water Treatment in Kenya" (www.stanford.edu/group/SITE/SITE_2008/segment_1/papers/de_ georgi_SITE_Trickle_Down.pdf).

Kremer, Michael, and Christel Vermeersch. 2004. "School Meals, Educational Attainment, and School Competition: Evidence from a Randomized Evaluation." Policy Research Working Paper WPS3523. Washington: World Bank.

Laibson, David. 1997. "Golden Eggs and Hyperbolic Discounting." *Quarterly Journal of Economics* 112, no. 2: 443–77.

Lalive, Rafael, and Alejandra Cattaneo. 2006. "Social Interactions and Schooling Decisions." Discussion Paper 2250. Skhirat, Mococco: Institute for the Study of Labor (IZA).

Levy, Santiago. 2006. *Progress against Poverty: Sustaining Mexico's Progresa-Oportunidades Program.* Brookings.

Madrian, Brigitte, and Dennis F. Shea. 2001. "The Power of Suggestion: Inertia in 401(k) Participation and Savings Behavior." *Quarterly Journal of Economics* 116, no. 4: 1149–87.

Maluccio, John A., and Rafael Flores. 2005. "Impact Evaluation of a Conditional Cash Transfer Program: The Nicaraguan Red de Protección Social." Washington: International Food Policy Research Institute.

Meuwissen, Liesbeth Emm. 2002. "Problems of Cost Recovery Implementation in District Health Care: A Case Study from Niger." *Health Policy and Planning* 17, no. 3: 304–13.

Miguel, Edward, and Michael Kremer. 2004. "Worms: Identifying Impacts on Education and Health in the Presence of Treatment Externalities." *Econometrica* 72, no. 1: 159–217.

Morduch, Jonathan. 1999. "The Microfinance Promise." *Journal of Economic Literature* 37 (4): 1569–1614.

Muralidharan, Karthik, and Venkatesh Sundararaman. 2007. "Teacher Incentives in Developing Countries: Experimental Evidence from India" (http:siteresources.worldbank.org/INTIN DIA/4371432-1194542398355/21543218/TeacherincentivesinDevelopingCountries.pdf).

O'Donoghue, Edward D., and Matthew Rabin. 1999. "Doing It Now or Doing It Later." *American Economic Review* 89, no. 1: 103–24.

Oster, Sharon M. 1995. *Strategic Management for Nonprofit Organizations: Theory and Cases.* Oxford University Press.

Pande, Rohini, and Christopher R. Udry. 2005. "Institutions and Development: A View from Below." In *Proceedings of the 9th World Congress of the Econometric Society*, edited by Richard Blundell, Whitney K. Newey, and Torsten Persson. Cambridge University Press.

Pandey, Priyanka, and others. 2007. "Informing Resource-Poor Populations and the Delivery of Entitled Health and Social Services in Rural India." *Journal of American Medical Association* 298, no. 16: 1867–75.

Parker, Susan W., Petra Todd, and Kenneth Wolpin. 2006. "Within-Family Program Effect Estimators: The Impact of Oportunidades on Schooling in Mexico" (http:/Athena.sus. upenn.edu/~petra/papers/sppaper/pdf).

Population Services International (PSI). 2006. "What Is Social Marketing?" (www.psi.org/ resources/pubs/what_is_SM.html).

Rosen, Sherwin. 1977. "Human Capital: A Survey of Empirical Research." *Research in Labor Economics* 1: 3–40.

Sachs, Jeffrey D. 2005. *The End of Poverty: Economic Possibilities for Our Time.* New York: Penguin Press.

Schady, Norbert, and Maria Caridad Araujo. 2006. "Cash Transfers, Conditions, School Enrollment, and Child Work: Evidence from a Randomized Experiment in Ecuador." Policy Research Working Paper 3930. Washington: World Bank.

Schultz, T. Paul. 2004. "School Subsidies for the Poor: Evaluating the Mexican PROGRESA Poverty Program." *Journal of Development Economics* 74, no. 1: 199–250.

Shastry, Gauri Kartini, and Leigh L. Linden. 2007. "Identifying Agent Discretion: Exaggerating Student Attendance in Response to a Conditional School Nutrition Program" (www. columbia.edu/~ll2240/shastry-linden-graininflation.pdf).

Thaler, Richard. 1980. "Toward a Positive Theory of Consumer Choice." *Journal of Economic Behavior and Organization* 1, no. 1: 39–60.

———. 1990. "Anomalies: Saving, Fungibility, and Mental Accounts." *Journal of Economic Perspectives* 4, no. 1: 193–205.

Thornton, Rebecca. 2008. "Demand for, and Impact of, Learning HIV Status." *American Economic Review* 95. no. 8:1829–63.

World Health Organization (WHO). 2005. *Deworming for Health and Development.* Report of the Third Partners for Parasite Control Meeting. Geneva.

———. 2006. *Bulletin of the World Health Organization* 84, no. 8: 589–684.

Comment by David N. Weil

M ichael Kremer and Alaka Holla's discussion offers a great deal of food for thought about four questions pertinent to randomized controlled trials. First, what are the effects of specific education and health programs on specified outcomes? This relates directly to their central topic. Second, what is the right model of household decisionmaking? This broader question underlies much of what is being said in this volume. Third, what should people do if they have the money or power and want to help the poor in developing countries? And fourth, why are some countries rich and some countries poor?

What Are the Effects of Specific Education and Health Policies on Specific Outcomes?

In focusing narrowly on how specific educational and health programs affect the behavior of households, Kremer and Holla make a real contribution. They summarize results from many different randomized evaluations. They categorize. They classify. They look for commonalities. Even when one is not doing experiments, this is the right scientific model for thinking about how to understand the world, yet it is often not what is done in economics. Every graduate student is encouraged to revolutionize the world with some fantastic new theory. As a field, economics underinvests in the type of thoughtful synthesis represented by Kremer and Holla's review.

Earlier in the book, Dani Rodrik raised the question of external validity, and of course the answer in large part is just to repeat. Keep doing this over and over in different settings and see what has been learned. But that is not so simple because one is not repeating exactly the same experiment. Every intervention takes place in a different country or region, is slightly different in its design, is slightly different in its target population, and so on.

One must then ask how to draw conclusions from looking at a set of these interventions. Kremer and Holla are right in thinking that drawing conclusions from these requires theory, but not the theory taught to first-year graduate students, which assumes there are n states of the world, m state-contingent commodities, and a page full of derivatives. Theory is needed in the sense of a sophisticated understanding of how the world works, with a scholar looking at these things in a sensible fashion. Economists are not going to be able to mathematically prove that this result does or does not conform with that other set of results. This is something that they will have to discuss like scholars in some broader social science sense.

The authors do a nice job of this, and they find a fair bit of external validity. One theme that runs through the results is that small fees, particularly in the health programs that they examine, do not yield substantial program benefits. That is, charging a small fee generally does not target the treatment toward the people who are most in need of it, and small fees do not recoup significant money compared with their administrative costs. This seems to be a real finding, although there are other reasons why programs might still want to have fees that Kremer and Holla do not address.

A second empirical regularity—one that the authors do not highlight—is that a lot of these strange findings apply much more to health programs than to education programs. The education programs, particularly PROGRESA, entail fairly large sums of money, so people are changing their behavior in response to powerful incentives. In the case of health programs, people seem to be making these large changes in behavior in response to extremely small monetary inducements.

What Is the Right Model of Household Decisionmaking?

Learning how particular programs work is a useful goal in and of itself. But scholars also want to extract from these experiments information that can be used in other settings. What, for example, does the literature summarized in chapter 4 convey about household decisionmaking? An initial fact that Kremer and Holla do not discuss directly is the surprisingly low uptake of what a pen-and-paper calculation would suggest to be good low-cost treatments. In the case of bed nets to prevent malaria, even when the subsidized price is sixty cents for a bed net that lasts five years and prevents a certain number of episodes of illness or possibly death of a child, the take-up rate is only 40 percent, which seems far too low.[1]

Of course, any behavior can be rationalized by some combination of discount rates, values placed on child health, and so on. But it is extremely hard to do so in this case.

The randomized controlled trials described by Kremer and Holla generate an additional prima facie fact, which is that there is extreme sensitivity to price, both at zero and at other prices. That is inconsistent with theory in the sense that sleeping under a bed net incurs some nonmonetary costs (such as discomfort and inconvenience) alongside all the usually discussed benefits, so there should be

1. An example of this calculation appears in Gollin and Zimmermann (2007).

some distribution of willingness to pay for a bed net. As the price changes, one should be moving through this distribution of willingness to pay. But instead when the price moves a little, there is a huge behavioral response. It is very hard to formulate a model that is consistent with such behavior.

When Kremer and Holla try to think of behavioral models with some kind of procrastination going on, I become less sympathetic to their argument, partly because of the very unusual things going on here. Would the typical persons in the subject population exhibit a lot of procrastination in other aspects of life? Are they people who fail to put their crops into the ground or to harvest them because they cannot get around to it? Or is this procrastination manifested only in the types of situations explored in these studies?

If it is the latter, that points to some other sources of the behavior, a prime candidate being some sort of information problem. That is, when I do the calculation, it is clear to me that the typical subjects in a trial should be buying this bed net for sixty cents. But maybe I have a different information structure than these persons do. Maybe they do not believe the net lasts five years, or that it works at all, or that mosquitoes cause malaria, or something like that. Maybe they are unable to tell the difference between legitimate public health workers offering them bed nets and charlatans offering them snake oil. Somehow these information problems are getting tied up with the behavioral response. So I am not ready to look to the full panoply of behavioral models to rationalize this behavior.

Similarly in the case of peer effects, I am reluctant to invoke strange utility structures to explain the findings. The peer effects that Kremer and Holla describe show up in odd ways. For example, there are positive peer effects for schooling and negative peer effects for the deworming medication. But "peer effect" is really just shorthand for something else. Again, it looks like some kind of information-processing issue. If I see my neighbors doing something, I come to the conclusion that maybe it is better (or worse) than what I am doing. The lesson here is that economists have to think more about what households know and what households think.

What Is a Good Thing to Do with Money or Power?

In Kremer and Holla's view, "more experimentation in these areas would aid in . . . generalizing about the most effective ways to deliver social services." This raises the question, how did economists get into the business of figuring out how to deliver social services to the poor?

The answer is, there is a community of interested parties out there who have decided that delivering social services to poor people is a good use of their money and power, and they have enlisted the help of economists in this endeavor. Many economists themselves feel that figuring out how to deliver social services to poor people is a more worthy use of their time than, say, figuring out how to get wealthy people to spend money on hair-care products.

The reason those interested parties (and economists) feel this way is that people in poor countries, especially poor people in poor countries, have very difficult lives. Anyone who is charitably inclined might reason that poor people's marginal utility of consumption is hugely higher than their own, and this may be sufficient to motivate them to spend money (or time, energy, and political influence) in trying to improve the lives of the poor. But why put these resources into providing services to the poor? Why not simply give them money? The literature seems to have given little thought to why nongovernmental organizations or governments should be providing these goods. As is well known, if there are externalities, then it is a classic public goods issue, and the government or someone else needs to be involved in supplying them. But when the take-up seems to be far too low even compared with the private benefits, as in the case of bed nets, this is not just an externality issue. Do economists know something that poor people in developing countries do not know and therefore plan to do something the poor would have done if they were more knowledgeable? Do economists have a different discount rate than they do? Do economists place a different value on the lives of their children, or some such thing? Being explicit about why one wants to be in the business of providing social services might help in designing policies that achieve one's goals.

Another issue that chapter 4 touches on is sustainability. Like Kremer and Holla, and others, I think that the quest for sustainability is often misguided.[2]

Looking from the outside, I find sustainability to be something of a fetish. If I want to do good in the world, I would certainly rather give money for a short period of time, get some program on its feet, and then see it become self-sustaining. But there is no theorem that says sustainability will follow. At least in some of the cases discussed here, it seems that to do good in the world one may have to provide bed nets with a huge subsidy or even free for the next fifty years.

Why Are Some Countries Rich and Some Countries Poor?

Kremer and Holla do not address this question, but it hangs over much of the discussion in this volume—although some would argue that it is not really a question for scientific inquiry because it cannot be addressed by replicable experiments, and because the event of economic growth occurs only once. On the contrary, a great deal of science consists of studying phenomena that can only be observed once, as in the study of cosmology or plate tectonics. People in these fields combine observation with theory and with results from other fields. In

2. See, for example, Easterly (2006) on the subject.

order to model the sliding of continental plates, for example, one will want information about the physical properties of rocks subject to high temperature and pressure that might be provided by laboratory experiments. Much of the current macrogrowth literature takes exactly this approach, applying evidence from other areas in economics (including a healthy dose of randomized controlled trials and other microeconomic evidence) to calibrate quantitative models to study growth at the aggregate level.

A further retort to the jibe that macrodevelopment is "not science" is that economists should get over their obsession with science. Historians do not wear lab coats or do experiments, but they have spent two and a half millennia trying to understand why events in the world have played out in the fashion that they have. Historians do not run cross-country regressions but learn how things happen in many other ways. Economists therefore need to look at a broader set of evidence. I would recommend the Engerman and Sokolof approach to reading the historical record as one example.

If it is not a waste of effort to look into why some countries are rich and some poor, what can one learn that is pertinent to this question from the many randomized trials discussed in chapter 4? People in poor countries seem to react to some of the price variations presented to them in experiments in ways that cannot be reconciled with normal economic optimization. If those people have the utility parameters that economists have hypothesized and if the economic calculus facing them is really what has been assumed and yet they are not doing what they are supposed to, then two possibilities remain: either the subjects are bad at optimizing, or they do not believe the world works in the way that economists think it does.

The first explanation is not very appealing. People in poor countries have strong incentives to think long and hard about their economic decisions because the consequences of wrong decisions can be so severe. Furthermore, I do not know of persuasive evidence from outside the experimental sphere indicating that people in poor countries are poor optimizers. The other possibility—that people in poor countries do not think the world works the way economists think they should see it (for example, see that malaria mosquitoes make a person sick and that a treated net will cut down on exposure for five years)—seems far more attractive. Even here, it is worth asking whether people in poor countries do an especially bad job of extracting the correct information from what is available in their environment.

Either of these explanations (people being bad at optimizing or being bad at figuring out the reality they face) could in principle partly account for why poor countries are poor. That is, if people are bad at figuring out what to do, this failing could be holding them back economically. That is not to say that being bad at figuring out what to do is an *ultimate* cause of poverty. Presumably, the ability to figure out what to do is itself endogenous, but it could be part of the mechanism that contributes to poverty. This is not a totally absurd theory. After all, if "being bad at figuring out what to do" were replaced with "having low years of formal education," this would be stating something that everyone believes.

Before one can take seriously the theory that people in poor countries are bad at figuring out what to do, it would be nice to have some evidence of whether this is even true. Nothing in the evidence summarized in chapter 4 says that people in poor countries are *worse* at optimizing than people in rich countries—only that people in poor countries are worse at optimizing than economists think they should be. Ample evidence is certainly available to show that people in rich countries are bad at figuring out what to do. This is where most behavioral economics starts.

Randomized controlled trials as described in chapter 4 cannot be done in the rich countries because, among other things, there is not much use for bed nets or water disinfectant there. But with the help of sensible economists like Kremer and Holla, trials can be done that are similar in spirit and the results can be compared with those for poor countries, the commonalities weighed, and patterns identified. Someday it may be possible to think of a way of putting the results of these trials in some consistent form and making a scatter plot of how the take-up of specific programs differs between rich countries and poor countries. This could not be expected to turn into a cross-country regression that is going to reveal something causal, but it might say something interesting about why some countries are rich and some are poor.

References

Gollin, Douglas, and Christian Zimmermann. 2007. "Malaria: Disease Impacts and Long-Run Income Differences." IZA Discussion Paper 2997. Bonn: Institute for the Study of Labor.
Easterly, William. 2006. *The White Man's Burden: Why the West's Efforts to Aid the Rest Have Done So Much Ill and So Little Good.* New York: Penguin.

Comment by Paul Romer

Economists can learn quite a bit about how to contribute to better policy in developing countries by looking at Milton Friedman's various contributions to monetary policy. In his monetary history of the United States, Friedman (together with Anna Schwartz) argued persuasively that money really does matter at a time when many economists were skeptical. Later, in his presidential address, he identified the key theoretical flaw in the prevailing understanding of the relationship between unemployment and inflation. These contributions (one empirical, the other theoretical) became part of the corpus of scientific knowledge that central bankers learn and rely on when they conduct monetary policy. In part because of this kind of progress at the level of basic science, monetary policy is, on average, much better today than it was fifty years ago.

But Friedman also ventured beyond the realm of science. He offered specific prescriptions for how central bankers should do their jobs with his famous k-percent rule for growth in some monetary aggregate. For good reason, no central banker ever followed this rule. The volatility on all time horizons in the demand for any specific monetary aggregate makes any pure quantity rule wholly impractical, perhaps even dangerous. Academic economists wasted much effort trying to come up with a definition of money that could justify this rule. Later in life, Friedman himself admitted that his emphasis on a quantity rather than the relevant price (the real interest rate) was misplaced.

The point here is that when Friedman crossed the line from scientist to amateur practitioner, he stopped being a good scientist. And because he did not take the job of practitioner seriously, he was not a good practitioner either. He became an academic nag.

In debates about policy, economists get into trouble when they are not clear about the differences between scientists and practitioners. Imagining themselves to be practitioners (or trying to dictate to them), they often tend to overstate the strength of their evidence or come under the influence of political views that can skew their reading of the evidence in ways that undermine both science and practice. If it were a question of running a firm, few economists would presume that an academic paper, even a very good one, would qualify its author to run the firm or dictate to someone who does. Yet when the task is running a government, it seems all too easy to slip into that presumption.

One of the subtexts of this volume is a critique by experimentalists of the quality of the evidence that macrodevelopment types have used to sell their prescriptions. I suspect that this complaint has some merit, but not because these economists are focusing on the wrong questions or using the wrong methods. The big questions they study are important and deserve continued attention, even if they do not lend themselves to experimental methods. Rather, the problem lies in their attempts to influence the political debate on development policy—to be nags—when they should have focused on the science. Moreover, if my diagnosis is correct, the experimentalists will overstate their conclusions if they too try to change what practitioners do. Experiments do not prevent overreaching, and the absence of experiments does not preclude honesty and humility.

What, then, can one learn from the evidence summarized by Michael Kremer and Alaka Holla? How should it be used? One option is to "overreach" and be the nag who tells the practitioners what to do. This naïve approach fails to take into account what people know about why government policymakers do what they do and about how one can influence policy. Policymakers are constrained, but rarely ignorant, at least no more so than the people who run firms.

A second option is to act as consultants to practitioners—to assume that the policymakers know things that we economists do not and that they are responding to constraints and forces that we do not understand. If they ask us to show them how scientific tools like experiments can help them do their jobs, we can make a difference.

The PROGRESA experiment is a good example of this. The practitioner who designed the program, Santiago Levy, reached out to academics for help in doing an evaluation so as to ensure that it would outlive the administration that created it. In this case, the specific policy selected for evaluation came from a practitioner who understood the political constraints on policy, not from an academic. The motivation for the evaluation was political, not scientific. It should come as no surprise that this particular policy, backed by experimental evidence, has been much more influential than experiments from outside the government. For some omnipotent benevolent dictator, treating worms might actually be a more cost-effective way to increase days of schooling for children, and from a scientific point of view, it is good to know this. But for most politicians, PROGRESA-type programs seem to offer a strategy that is more durable and effective, given the constraints they face.

In addition to being the nag ("go treat worms" or "get people to use bed nets") or the consultant ("sure, we can show you how to use random variation to evaluate PROGRESA"), academics can play a third role, which is alluded to by Kremer and Holla and is one that I endorse forcefully. It is, of course, the role suggested by the positive contributions made by Friedman: the role of the scientist. As such, economists can use experimental evidence to change society's basic scientific understanding of behavior and thereby inform, indirectly but powerfully, the decisions undertaken by the practitioners who will make policy in the future.

It is becoming increasingly clear that experiments can be a very powerful way to revise and improve theories. (Odd really, how long it took economists to come to a point that all other scientists take for granted.) For example, the experimental evidence on the ultimatum game is forcing economists to reexamine some of their most basic assumptions about what motivates human behavior. As Kremer and Holla suggest, the experiments they summarize may ultimately have the same effect. In important contexts, there may be a discontinuity at zero in the choices that people make in response to various prices.

These authors do not take much of a stand on what model might rationalize this kind of behavior. Progress here will depend on devising models that complement the evidence. The existing models, such as those based on hyperbolic discounting, do not seem up to the task.

I hope that this kind of experimental work goes hand in hand with serious, open-minded theorizing designed to make sense of what the experimentalists find, but in this partnership I am quite happy with the role that experimentalists have carved out for themselves in development as first-movers. There is no reason for them to wait for theorists to come up with a prediction that needs testing.

The experimentalists will uncover much more if they look at types of behavior that are of great practical significance—such as the decision to buy or use a bed net. It makes good sense for the theorists to come along later and try to make sense of the accumulated evidence, as they are doing for the ultimatum game. Still, I hope that in the process the experimentalists based in academic institutions will remember that their most durable contribution will probably come from progress in basic science, not from some silver-bullet policy intervention that will sweep through the developing world if they nag often enough and loud enough.

Now and then economists have discovered policies that have had a big impact throughout the world as in the case of Santiago Levy's work on the PROGRESA program in Mexico and Muhammad Yunus's microfinance approach at the Grameen Bank. But these policy innovations came from economists who fully made the leap into the role of practitioners, who understood that they were innovators, not scientists, and who came up with their innovations because of the knowledge they had acquired as practitioners. If this is your ambition, by all means pursue it and become a practitioner.

Recognizing that economists are professionally committed to the notion of a division of labor, I believe that it is good that some are willing to shift into the role of consultant or practitioner, often after a productive career as a scientist. Of course, I also believe in the power of pure scientific inquiry and support economists who stay devoted to this kind of work. It seems to me, however, that the role of the academic as nag is a distinctly less helpful one because it blurs the very different roles of the scientist and practitioner.

5

The Policy Irrelevance of the Economics of Education: Is "Normative as Positive" Just Useless, or Worse?

LANT PRITCHETT

Economists have an excellent positive model of the individual/household demand for schooling—in part because it is a straightforward extension of their positive model of everything else. Utility-maximizing people will invest now by sacrificing time, effort, and money on education/schooling/training to gain benefits in the future. Schooling choices depend on the usual factors of preferences, endowments, technologies, relative prices, and budget constraints. Likewise, economists have an excellent normative theory of schooling policy that is a straightforward extension of their normative model for other policy areas. Normative (welfare or public) economics is devoted to the question "What public sector actions would be either (potentially or actually) Pareto improving (by solving a market failure) or, for a given social welfare function, welfare improving (by addressing an equity concern) over the 'no intervention' outcome?"

But economists have no general positive model of schooling policy. The following passage from a World Bank website on education is typical of educational policy discussions: "Governments around the world recognize the importance of education for economic and social development and invest large shares of their

I thank Louis Crouch, Jeff Hammer, Ricardo Hausmann, Emmanuel Jimenez, and Gunnar Eskeland for helpful pre-draft discussions and Amanda Beatty, Michael Clemens, Susan Dynarski, Bill Easterly, Deon Filmer, Jonah Gelbach, Michael Kremer, David Lindauer, Nolan Miller, Emiliana Vegas, and Larry Wimmer for comments on previous versions. Comments made at the Brookings conference by Nancy Birdsall and Ben Olken were also particularly useful and are incorporated into this version.

budgets [in] education. The reasons for state intervention in the financing of education can be summarized as: High returns, Equity, Externalities, Information asymmetries, Market failure."[1]

In the absence of a positive model, the use of normative as positive (NAP)—assuming actual governments do what they do because of market failure(s) or equity concerns—is an apparently irresistible temptation. When pressed, economists immediately see the obvious mistake of confusing normative rationales for actions of a hypothetical welfare-maximizing social planner with positive reasons for the actual actions of real governments. Nevertheless, this does not prevent NAP from lurking as the default positive model when economists discuss the "policy relevance" of their work on the economics of education. This chapter offers three arguments for fending off this temptation.

First, NAP is not a useful first approximation with some flaws: it has only failures and no real successes. The standard rationales for public sector interventions provided by normative models do not predict anything about what governments actually do. NAP does not explain

—the government's largely direct-production support for schooling as opposed to other instruments such as mandates, subsidies, entitlements, vouchers,

—the nonprogressive incidence of schooling or the role of displacement effects in public sector supply decisions,

—the observed productive inefficiency, in comparison with private schools, in the allocation of budget across inputs, or in the adoption of innovations,

—the variation across countries in the allocations of public sector support either in total or across the levels of education (primary versus secondary versus tertiary), or

—the scale of the control of schooling systems.

Second, alternative positive models of schooling policy do a much better job of accounting for observed policies. I have developed one such model, which is a formalization of what everyone, except economists, acknowledges are the important reasons for government engagement in schooling.[2] This model has three simple features: (1) skills and beliefs are jointly produced in formal schooling, (2) the verifiability of the inculcation of beliefs is very costly and hence there is incomplete third-party contracting for schooling, and (3) the "state" as an actor has a desired ideology and hence cares directly about the socialization schooling provides. This model, which I call State Ideology and Incomplete Contracting on Socialization (SI-ICS, sounds like SIX), can easily explain everything NAP cannot. Certainly this is not the only alternative to NAP but is presented to stress that there are viable alternatives.

1. World Bank (2008).
2. Pritchett (2003).

Third, if NAP is false, then there is no way for a researcher to defend positive claims about the policy relevance of research in the economics of education. Four distinct points can be made about the body of empirical work in the economics of education:

1. A large part of the economics of education is explicitly about the development of a positive economics of the demand for schooling that has no policy implications, even if NAP were true.

2. If NAP is not demonstrated to be true, there is no way to prove that the conventional economics of education is not irrelevant to policy as its claims to policy relevance hinge on NAP.

3. If, as I argue, NAP is in fact false, nearly all of the conventional economics of education—whose policy relevance, if grounded at all, is premised on the truth of NAP—is policy irrelevant (which is stronger than argument 2, that it cannot be *proved* to be relevant).

4. In alternative positive models of schooling policy, devoting time and effort to the conventional economics of education in the pursuit of NAP-relevant research might be worse than useless and might actually lower social welfare by aiding and abetting the adoption of welfare-worsening policies.

These four points about policy relevance are increasingly difficult to defend, but fortunately rejecting the stronger one does not imply rejecting the weaker. The first is obvious (if elided a bit in practice). The second only requires accepting that NAP has not been *demonstrated* to be true. Most economists easily abandon NAP, but if one jettisons NAP, there is no way to defend the claim that research that would be policy relevant if NAP were true is, in fact, policy relevant even though NAP is false. The third actually accepts that NAP is false (and again, most economists are willing to concede this), which then implies that the conventional economics of education, which addresses questions relevant only within NAP, has no intuitive basis for claims to policy relevance, as it depends on asserting a positive model in which one can assess the actual impact of research. The fourth illustrates that there is no basis for claiming that, even if NAP is false, policy research or "recommendations" that would be welfare improving under NAP are beneficial. There is no reason to believe that the positive model does not matter and that "good" recommendations or "good" research have robustly "good" effects on policy or well-being.

The difference between research that is thinking big and research that is thinking small depends in part on how one imagines the process by which research findings are translated into practice. The phrase often used about innovation is "build a better mousetrap and people will beat a path to your door," which reflects a positive model of the world in which people have a demand for better mousetraps. The key constraint on the adoption of new mousetrap technology is the existence of a demonstrably superior mousetrap. In this case, "thinking small" on the engineering of mousetraps is already thinking big, as the innovation will scale itself (or the systemic mechanisms for scaling exist and are functional).

However, if the problem is that educational systems are structured such that there are few, if any, incentives to adopt better mousetraps (or even acknowledge that there are mice) and few organizational and institutional structures for the dissemination of better mousetraps when discovered, then thinking small is just thinking small. Demonstrating the efficacy or lack of efficacy of various new (or old) technical or policy innovations in schooling may have little or nothing to do with whether these will be adopted at scale. It all depends on a postulated positive model of schooling policy, and as part of that, on the diffusion of productivity-enhancing innovations.

This potential policy irrelevance of the empirics of the economics of education is not mitigated by the use of rigorous methods, such as randomization. If an empirical parameter is only policy relevant under a given hypothesis (H_0: NAP is true) that is in fact false, then a more rigorous and precise estimate of that parameter remains just as policy irrelevant—and as unlikely to lead to scaled-up impacts—as a less rigorous estimate.

To lay out my case against NAP's policy relevance, I begin with a formal statement of "normative as positive" and a brief statement of the State Ideology and Incomplete Contracting on Socialization (SI-ICS) model, which has at least surface plausibility as a positive model. I then show that nearly all existing economics of education, both theoretical and empirical, are not policy relevant and that, if anything, NAP-relevant research has led economists to support welfare-worsening policies.

Normative as Positive

To be a fully specified positive model, NAP must explain that policy P is chosen because policy P is the optimal choice over a suitable aggregation of citizen preferences (social welfare function) and over the feasible policy instruments, subject to all the constraints the decisionmaker faces, for the economic model maintained by the policymaker. Normative analysis shows that, in the presence of a market failure, there exists a (potentially large) set of policies $\mathbf{P}$ such that any policy P from this set produces higher maximized social welfare than a policy of "no action." For NAP to serve as a complete positive explanation of the observed policy, the policy P cannot be just one of the possible policies $P \in \mathbf{P}^{Beats\ no\ action}$ but should be the optimal response to the invoked market failure(s)/equity concerns. Without the claim of optimality, NAP is underspecified as a positive theory. If NAP only proposed that P was chosen because it was one of many possible policies that led to welfare improvements over "no action," then it would have to be supplemented by another model explaining the choice of the particular policy P from among the set of all welfare-improving policy instruments.

An analogy with automobiles is perhaps useful. Automobile ownership creates numerous externalities: traffic congestion, safety risks to other drivers, polluting emissions. One could almost certainly formulate a normative model in which government ownership of car factories and distributors allowed them to address externalities through control of the production and pricing of cars. But as a positive explanation of why a particular government owned and operated a car factory, the answer "because there are externalities in consumption of automobiles" is obviously inadequate. One would need to show why ownership of factories was chosen over other alternative instruments such as taxes, subsidies, or regulation. A formal statement of NAP requires an objective function as a suitable aggregation of preferences, the policy choice set and constraints, and the maintained economic model of the policymaker.

Preferences

The utility of each of the C citizens depends on consumption of all non-education goods taken as an aggregate over goods and time, their child's school, and the schools chosen by their fellow citizens. The utility of the cth citizen with consumption of non-education goods X^c, whose child attends the jth school while the $C-1$ other citizens attend the (vector of) schools j^{-c}, can be written as

$$(5\text{-}1) \qquad\qquad U^c(X^c, j^c, j^{-c}).$$

A school is defined as a set of skill objectives (N_A dimensional vector), set of belief/value objectives (dimension N_B), and a pedagogical approach to convey those skills and beliefs (dimension N_T)[3] so that each school j is specified as a $N_A + N_B + N_T$ dimensional vector.

Each citizen's utility from schooling depends on the discrepancies between his or her ideal and actual schools. Each parent/citizen c has a different metric $(\| \ \|_c^{A,B,T})$ that maps from deviations in each of the subvectors of schooling into a single cardinal number, which represents for each citizen c the welfare loss from a child being in school j versus the optimal school in that dimension (some parents might care only about mathematics, others only creativity, others only religious doctrine). The function f maps from these three subcomponents to a single (positive) number.

$$(5\text{-}2) \qquad\qquad j^c = -f^c \left(\begin{array}{c} \|A^{c^*} - A^j\|_c^A \\ \|B^{c^*} - B^j\|_c^B \\ \|T^{c^*} - T^j\|_c^T \end{array} \right).$$

The third component of each citizen's utility is the direct effect of ideological choices that other citizens/parents make for their children. I assume that each cit-

---

3. I assume all schools are "feasible" such that the pedagogical approach is consistent with production of the skills and beliefs and that this feasibility is common knowledge.

izen c cares about the skills of other citizens' children only insofar as there are externalities that affect citizen c's consumption (X). But with beliefs there are two possible effects. One is that beliefs acquired by others may affect c's consumption by affecting productivity.[4] The other is that citizen c directly cares about other citizens' beliefs. The typical citizen c might not like having other people's children taught that c's own ethnicity/religion/political beliefs/gender/nationality are inferior or stupid or evil—whether or not these beliefs directly affect c's measured consumption of goods. Exactly how each citizen might care about the beliefs of others is complex, and there is no presumption that the function is linear or symmetric as some citizens may be indifferent (tolerant) in a broad range and yet care strongly when beliefs cross a certain threshold of ideological difference. Others may object strongly to even small deviations in certain directions. For simplicity, I assume that each citizen c has a different optimal belief for all others (B^{c*}) and has some metric $(\| \ \|)$ over the $N_B \times (C-1)$ stacked vector of ideologies received when children attend schools j^{-c} (where the notation "$-c$" indicates a $C-1$ dimensional vector that excludes c):

$$(5\text{-}3) \qquad j^{-c} = \begin{array}{c} \| \ B^{c*} - B^{j^1} \ \| \\ \| \ B^{c*} - B^{j^{c-1}} \ \| \\ \| \ B^{c*} - B^{j^{c+1}} \ \| \\ \| \ B^{c*} - B^{j^C} \ \|_c \end{array} .$$

Aggregate Individualized Social Welfare

The social welfare function aggregates citizen utility. I impose the common constraint that the social welfare aggregation is "inequality averse." I also impose the common, but often implicit, assumption that the social welfare aggregation is "individualistic." This means only the utility of citizens from their own consumption of goods and schooling is considered in the technocrat's aggregation of well-being. That is, if citizen c's neighbor Mr. $c+1$ plays jazz on his stereo sufficiently loudly that c can hear it, this is part of c's consumption vector and that does enter the technocrat's utility function. But utility from existence values are ruled out: citizen c may dislike it if Mr. $c+1$ plays jazz (or worships Satan, or tells racist jokes, or watches pornography, or is homophobic) at all, ever, even in the privacy of Mr. $c+1$'s own home.[5] The assumption is ubiquitous but usually made implicitly by dropping this element from the specification for individual utility. There is a long tradition of liberal individualism that rules out as inappropriate for policy consideration all such interpersonal existence values (for example, envy, prudery, religious intolerance, jealousy, sadism).

---

4. See, for example, Gradstein and Justman (2000), who assume homogeneity in beliefs promotes interpersonal trust, which promotes higher output.

5. This same distinction is made in the discussion of environmental externalities between *use* values (that I value a clean environment because I may use it someday) and *existence* values (that I value the very existence of some unspoiled environment even if I personally never see it).

In the context of education, the interpersonal concern about beliefs is empirically important, but one needs to sharply differentiate policies that can be justified within the standard NAP approach using an "individualized social welfare" (ISW) function (which, again, may include indirect effects of beliefs via propensity to trust and cooperate that affect consumption via impacts on aggregate production) and those that invoke direct consideration of interpersonal concern about beliefs (which are a subset of the positive models presented in the following sections).

$$ISW = SW(U^1(X^1, j^1, j^{-1}), ..., U^C(X^C, j^C, j^{-C})),$$

Individualistic

(5-4) $$\partial SW / \partial U_1^c \geq 0, \partial SW / \partial U_2^c \geq 0, \partial SW / \partial U_3^c = 0 \; \forall c$$

Inequality averse

$$\partial^2 SW / \partial U_1^c \leq 0, \partial^2 SW / \partial U_2^c \leq 0.$$

Policy Choice Set and Constraints

Policy choices consist of two elements: the policy instruments under consideration and the constraints on those instruments.

INSTRUMENTS. If the causal explanation of "Why policy *P*?" is that "*P* was normatively optimal," then policy *P* should not just be better than the alternative of "nothing" but should be the best feasible policy. So if market failures lead to an inefficiently low level of education with "no intervention," then there are a variety of possible instruments to raise the level: mandates, entitlements, universal subsidies, targeted subsidies, subsidies to providers, direct production, and so on. The feasible policy set is limited by implementation constraints, but these should be modeled explicitly either as limitations on the feasible instrument or as constraints on the instrument.

(5-5)   P ∈ **P**{*set of all feasible instruments*}.

CONSTRAINTS. The policy chosen must satisfy a variety of constraints. For instance, any policy that involves positive public expenditures should satisfy the budget constraint—so that expenditures are matched to mobilized revenues. These constraints can also impose feasibility constraints on various instruments. For instance, targeted subsidies may be a possible instrument, but the efficiency of targeting might be limited by the public sector's ability to observe household outcomes (for example, current income might not be observable). These two elements, feasibility and constraints, are obviously intertwined; if an instrument is included in the choice set, the relevant constraints need to be imposed, and if the constraints imply that a certain instrument will never be chosen, this can be incorporated by eliminating the instrument from the feasible set.

(5-6)   P *satisifies* $\mathbf{C}$ = {*policy instrument constraints*}.

ECONOMIC MODEL. An economic model is a mapping between possible policy actions (including no action) and the resulting equilibrium of the choices by individual citizens (as consumers and producers), which determines the income/consumption for each citizen and schooling outcomes for each of the C citizens. This dependency of policy outcomes on the maintained model is denoted by indexing the outcomes by model M:

(5-7) $(X^c, j^c, j^{-c}) = X_M^c(P), j_M^c(P), j_M^{-c}(P).$

A great deal is packed into model M: behavioral functions of producers and consumers, market-clearing mechanisms, production functions, and so forth. The standard welfare theorems often specify a general equilibrium model (specifications of production functions, utility functions, behavior of consumers, market clearing) under which no Pareto-improving policies exist. A rationale for public sector intervention usually takes the form of some assumption about externalities or other market failure. One common assumption is that governments promote schooling because there are externalities to skills (of some type—perhaps literacy). In NAP the relevant model is one that the policymaker believes and hence translates into policy choices.

The normative-as-positive answer to the question "Why did the government do P?" is "Because P was P_{ISW}^*—the optimal feasible policy to maximize the aggregation of citizen preferences ISW under the policymaker's maintained economic model M, subject to the constraints C."

Normative as Positive (NAP) : Policy P is chosen because P is P*,

(5-8) $P_{ISW}^*(\mathbf{C},M) = \overset{\text{argmax}}{\underset{\mathbf{P}}{}} ISW\,(U^1(X_M^1(P), j_M^1(P), j_M^{-1}(P)),...,$
$$U^C(X_M^C(P), j_M^C(P), j_M^{-C}(P)))$$

subject to Constraint set $\mathbf{C}$ *and* $M^{Policymaker} = M$.

An Alternative Model: State Ideology and Incomplete Contracting on Socialization

Attacking NAP against an unspecified alternative is easy, but I want to go further and pose a concrete alternative, which is handy to have in illustrating the policy-irrelevant consequences of NAP. Nothing in this discussion hinges on accepting this alternative, and readers should feel free to propose their own NAP alternative (more on this later in the chapter). My alternative combines state ideology and incomplete contracting in the inculcation of beliefs. Ask anyone but an economist—either those in other disciplines (historians, sociologists, political scientists, educationists) or practitioners (educators, politicians)—why governments produce schooling, and they will say it is because schooling plays a crucial role in socialization, in the formation of a mass public culture, and in the control of the ideology transmitted. Moreover, this is explicitly what governments say they are doing, both historically and today. What an early Meiji-era minister of education had to say about the administration of schools—that "what is to be done is not for the sake of the pupils, but for the sake of the country"—is not far from the comment that Turkey's Ministry of Education recently posted on its website: "The Turkish education system aims to take the Turkish people to the level of modern civilization by preparing individuals with high qualifications for the information age, who . . . are committed to Atatürk's nationalism and Atatürk's principles and revolution."[6]

An alternative positive model entertains the notion that governments really mean what they say (and that in this case other disciplines might actually have it right) and takes seriously the role of socialization as a key function of schooling. This alternative model differs from NAP in two key respects. First, there is an actor called "the state," which chooses policies. The state as an autonomous actor has its own objective function, which in general is not simply an aggregation of individual preferences (although in a super special case of a political system that perfectly replicated an aggregation of preferences, it could be). The state's objective function has as a direct argument the beliefs inculcated in schools. The history of schooling is replete with explicit battles for control of the ideological content of schools: communists wanted their schools/ideology to build the new socialist man, nineteenth-century liberals wanted to reduce the influence of Catholics, Napoleon called on schools to build a national French identity over regional affiliations, Atatürk wrested control of schooling from the clerics to form a distinctively Turkish (as opposed to either Ottoman or Islamic) identity, and Suharto in Indonesia used schools to promote his philosophy of *panchasila*. Therefore the first element of this non-NAP model is "state ideology" (SI)—the state chooses policies to maximize its own objective function, and the discrepancy between the beliefs inculcated in the schools children attend and the state's "ideal" beliefs enters directly as an argument in its objective function.[7]

The second element is that the effective inculcation of beliefs, unlike the teaching of skills, is very costly for a third party to observe because one cannot pretend to have skills one does not have, but it is relatively easy to pretend to have beliefs one does not have. If the state desires the inculcation of an ideology that a significant fraction of the population does not share (for example, communism, secularism, Catholicism, nation-state loyalty over ethnicity), then verification costs are potentially high enough that the third party contracting for schooling (as when

6. See www.mob.gov.tr/english/indexeng.htm.

7. The emphasis on the ideological role of schooling is similar to Lott (1999), but the approach is different in two respects. First, his model focuses on the attempt of particular "regimes" to stay in power rather than on the interests of "the state." Second, he models the regime concern about ideology not as a direct argument in the objective function but rather as exclusively instrumental to perpetuation of the regime in power. My approach is much more general as I allow for "states" to have sincere beliefs.

the state gives a voucher) does not accomplish the state objective, as it is undermined by collusion between teacher and student for insincere teaching. A student with the incentive to be able to pass himself off as a communist or Catholic or nationalist but with no desire to actually believe the ideology could contract with an instructor to "teach me to pass the exam and mimic communist/Catholic/nationalist beliefs while at the same time teaching me these beliefs are false." This second element is therefore the technological constraint of "incomplete contracting over socialization" (ICS).

In the SI-ICS model, policy P is chosen to maximize the state's objective function, which has as a direct argument the beliefs in schools attended subject to the observational constraints on socialization and political constraints on state viability. The constraints on state viability depend on the political model of both the "state" (which is broader than the control of any given regime) and the "regime" (the entity that controls the state). Constraints on the state depend on the citizens' ability to monitor and hold the state accountable—which can vary from next to no control by citizens in authoritarian regimes to tight control of regime behavior by electoral accountability in others. This assumes some discrepancy between the interests of the citizens in maximizing their own welfare (which includes the degree to which their children's school conforms to their desired socialization and pedagogical approach) and the state; it also assumes that citizen well-being, rather than being an objective of the state, is a constraint on the state's pursuit of its own interests, of which ideological control is one element.

As Ben Olken has pointed out, this SI-ICS is in some respects just a special case of the general point that actual governments, to the extent they have preferences that can be expressed as a function, have a social welfare function SW^G that differs from the usual notions of a standard social welfare function—it may care more about rich government donors, or the well-being of key constituencies (such as public sector unions), or may simply care only about a narrow clique and have zero concern about others.[8] This is true, and this point will arise again, with the proviso that incomplete contracting on the inculcation of beliefs is an additional, technological, constraint that is not about the welfare function of the state/regime/government per se.

As a Model, NAP Has No Successes and Many Failures

The NAP is inconsistent with, or at best does not explain, five common facts about schooling policy in countries around the world. I stress "countries around the world" so as not to dwell on what is true of the United States or Denmark, for example, but to recall that a range of governments is present around the world, from Moldova to Mozambique to Mexico to Morocco, and that all of these governments

8. Benjamin Olken, comments at the Development Conference, Brookings (May 29–30, 2008).

have schooling policies. SI-ICS provides a general alternative model that, if fully elaborated, at least would have the potential to explain everything NAP cannot. Again, this is not to argue that SI-ICS is the only alternative to NAP, as there are explicit political economy models of some aspects of schooling, and one can accept that the arguments against NAP can be leveled against an unspecified alternative positive model without accepting SI-ICS as the alternative.

—The first fact is that support to schooling comes about predominantly (if not only) through direct production, and there is strikingly little reliance on other instruments that would appear to be economically more efficient instruments for the ISW objectives.

—Second, the overall benefit incidence of education spending is not progressive (relative to say, a uniform transfer), and governments do not minimize displacement effects.

—Third, allocation of total budget to education and across levels of education (for example, primary versus secondary) varies widely across countries.

—Fourth, government production of schooling is inefficient in that (a) allocation of budget across activities (for example, teachers versus buildings versus chalk) often seems biased toward wages, (b) at least in some instances government-operated schools are economically far less efficient than private schools, and (c) adoption of innovations seems slow.

—Fifth, the scale of the jurisdictions responsible for the production of schooling is much larger than any economics would suggest.

NAP and the Policy of "Only Direct Production"

NAP is useless with regard to the most basic and common feature of schooling policy—that nearly all governments not only directly produce schooling but that, to first order, direct production is their only support to education. Mark Blaug's review of the economics of education, although compiled more than thirty years ago, remains roughly true: "What needs to be explained about formal schooling is not so much why governments subsidize it as they do, but why they insist on owning so much of it in every country. On this crucial question we get no help, and cannot expect to get help, from the human capital research program, even when it is supplemented by the theory of externalities and public goods of welfare economics."[9]

Three distinct arguments can be put forward to demonstrate NAP's uselessness. First, the usual normative economics of education does not lead to a positive prediction of "only direct production" as it stops short of showing why production is superior to other instruments for achieving the same objective. Second, NAP cannot be made to plausibly predict "only direct production." Third, even

9. Blaug (1976, p. 831).

if in some special case NAP could predict "only direct production," it does not work as a general explanation of government behavior.

NAP DOES NOT PREDICT "ONLY DIRECT PRODUCTION." Positive externalities, both economic and noneconomic, to a minimal level of basic education are often cited as a normative rationale for government intervention in the market for basic schooling. Some might argue: (a) many believe externalities exist, and (b) that governments produce schooling is itself a "successful" prediction of NAP. Although I use this example to illustrate the difficulties with NAP, the arguments can be extended to other market failures (such as credit constraints and information asymmetries).

Suppose the policymaker's model has Externalities to Basic Schooling (M^{ETB}); then the socially optimal amount of basic education exceeds private demand in a "no intervention" equilibrium. But to be a positive model with any predictive content, NAP must show not merely that more than "only production" is one of many instruments that could lead to welfare improvements, but that it is the optimal instrument.

$$(5\text{-}9) \qquad\qquad P^{Only\ Production} \overset{?}{=} P^*\,(C,M^{ETB})\,.$$

In judging the relative merits of potential policy instruments for addressing normative market failure or equity concerns, I assert that economists have four general propensities. While each of these could be proved as theorems in specific contexts, here I just assert them as broad propensities among policy alternatives (PAPAs).[10]

PAPA I (Choice): In choosing between two policies that can address the same problem, the policy that allows greater scope for individual choice is more likely to be optimal.

PAPA II (Entry and Exit): In choosing between two policies, the policy that produces freer entry and exit of producers is more likely to be optimal (as this is more likely to result in productive efficiency and diffusion of innovation).

PAPA III (Tax Minimizing): In the choice between two policies, the policy that minimizes the distortions induced from mobilizing public sector revenue is more likely to be optimal.

PAPA IV (Instruments to Targets): The optimal solution matches as closely as possible the instrument to the objective.

Can NAP show the optimality of a policy of "only direct production"? An alternative policy to address externalities to basic education is to enforce a mandate that every child must receive at least some minimal standard of education

10. I would argue that most trained economists are sympathetic to these propositions and might even believe them to be generally true—by which I mean these propositions can be stated technically and proved as theorems under certain conditions and economists tend to believe that the conditions are empirically quite widely applicable—though there will be important exceptions to each.

(with the minimum specified either in terms of passing a minimal number of years, attending until a certain age, or achieving some level of actual performance—say, literacy). Mandates are widely used as a policy instrument to address externalities in other domains (emissions testing, food safety requirements, occupational certification, zoning restrictions, immunization requirements, and so on). Mandates are plausibly a better response to positive externalities than direct government production because mandates (a) maintain consumer choice of provider (PAPA I), (b) allow for competition in production (PAPA II), (c) use fewer tax resources as there are expenditures only in enforcement (PAPA III), and (d) can be directly matched to the externality—if the externality pertains to a particular level of education (basic) or set of skills (such as literacy), then the acquisition of those skills is mandated while leaving the other content of schooling and the total level achieved to citizen choice (PAPA IV). This argument is not intended to prove mandates are the optimal response, but only to show that the existence of externalities alone does not imply NAP predicts any public production (much less only production) unless it is shown to be superior to mandates (and all other alternatives).

To get NAP with the policymaker economic model M^{ETB} to explain only direct production, one might add features to the constraint set on policies or restrict the range of feasible policies. For instance, one could assert that mandates are not the optimal instrument because some parents "cannot afford" the mandated minimal standard. To formalize this, one might add a constraint on the policy set such that the mandated expenses not exceed some fraction of household expenditures.[11] With both externalities and affordability constraints, a policy of a mandate supplemented by targeted transfers or fee waivers (again, commonly implemented in other policy domains) is arguably superior to production (again by invoking PAPA I–IV). Further complications might be added—perhaps some people cannot afford the mandated standard and governments do not have information to target household ability to pay. The policy choice problem is now ($M^{\text{Policymaker}} = M^{ETB}$) and the constraint set is {"Mandated expenditures cannot exceed threshold" and "Cannot target on ability to pay"} $\in C$. With externalities and affordability constraints and inability to target, a mandate plus a universal "demand-side subsidy" (for example, vouchers) might still be superior to direct production as it allows consumers to choose their schools (PAPA I), allows for competition (PAPA II), and reduces public resource use (in the absence of cost recovery).

$$(5\text{-}10) \qquad\qquad P^{\textit{Only Production}} \overset{?}{=} P^*\left(C^?, M^{ETB}\right).$$

The first point, then, is that NAP typically fails because it does not constitute a fully articulated positive explanation of the widely observed policy of only direct

11. Of course, if the policymaker has access to lump-sum taxes and transfers, the "instruments to targets" argument would suggest implementing the joint policy of optimal transfer to address the "equity" issue and the use of the mandate to address externalities. But I have excluded lump-sum taxes in PAPA III.

production. The model and constraint set under which this is the optimal policy instrument are not specified.[12]

NAP CANNOT BE MADE TO PREDICT "ONLY DIRECT PRODUCTION." Taking this argument further, Caroline Hoxby has shown that essentially anything direct production can do (that is observable) vouchers can do better.[13] In particular, one might imagine that in addition to standard externalities, perhaps schooling has social objectives, such as achieving social integration. Hoxby shows that even for schooling goals such as encouraging racial or ethnic diversity, well-designed vouchers are still superior to government production. Her argument is an extension (and formalization) of the heuristic arguments made as PAPA I–IV.[14] Under standard normative public economics, as reflected in propensities among policy alternatives (PAPA I–IV), one can make the bold assertion that "anything q can do, p can do better," or that there is always a policy superior to only direct production and hence NAP cannot predict the world's most widely observed schooling policy.

(5-11)   (Conjecture) $\forall\ C,M\ \exists\ P$ such that $ISW(P) > ISW(P^{Only\ Direct\ Production})$.

The fundamental difficulty with constructing a positive model that predicts government production is that the market failures for schooling are nearly always on the demand side (owing to factors such as externalities, credit constraints, and information asymmetries), but it is the characteristics of production that usually occasion government ownership as an economically optimal response. Governments often directly produce pure public goods (nonrival and nonexcludable). Governments also often end up owning assets that provide services for which excludability is difficult, as in the case of urban roads, although interurban highways are at least in some instances served with toll roads. Governments also end up owning industries considered natural monopolies—that is, industries having either network externalities in the delivery of the service (for example, urban sanitation, natural gas) or large economies of scale, or both when vertically integrated (for example, power). In these cases the "make or buy" choice between government ownership and private ownership with regulation is complex.

In contrast, on the supply side, schooling (certainly primary and secondary and nearly all of tertiary) is a garden-variety, plain vanilla, private good. Schooling is

12. Many developing countries have at some point banned the private production of education at the primary or secondary level (and some even banned it at the university level). Reconciling a ban on private education with NAP is perhaps not impossible—but no one has, and it would require some ingenuity to show why a technocrat with the objective to increase skills through education would prohibit voluntary, skill-enhancing, public budget-reducing agreements between parents and providers. Perhaps there is a model with important peer effects in which the only way to preserve the positive externalities of "high-quality" students is to force them into public schools.

13. Hoxby (2001).

14. Which are roughly the same as famously presented by Milton Friedman (1962) in his argument for school vouchers more than forty years ago.

fully excludable. Schooling is rival.[15] Except in very small and remote places (such as Pakistan's rural Punjab, which now has many public and private schools), the economies of scale are small in relation to the total market, and there are few infrastructure-like network externalities.[16] The supply of basic schooling is probably almost infinitely elastic.[17]

Few markets, when left to their own devices, look more like the economist's model of competitive markets with atomistic producers than does for-profit training. Take markets for language or computer instruction, tutoring, or "lessons" (say, in athletics or music). Walk down a street in any medium-sized town in a developing country and prepare to be bombarded with advertisements for these services from a multitude of suppliers. If one thinks of schooling as sequenced multi-topic training, then one at least suspects the same competitive nature of the industry would apply when entry is allowed—which is consistent with the evidence of many small producers rather than large market players when there is significant private sector entry.

THE "ALL-COUNTRIES" PROBLEM WITH DIRECT PRODUCTION AND NAP. Economists can be simultaneously clever and stubborn in ignoring the obvious. If taken as a theorem, that no NAP model could explain "only production" as an optimal policy, a sufficiently clever economist might take a proof by a counterexample approach. Perhaps by tweaking assumptions here and there, one might concoct a model in which NAP does predict production in some configuration of economic and political circumstances.[18] But to be a general model, NAP would have to deal with the "all" problem. Think of any list of developing countries: Bolivia, El Salvador, Haiti, Morocco, Egypt, Kenya, Malawi, Côte d' Ivoire, Nepal, Pakistan, Malaysia, Vietnam. The government produces schooling in all of these countries and at all levels—from primary to tertiary—and in all of them public schooling has expanded massively. But it is difficult to believe that the predominant motivation behind any of their schooling policies has been the maximization of social welfare.[19] So even if one had a counterexample in which a com-

15. This is a little complicated: over some ranges of class size, one additional student may impose only small costs on other children, but this is over a very narrow range compared with the market.

16. Especially if one divides the overall production of schooling into components, such as curriculum, setting standards, creating textbooks, external assessment, and those parts of the daily operation of the school. See Pritchett and Pande (2006). Since these can easily be separated in practice, vertical integration is not a necessary feature of the industry.

17. At least where the main input (potential teachers) is readily available. Andrabi and others (2008) show that in Pakistan women do not move across villages easily, and locally available teachers created by past public schooling strongly influence the *supply* of private schools.

18. Epple and Romano (1996) also have a model that explains direct production in a voting game in which some mix of market and public provision (with private supplements) is observed. Whatever its merits as a description of some current situations (for example, voting in the United States), these models can hardly be robust general models of schooling policy. Epple and Romano never suggest their model is general or extends beyond the United States.

19. Official statistics for Ukraine provide a particularly strong example: the number of children aged eight to fifteen in Ukraine schooling almost doubled from 1928–29 to 1932–33, and enrollment reached

plicated variant of NAP did appear to be correct, it would likely be a special case and would not vindicate NAP as a general model.

Although a disinterested social welfare maximizer is a useful imaginary device for normative analysis, it cannot offer a positive description of the behavior of any real agent since it is obviously inconsistent with both the facts and the rest of the economics, which assumes self-interested maximization by all other agents. Moreover, it is obviously inconsistent with the actual behavior of most governments of the world—all of which do produce education.

SI-ICS DOES NATURALLY WHAT NAP CANNOT DO: PREDICT "ONLY DIRECT PRODUCTION" EVERYWHERE. First, the cost of third-party observation of the sincerity of socialization is the key assumption that drives government production, which is a supply-side assumption and hence naturally predicts production. Second, since the objective is to control socialization, production is preferred over other instruments that would increase the total amount of schooling but would do so outside the control of government (as mandates or vouchers would) and thus would not advance the objective function of the state. Third, since (nearly) all governments—including democracies[20]—seek to control socialization in schooling, the SI-ICS model easily handles the "all" problem as democracies are a special case.[21] Fourth, SI-ICS can explain the deviations from "only direct production"—in which suppliers are provided public support and (very few) countries actually adopt widespread voucher-like programs.[22]

Displacement and Benefit Incidence

The second most widely known fact about education is that around the world children from richer households complete substantially more schooling than children from poorer households because they are more likely to enroll, more likely to enroll at an early age, and less likely to drop out.[23] Nearly the entire government budget for education goes to direct production, and the structure of the

---

4.5 million. A purge of the Ukrainian elite in 1932–33 together with "nationalist" sympathies and a famine cost somewhere between 3 million and 5 million lives. Was Stalin of two minds about the region—expanding schools for benign normative motives and yet killing, deporting, and confiscating food for malign motives? Of course not. The expansion of schooling, the purges, and the famine had the same objective: to suppress Ukrainian nationalism and opposition to Stalin's policies.

20. Kremer and Sarychev (2000).

21. Other models besides Pritchett's (2003) stress the inculcation of beliefs in the education process in explaining government production (Kremer and Sarychev [2000]; Gradstein and Justman [2000]). These are special cases that invoke an actual production externality to beliefs (Gradstein and Justman) or democracy or a distribution of beliefs (Kremer and Sarychev), neither of which is general.

22. In some predominantly Catholic countries (for example, Argentina and Venezuela), public funds are allowed to flow to Catholic schools—but only Catholic schools. In some predominantly Muslim countries (for example, Indonesia), public funds are allowed to flow to Muslim schools. The only country that has historically provided resources to public and private institutions on a (more or less) comparable footing is Holland. Its policy is clearly rooted in the population's mixed religious denominations.

23. Filmer and Pritchett (1999).

cost of that subsidy per child is X if the child is enrolled in a government school, zero otherwise. If the gradient of enrollment in private school is not sufficiently large, then in most of the world the public sector cost incidence of overall education spending is less progressive than a uniform transfer.[24] Education spending tends to follow enrollment so that as enrollment at any given level (primary, secondary, tertiary) increases, the marginal incidence is higher than the average incidence (as the richer enroll first), and thus incidence "improves" as enrollments expand.[25]

This pattern constitutes an enormous puzzle for the NAP model in that if the goal is to increase the level of schooling, then all costs on students who would have otherwise enrolled in the private sector are inframarginal. Inasmuch as inframarginal subsidies imply public costs, with all the attendant costs of mobilizing public sector funds, these subsidies are inefficient. Under NAP, one would expect public policies to be consciously designed to minimize displacement from the private sector. The most obvious way to do so would be to have public support flow to poorer households.

This question of displacement sharply distinguishes the NAP from the SI-ICS model. In SI-ICS, the state's objective function can increase when a student moves from the private to the public sector, since the conformity with the desired socialization is higher. If NAP were true, one should observe governments designing policies to minimize displacement and maximize total, not just public sector, enrollment per public sector dollar. The goal would be to see that all students receive schooling. If SI-ICS were true, one would expect governments to maximize public sector enrollment—even at times when they are actively discouraging private schools. The goal is to see that students who get schooling receive publicly produced schooling. This difference regarding displacement explains many commonly observed empirical facts.

First, it explains the widely observed patterns of the incidence of benefits. If the state wants to control the schooling of those getting educated, and if those come from richer backgrounds, then the incidence will follow rather than lead the private demand for schooling.

Second, this difference explains the lack of other instruments (such as mandates, entitlements, and vouchers) as the state does not wish to push demand ahead of the publicly available supply. Although the government production of schools is sometimes used as an argument for government commitment to universal schooling, the simple plausible argument is that governments produce schooling as their only support precisely because they are *not* committed to universal schooling. It is commonly accepted that there is almost no developing country in which the enforcement of a legal mandate accounts for a significant

24. I use the phrase "cost incidence" rather than the more common "benefit incidence" since, for a variety of reasons, the public sector cost per child may not even approximate the benefit to the child.

25. For an example, see Lanjouw and Ravallion (1999).

increase in the amount of education.[26] While a mandate with no production would not be a puzzling response to an externality, direct production with no mandate is truly a puzzle for NAP. Suppose, however, the government had a limited commitment to education and really only wanted those who would go to school in any case to attend publicly produced schools and was willing to devote only X percent of its budget to education. Support only through direct production allows a convenient way to ration the exogenously determined budget, not to those who would not have attended but to all, including those who would have had private schooling.

Third, this difference explains the historical phenomenon of the state's creating a public sector educational system by absorbing and controlling existing schools (which is the origin of the government system in nearly every currently developed country). In Japan, a decade after the consolidation of schooling into nationally controlled schools, enrollments are said to be roughly the same—so the government's expansion of schools amounts to 100 percent displacement.

Fourth, many countries forbid private schooling. For instance, in the 1970s Pakistan nationalized existing schools and banned private schools as a deliberate policy to push children into government schools.[27] This is hard to reconcile with the goal of maximizing enrollment (NAP) but easy to reconcile with the goal of maximizing the fraction of those who enroll in a publicly controlled school (SI-ICS).

Fifth, this explains the general lack of calculations of displacement in building new schools. Suppose that the government builds a new school and attendance at that school is 100 children. By how much did the "public sector intervention" increase enrollment? The answer could be 100, or it could be 0. If NAP were the correct description of behavior, then the magnitude of displacement effects would be a huge empirical issue, both in assessing overall support to education and in deciding on the location of individual schools. But the contrary is true; only two studies, and both quite recent, seem to have tackled the subject. The lack of interest in displacement effects is consistent with an objective function increasing in the proportion enrolled in publicly controlled schools.

Total Support and Allocation of Support across Tiers of Schooling

In principle, NAP would explain total support to and the variation across the levels of schooling from basic right up to tertiary—both in terms of instruments (for example, subsidies versus direct production) and budget allocations—as functions of an economic model and set of constraints that led the choices to be welfare

26. Basu (1998). If a mandatory age were effective and binding, one should see a discontinuity in the enrollment profile by age around the mandatory age, as those held in the system by the mandate would drop out as they neared the age limit. While there is some evidence of this type for countries of the Organization for Economic Cooperation and Development (one being Britain), even countries with a mandatory age on the books show no empirical evidence of impact.

27. Farooqi and Pritchett (2003).

maximizing. Despite the substantial variation both across countries/jurisdictions and across time in budget allocation, however, a relationship in total and across the tiers of education has never been established between the empirical magnitudes of market failures/equity concerns and (a) the level of allocation in any single country, (b) the variation over time within a single country/jurisdiction, or (c) the variations across countries.

Moreover, at higher levels of schooling the question of choice between direct production and vouchers also arises. The extent to which higher education is carried out by publicly controlled versus private institutions varies substantially across countries. This variation in instruments has never been explained across contexts in the underlying market model or in constraint sets across countries. The SI-ICS model can be extended to take into account socialization/ideological control at both the mass and higher levels—which would explain the government engagement in this area (even without invoking any market failures), as well as cross-country variations in support across levels of schooling (depending on whether governments wish to control ideology most at the mass or elite levels).

The Efficiency of Production

NAP implies that if the technocrat chooses government production of schooling to promote skills, then these government schools should be productively efficient (cost minimizing). Productive efficiency would have three implications: (a) budgets are allocated efficiently across inputs, (b) public and private schooling are equally efficient, and (c) to remain efficient, government schools must also adopt innovations.

BUDGET ALLOCATIONS. An earlier study has demonstrated there is no evidence for productive efficiency of the allocation of inputs.[28] No one has ever tested the proposition that schools were productively efficient and not been able to reject it. Note, too, that the increment in measured skills per expenditure across inputs (for example, books versus class size), which of course should be equalized in productively efficient units, often differs by one, two, or even three orders of magnitude. Cumulatively, the evidence suggests deviations from productive efficiency that are systematic and inconsistent with NAP. The deviations from efficient budget allocations are consistent with positive models in which the objective functions of policymakers put substantial weight on factors other than maximization of social welfare.[29]

PUBLIC VERSUS PRIVATE SCHOOLS. There is much evidence that, even if one controls for selection effects, private schools are enormously more cost-effective in learning achievement per expenditure than government-run schools. This is not to say that private schools will be uniformly more effective at producing learning

28. Pritchett and Filmer (1999).
29. Filmer and Pritchett (1999).

outcomes—in many countries with effective governance and tight democratic control the differences between public and private school efficiency might be small. But in cases with weak governance, the estimated gap between public and private schools in measured learning gain per dollar is large (and can be as large as a factor of two).[30] This is usually because unit teacher costs are enormously higher in government schools either because teacher wages are high (and not well structured) or class sizes are inefficiently low (compared with other inputs).

DIFFUSION OF INNOVATIONS. A third implication of productive efficiency is that schools should be at the productive frontier, including in the adoption of whatever existing innovations there are (with some lag for diffusion). One thing the series of randomized experiments that have been carried out in education over the last few years have definitively established is that a number of easily available, "common sense" interventions (such as tutoring for those behind in reading or introducing "community" teachers) have not been widely adopted.[31] This is consistent with the commonly observed phenomenon of wide gaps in the effectiveness of individual schools and, at least in some environments, the very wide variation across government schools in effectiveness.[32] Since what government is doing under SI-ICS is not in fact attempting to address market failures, there is no particular reason to expect it to be productively efficient in producing learning outcomes.

Scale of Government Jurisdiction Responsible for Production

Even if it were decided that "only direct production" by the government were the optimal policy, there would still be a question of which level of political jurisdiction should be endowed with control over which aspects of schooling. If one were imagining that schooling policy were chosen optimally, what would be the relative roles of national, provincial/state, municipality, and local governments in schooling? Moreover, would schooling be controlled by quasi-parallel organizations (such as autonomous school boards) or directly as a line ministry function?

The prevalence of national or state/provincial control of the production of schooling over more local bodies is another common feature of schooling for which NAP has no explanatory power at all. There is no suggestion that this could possibly be explained by economies of scale. SI-ICS has a coherent answer: the level of jurisdiction is a political issue and depends on battles over the control of socialization—national control, the preservation of state/provincial autonomy

---

30. Jimenez, Lockheed, and Paqueo (1991). Das, Pandey, and Zajonc (2006) find that after adjusting for student characteristics, the private-public gap is 73, 92, and 143 points in Math, Urdu, and English, respectively, in rural Pakistan even though private schools have substantially lower costs per student. A recent study finds the same gap for schools in Orissa and Rajasthan in India. A small survey of schools in urban areas of India finds the same phenomenon—substantially higher scores (adjusting for background) with lower unit costs (Tooley and Dixon [2002]).

31. Duflo, Dupas, and Kremer (2007).

32 . On individual schools, see Crouch and Healy (1997); on the variation across government schools in Pakistan, see Das and others (2006).

in federal systems (as in India and Germany), and even less commonly, local control (as in the United States).

Summary of Empirical Validation of NAP

There is not a single aspect of actual educational policymaking that normative welfare economics taken as a positive model elucidates correctly (table 5-1). By contrast, the SI-ICS alternative has the potential to explain easily the "puzzles" NAP must work itself into contortions to accommodate.

Other political economy models of schooling attempt to explain the rise of schooling without NAP as well, but most explain the expansion of education historically as the result of the expansion of the franchise, with the "elite" extending schooling under pressure from the "masses" to forestall even larger changes.[33] Although these models elucidate some elements of the political economy of schooling, they cannot act as general models of schooling policy unless they explicitly incorporate the role of socialization. Without that input and incomplete contracting, they are unable to deal with the "only direct production" versus alternative instruments, the rise of schooling in nondemocratic environments, the displacement issue, or efficiency problems.

Many models of the political economy of education policy focus on other ways (besides concern for ideology) that the government welfare function may differ from a standard social welfare function. For instance, the role of teachers and teachers' unions looms large in discussions of education reform. Also, the role of elites and social stratification in education policy is an important element in the social welfare function SW^G for many governments that does not fit the standard social welfare approach.

What Is Policy Relevant?

Some may think the previous section administered a vicious beating to an already dead horse. It is easy to admit that NAP is wrong, and surely no one believes that the normative model of welfare economics is appropriate for the political economy of policymaking (and not just schooling policy). But however much economists may claim not to believe NAP, when it comes to defining what research is "policy relevant," they have no other standard. For instance, in reviewing the empirical basis of education policy in the United States, James Poterba points out: "There is virtually no evidence on the empirical magnitudes of many of the key parameters needed to guide policy in these areas," and "because externalities are invoked to justify intervention . . . there is a pressing need to document the magnitude of the externalities, particularly those associated with the consumption of education."[34]

---

33. See, for example, Acemoglu and Robinson (2000); Lindert (2004); Bourguinon and Verdier (2001).

34. Poterba (1996, pp. 278, 301).

Claims about what research is "needed to guide policy" or about the "policy relevance" of research are implicitly claims about a positive model of policy. A sensible definition of "policy relevant" research is that the research would change the distribution of beliefs in such a way that resulting policy would lead to a welfare superior outcome, as follows:

> Definition of "policy relevant" research :
> $F^i(\Theta)$ is the distribution function over a set of parameters of each of i actors.
> Research is policy relevant under positive model PM iff :
> $ISW\,(PM^{True}\,(F^i(\Theta\,|\,Research\,),...,F^N\,(\Theta\,|\,Research\,)) >$
> $ISW\,(PM^{True}\,(F^i_0(\Theta),...,F^N_0(\Theta)).$

As an alternative definition of hypothetical policy relevance, one could make the set of relevant parameters specific to any given positive model of policy as Θ^{PM} and then do research into the parameters that would be relevant if the model PM were the true model:

> Definition of hypothetically "policy relevant" research :
> $F(\Theta^{PM})$ is the distribution function over a set of model specific parameters.
> Research is hypothetically policy relevant iff :
> $ISW\,(PM^A\,(F(\Theta^{PMA}\,|\,Research\,)) > ISW\,(PM^A\,(F(\Theta^{PMA})).$

These simple definitions allow one to distinguish three possibilities for theoretical or empirical research into the economics of education. The first would be research that is explicitly not "policy relevant" (under NAP or any other model) but is relevant to a positive behavioral model of education. Thousands of studies using hundreds of data sets in more than sixty countries have firmly established a quite general positive empirical association of schooling and earnings. After Engel's curve, this is now the most widely replicated and accepted empirical fact in economics. The more sophisticated part of this literature uses a variety of identification techniques (such as mandatory attendance laws and geographic spread of schooling) to account for other possible explanations of an earnings–schooling association (such as signaling models or ability bias) and to estimate the causal connection between additional years of schooling and additional earnings for the average or marginal attendee.[35] But this research makes no claims to being NAP policy relevant.[36] The earnings increments to individual schooling are relevant to

35. On these respective topics, see Angrist and Krueger (1991, 1992); Duflo (2001); and Spence (1973).

36. One of the most confused episodes in the intellectual history of development economics is the misuse of the tables of "social" rates of return published in a series of review articles by Psacharopoulos (1994), updating versions beginning in the 1980s, in which, owing to a quirk in one organization's policies, the difference between *investment* and *consumption* was confused with the existence of a *rationale* for public sector intervention (which can be justified for either production or consumption). That is, the World Bank's Articles of Agreement specify that the World Bank should finance only *productive* investments and not consumption. As the World Bank wanted to lend for education and countries wanted to borrow, there was a

Table 5-1. *Not a Single Redeeming Virtue to NAP*

Aspect of actual policies	Normative as Positive (NAP)		State Ideology-Incomplete Contracting Socialization (SI-ICS)	
	Theory/prediction	Reality	Theory/prediction	Reality
Direct production	Array of instruments (for example, mandates, vouchers); direct production rare.	Only direct production common; other instruments rare.	Direct production universal; mandates, vouchers rare.	Direct production universal; other instruments rare.
Benefit incidence/displacement	Displacement minimized; progressive benefit incidence.	Displacement ignored or maximized; benefit incidence neutral.	Displacement maximized; benefit incidence passively responds to demand.	Existence of active displacement (nationalization, bans on private); benefit incidence evolves with demand.
Productive efficiency	Productively efficient; efficient allocation of spending across inputs.	Production frequently inefficient (compared with private); input allocation inefficient.	No strong prediction on efficiency in learning since socialization strong element of production.	Little or no attention to efficacy or efficiency of learning; rarely measured.
Allocation of budget across level	Based on magnitude of market failures/equity concerns across levels of education.	Huge variations in allocation across countries; no demonstrated connection with market failures or equity.	Allocation across levels dependent on need to control mass versus elite education.	Yet to be investigated.
Scale of production	Based on optimality of productive efficiency.	Control at a very large scale (national, state/provincial); politically driven; demonstrated effectiveness of community control has no impact.	Based on scale of political jurisdiction, which gains control of socialization (national versus state/provincial).	Control at a very large scale (national, state/provincial); politically driven; no community control.

a positive theory of schooling in exactly the same way that accurate estimates of returns to the marginal investor in various financial investments are relevant to a positive theory of investing but have no obvious and immediate policy implications in a standard normative policy model.[37]

Alternatively, research might be claimed to be NAP hypothetically policy relevant—but without any real assertion that this constitutes actual policy relevance. Or one might claim research is actually policy relevant; to do so one must assert a particular positive model as an accurate representation of policymaking. This distinction is usually ignored, and NAP hypothetically policy relevant research is said to be policy relevant—but without any assertion of the empirical soundness of NAP—which is an inconsistent set of claims.

Take the research into the magnitude of externalities in education of the type Poterba refers to.[38] These are unambiguously NAP hypothetically relevant. But can a case be made that they are actually policy relevant—that better estimates of externalities would lead to better policy? Since it has never been demonstrated that empirically observed differences in policy are driven by differences in policymaker beliefs (either across countries or over time) about externalities, that claim would simply have to be taken on faith. Moreover, there are alternative models with at least as much plausibility as NAP (one being SI-ICS) in which externalities play no essential role. Hence it is impossible to conclude that this research is "needed" for actual policymaking.

Some might counter that the argument about NAP is a quibble, and that while SW^G is not the economist's usual conception of a social welfare function, one would somehow expect research that was ISW maximizing to also move policy in a similar direction across a variety of positive models of policy (different SW^G). But this has never been defended as a serious conjecture, that the policy relevance of research is "robust" across alternative positive models, and many examples showing conflicts of interest in policymaking easily come to mind—among them, reforms that improve parent well-being but at the expense of teachers (unions).

---

question of whether education was within the scope of a "productive" investment. So a series of review articles showed that education was "productive." Moreover, to show that this investment had a return even accounting for the cost borne by the public sector, these private rates of return were adjusted for public expenditures to get a "social" rate of return. Obviously, since nothing was added to the private return to reflect putative externalities and costs were deducted, the social returns were consistently *less* than the private returns. These tables showing a higher private than social return were then used repeatedly to justify continued (even increased) *public sector* investment in the production of schooling—which is, of course, analytically completely backwards, as the rationale for public sector intervention justifies actions in which the social return is *higher* than the private return.

37. This might be considered "conditionally policy relevant" in the sense of predicting how an expansion in schooling induced by policy would affect wages, without any implication that this would be a normative welfare-maximizing policy.

38. Poterba (1996).

Indeed, this is why SI-ICS is a good alternative: in many cases there is a direct conflict of interest between the state and its citizens over control of the socialization process in schools, and hence research that "proved" private schools to be superior in promoting skills outcomes would be not only policy irrelevant to a regime that had banned private schools in order to control socialization (as many have) but would be expected to have no impact on policy at all.[39] If NAP is empirically inadequate, then there is no way to defend the policy relevance of any of the existing economics of education without asserting some alternative positive model.

The third possibility therefore is actual policy relevance postulated with respect to a plausible (perhaps even empirically validated) positive model of policy. But this involves the explicit recognition that claims about policy relevance of research are empirical claims about positive models of policymaking. However, such empirical claims are often made in the absence of evidence.

NAP with Error and Uncertainty and the "Randomization" Agenda

A fundamental problem with most assertions about the policy relevance of research is how to explain the need for the research in the first place. After all, if agents were optimizing overall actions, including the acquisition of information, then they should have already devoted resources to estimating the value of the relevant parameters. The usual, casual, response is that knowledge is a public good and hence people underinvest in research—but this of course is not true of a welfare-maximizing planner who is assumed to internalize externalities. Economists tend to be cavalier and describe information relevant to a normative policy and assume that policy is not already optimal because of exogenously assumed policymaker error or uncertainty about the relevant model. They are tempted to use NAP with errors and uncertainty (NAP-EU) because it gives them an easy and attractive role to play. The heroic role for the economist is to do the solid research that provides the policymaker with the correct and reliable information that tightens the policymaker's priors around correct parameters and leads to optimal policies.

At first blush, the case for randomized evaluations of interventions in schooling as a means to improve schooling policy glows with the possibility of combining good science with good work. However, randomization per se as a new policy-relevant endeavor seems self-refuting. The randomization agenda in current favor reflects hypersensitivity about the internal validity of empirical work that estimates impacts of various interventions, yet it fails to offer any plausible positive model of policy.

This leads to a glaring inconsistency. On one hand, advocates of randomization firmly believe that empirical estimates of impact rooted in nonexperimental data (regardless of how those are identified) are unreliable. This reflects skepticism

---

39. See Pritchett and Viarengo (2008).

(Bayesian priors are centered on "no-effect") and a methodological stance (Bayesian posteriors are influenced only by evidence from randomized experiments, with perhaps some exceptions for other clean identification). As an argument for the rules of the language game (in the sense of Wittgenstein) internal to an academic discipline, the position is perhaps defensible.

On the other hand, advocates push randomization not just as a purely internal disciplinary game but as a means of improving policy. This is itself an empirical claim: that evidence from randomized experiments will improve policy by more than existing evidence or other research techniques. What is the rigorous scientific basis for this claim? Where is the randomized experiment that shows evidence from randomized experiments influences policy more than evidence from other sources? Moreover, where is the empirically plausible positive model of policy in which information to policymakers (of any type, randomized or not) plays a key role and in which randomized information plays a larger role?

So the randomization supporters would reject all existing empirical claims about the impact of, for example, reducing class size on academic performance and would only fund (and believe) randomized estimates—but act on the premise that estimates of class size are "policy relevant" (an empirical claim) and that randomized estimates are of more policy use than others (an empirical claim), when both premises lack not only rigorous evidence but any evidence, or even any surface plausibility once explicitly stated as empirical claims.

The first drawback of this approach is that it treats policy relevance as an analytical issue, which is only true of hypothetical policy relevance. Actual policy relevance is an empirical question. So far, no evidence has shown that policymakers' "lack of knowledge" of key policy parameters has in fact been a principal constraint on educational policy. Most experienced practitioners reject this notion explicitly.[40] Moreover, the experience to date with randomized evaluations does not suggest that policymakers are keen to create or act on the evidence that is being generated.

Second, particularly problematic is the assumption that the lack of knowledge is exogenous. Randomization is a well-known technique and actually makes empirical analysis much easier than research using nonexperimental analysis; much of the sophistication of econometric technique compensates for the lack of experimental data. So one cannot say that the new research agenda represents a technological advance creating knowledge previously unobtainable. If policymakers had wanted reliable estimates of impacts, they could presumably have performed the relevant experiments. But the usual reason given for the lack of randomization is not the lack of technical expertise, but the lack of political will. Hence the claim that estimates from randomized studies have relevance depends on remedying ignorance that is the result of policymakers' deliberately choosing

40. See, for example, Crouch (2000).

not to carry out randomized studies, though these have been within their technical and administrative capability for many decades.

Third, in nearly any other industry economists would be interested in the empirics of the "inside-the-firm" production process, either to test the underlying theory of the firm (for instance, the first-order conditions emerging from cost minimization) or to examine whether production conditions themselves (such as economies of scale or mark-up) suggest "supply-side" market failures. If one were estimating supply-side conditions that might occasion policy action (such as economies of scale), this exercise might be construed as economics. But no economist imagines that estimating the relationship between restaurant inputs and outputs (type of vegetable oil and crispiness of fries), or between shoe inputs and shoe outputs (leather and soles), or between law firm inputs and outputs (how many associates per brief) is a foundation for giving advice to these firms. But somehow the most routine of production decisions of no economic relevance at all (for example, about class size, textbook availability, or ability tracking) are somehow considered interesting areas for "policy-relevant" research without any coherent explanation of how this knowledge will lead producers to change their behavior to scale.

On these scores, randomization is plausibly no worse at influencing policy than other forms of research. However, the topic of whether it is better has not actually been broached in the context of any articulated positive model of schooling policy, much less one that is empirically validated in any way, or validated by the rigorous standards that its advocates propose for all other approaches.

Is NAP Worse than Useless?

Although NAP's inadequacies should by now be clear, some may find the foregoing points academic (in the bad sense) inasmuch as roughly the same things would be recommended by "practical" policy people no matter what the positive model because, after all, what is recommended is the normatively best policy. But the "common sense" view that introducing political considerations is a marginal change that leaves the policy recommendations roughly unchanged from the apolitical analysis is simply not defensible. For instance, there is a "politically naïve" model of targeting in which policy recommendations that ignore political constraints are not only suboptimal but pessimal for the poor, the group the "policymaker" in the model was intending to help.[41] Note that court attempts to impose fiscal equalization in spending across districts in California to support schooling without understanding the political economy of taxation in this regard reportedly turned voters against property taxation that supported educational spending and

41. See Gelbach and Pritchett (2002). Gelbach and Pritchett (1997) have also shown that recommendations on targeting that emerge from a "naïve" political economy in which budgets for transfers are fixed independently of the targeting transfers are in fact the recommendations that, if implemented when there was voting over the budget, would be not only suboptimal but welfare *minimizing* for the poor.

helped undermine educational budgets in that state.[42] There is no general presumption that changes in SW and changes in an appropriately specified SW^G have the same magnitude or even direction in response to policy or research.

The fundamental problem with NAP lies in two of its basic notions. First, it treats the objective of schooling as exclusively "skill acquisition," either ignoring the socialization component or assuming that state control of socialization is legitimate and needs no further attention. Second, it assumes that the policymaker is maximizing welfare and hence is the focus of potential improvements in schooling—in other words, the agent who lacks information is the "policymaker" and the "scaling" of interventions is a top-down process of dissemination and diffusion from above.

Consider, now, the following provocative example of ignoring actual consumer welfare. Basic consumer theory suggests that if new goods acquire market share, it is because consumers find them superior to old varieties, and hence there is an increase in social welfare—a gain that may not be adequately reflected in price indexes that fail to account for the value of product variety. The welfare gains in the United States of introducing Apple Cinnamon Cheerios cereal (given the existence of other varieties from the same company, such as Cheerios and Honey Nut Cheerios, and varieties from other brands such as Apple Jacks) are estimated to be on the order of $60 million a year (and, when extrapolated, imply that the component of the consumer price index for ready-to-eat cereals is understated by 20 percent).[43]

Contrast this with the overall small gains from Chile's privatization of schools, taking into account some gains from individuals shifting from public to private schools and peer effects.[44] Over the course of the privatization, the share of students in private schools increased by roughly 20 percentage points—from 28 to 48 percent of all students. This suggests that roughly one in five parents moved to a different school because of vouchers, which, by revealed preference, suggests that they are better off in terms of their own rankings of well-being. Where are the calculations of the welfare gains of this massive shift across varieties of schools? To the best of my knowledge, there are none. The reason is that the existing economics of education does not seem to accept the concept of consumer sovereignty. Suppose that public and private schools were equally productive in skill outcomes but not in socialization, where some private schools were more Catholic, some were more left-progressive, and so on. Then by any standard approach to economics, there are welfare gains to allowing choice. Valuation of these gains is not too difficult as many people, in the absence of vouchers, enrolled their children in private school,

42. Fischel (2001).

43. Hausman (1997). These calculations are themselves controversial (see, for instance, the interchange between Hausman and Breshnahan) as they rely on particular identification assumptions, but the fundamental approach to consumer welfare and price indexes is standard.

44. Hsieh and Urquiola (2006).

and hence the marginal household choosing a private school was just indifferent between a low-cost publicly provided education with socialization content that was not their preferred variety and a full-cost private education for a more preferred variety (plus perhaps some learning gains, which may be peer-effect influenced). Therefore the estimate of the valuation difference for the marginal switcher is the difference in the prices of the two alternatives. This is a huge number, crudely around 0.5 percent of GDP, which makes Chile's move to a voucher-like scheme a massively successful policy.[45]

To reiterate, the existing economics of education ignores the household's valuation of the "school match" on socialization and pedagogy and values only the "skills" component as "output" of schooling, the underlying view being that the socialization role of schooling is of no consequence or that only the state's views on socialization are worthy of consideration. This is indeed the precise view of governments that assume the expansion of schooling is an integral part of "modernization," which in their view calls for new affiliations (to the state and nation), respect for new institutions, and acceptance of the ideology of the state. In other words, it is acceptable to explicitly override the preferences of perhaps a majority or only a substantial minority of citizens. Why did economists, who are typically staunch defenders of consumer sovereignty, ever buy into this?

One reason, at least in the developing world, is that this was part and parcel of the modernization agenda, which promoted the creation of strong, centralized, nation-states in former colonies where, in many cases, none previously existed. This agenda, which James Scott refers to as "bureaucratic high modernism," was so widely supported in the "development" world that it became invisible.[46] The "development" discourse was constructed as an "anti-politics machine" so as to make policy decisions seem the realm of technocrats and experts, not actual citizens.[47]

As a result, citizen preferences took a back seat to "national" development. Yet school choice was so obvious a principle that it was included in the 1948 UN Charter, under Article 26(3): "Parents have a prior right to choose the kind of education that shall be given to their children." This statement, combined with a commitment to free elementary education, implies a fundamental right to state support of the schooling parents choose. In the subsequent pushes to achieve "universal" schooling, however, the norm came to be universally government-produced schooling.

---

45. Here is a crude, back-of-the envelope calculation. Public cost per child in school is roughly 12.5 percent of GDP per capita (assume teacher wage two times GDP per capita, twenty-five students per teacher, teacher costs 80 percent of total); if 20 percent of the population are school-aged children, and 20 percent of those switched, then the total welfare gain (attributing the full difference in cost as the gain to the marginal switcher, applied to the average switcher) is 0.5 percent of GDP.

46. Scott (1999).

47. See Ferguson (1990).

Arguments for the superiority of vouchers (both in learning and in welfare) need not rest on the usual line that the "policymaker" is the locus of decisionmaking and "learning" is the primary goal of schooling. Nor should one conclude that if vouchers are a superior instrument for improving welfare, this constitutes a "policy recommendation" that governments adopt vouchers. Rather, if governments were actually concerned about the educational issues posited in normative models (such as maximizing welfare, addressing market failures, improving equity), then they would have already adopted vouchers. But they have not. The conclusion is not that therefore governments do not know about vouchers (vouchers or voucher-like money-follows-the-student instruments have been around for hundreds of years) or their potential impacts. The Netherlands has had a functional choice-based system since the nineteenth century. Chile adopted a choice-based system in 1981.[48] Hundreds of countries in the world could now adopt a voucher-like system if they so chose. Governments are not making "policy mistakes" because of error or uncertainty regarding the impact of vouchers that more and better research on the impact of vouchers on learning could possibly remedy.[49] If governments do not produce schooling because of the "normative" issues of market failures or equity concerns but because of a desire to control socialization, then the "policy-relevant" research agenda is the one that informs parents as citizens on how to achieve superior welfare outcomes, not that informs policymakers.

How, then, can the economics of education be worse than useless? Suppose that the SI-ICS model is a reasonable representation of the formation of schooling policy. In this model, the state is pursuing its own interests, subject to political constraints. The main pressure for more and better schooling comes not from "policymakers" but from parents. It is perfectly possible that the usual economics of education—by assuming that the beliefs of the policymaker are the key constraint to better policy and using hypothetical NAP as the frame for deciding which issues to research—has two deleterious effects.

First, this economics legitimizes and, to the extent that economists have leverage with development assistance in the context of emerging countries, adds resources to a system of state control that may, or may not, have any benign objectives. The view that schooling is a "public good" rationalizes the exclusion of parents from decisionmaking in schooling.

Second, it focuses the provision of research and information on the "policymaker" rather than on citizens and communities. In doing so, it may delay the formation of the coalitions pressing for better schooling. For instance, many of the assessments of learning quality have been carried out in close cooperation with "policymakers" (for example, ministries of education), and hence the results

---

48. The Czech Republic adopted a choice-based system in the 1990s (Filer and Munich [2000]).

49. It is intriguing that the "best" evidence for the superiority of voucher-like programs (in that it comes from a randomization-like study) comes from a program in Colombia *that has been eliminated* (Angrist and others [2002]).

may never be disseminated to the public. When Mexico participated in the Trends in International Mathematics and Science Study (TIMSS) in 1995, it refused to allow the results to be published. In other, plausible positive models, improvements will come from expanding citizen access to information, for that is what will change the constraints states face, lead parents to have more power, and reduce the state's latitude.

Third, the current economics of education perpetuates false notions about how innovations are going to go to scale. An apt metaphor suggested to illustrate the differences between top-down-directed action in organizations is that of the spider (at the center of a web receiving information and reacting) and the starfish (distributing localized information and response).[50] Economists usually treat the diffusion of innovations in a starfish way: there are many organizations, each trying to improve, and when one discovers something superior it expands its share of the market; others are then quick to imitate, respond, so that the innovation diffuses as an emergent property of a set of incentives created by decentralized decisionsmakers, no one of whom pursues as a goal the system properties (diffusion of information is nonteleological).

In the spider model of innovation, someone "learns" (perhaps through a randomized experiment) and then mandates the adoption of innovation as a "policy"—so one could discover some parameter about the world (for example, the impact of class size on performance is such that reducing class size is a cost-effective means of improving learning) and then enshrine this parameter in policy for an entire organization (say, in actions to reduce class size).

However, this may not be a very useful model about how innovations that are relevant to improving schooling are going to be discovered, validated, and diffused. In particular, if the "spider" model of the control of schooling is adopted not because it is regarded as a superior way of achieving learning performance but because of the desire to control socialization, then it may well be that the key constraint is a complete lack of interest in innovations that improve learning. The longer this goes unacknowledged and unspoken—particularly by researchers pretending the spider has motivations it does not—the longer it might take for needed reforms to be adopted.

Conclusion

Now for the big question. Who cares? Everyone should. How societies organize themselves—socially, economically, politically, and administratively—to prepare the young for the future is perhaps the most important driver of long-run well-being. Solid science that contributes to that goal is therefore a win-win pursuit. Only two agendas within economics (although there appear to be three) really

50. See Brafman and Beckstrom (2006).

address the efficacy, efficiency, and quality of service delivery in developing countries in general, and certainly in education. One is the traditional economics of education, and the other, for lack of a better term, is the "accountability agenda."

The economics of education is either a positive science of the behavior of consumers of, or investors in, education or a normative analysis of how a hypothetical agent (a "planner" or "policymaker") endowed with a particular objective function ought to behave. But actual policy relevance—predicting which actions, including self-referential analysis of the impact of more and better research, will change actual policy—requires a serviceable general positive model of policy. Normative analysis as a positive model is completely worthless. This means that estimating parameters that would be relevant if NAP were true is not (or at the very least cannot be defended as) policy relevant—irrespective of the methodological purity of those estimates. Assertions that estimates of the externalities to education or the credit constraints to financing education or the "production function" will improve policy by altering the social planner's Bayesian posterior distribution over NAP-relevant parameters are empirical claims about a positive model that have never been validated and do not even have a patina of plausibility.

An alternative positive model, SI-ICS, outperforms NAP in predicting the key observed features of schooling policy. In this model, none of the NAP parameters are essential and may well be irrelevant. In fact, under SI-ICS it cannot be ruled out that the same research that is policy improving if NAP has no impact could make citizen welfare worse. Even if one chooses to reject SI-ICS (and its variants), the illustration holds true: there is no basis for a general claim that hypothetical-NAP-relevant research is welfare improving if NAP is false—this depends on which positive model is true.

As for the "accountability agenda," it attempts to construct a complete positive model of the efficacy of services as the endogenous result of the operation of accountability relationships between the major actors involved in the public provision of services. This agenda takes the words of the founder of welfare economics, Arthur Pigou, seriously: "It is not sufficient to contrast the imperfect adjustments of unfettered enterprise with the best adjustment economists in their studies can imagine. For we cannot expect that any State authority will attain, or will even wholeheartedly seek, that ideal. Such authorities are liable alike to ignorance, to sectional pressure, and to personal corruption by private interest."[51]

In grappling with the systemic incentives embedded in politics, administration, and markets, the accountability agenda is messy and imprecise and does not lend itself well to small-scale experimentation—but it is attempting to be policy relevant. The agenda does not depend solely on changing the views of a "policymaker" but is open to considering which change in power or the availability of information to which actor will actually improve outcomes for children.

51. Pigou (1920).

The seemingly third option, the "randomization" agenda, is concerned with the lack of rigorous evidence, primarily from randomized field experiments, about the impact of a variety of potential public sector actions. That lack is said to be a key constraint to improved policy and hence to outputs and outcomes. However, randomization is merely a methodology and does not, in and of itself, specify the interesting questions to which it should be applied. If randomization is taken exclusively as a proposal for the internal disciplinary logic or "rules of the game" for the traditional practice of the "economics of education," it is of almost no real interest to anyone outside of a few engaged in a picayune dispute over proper methods of identification. If this is only a methodological twist on estimating standard questions of the economics of education (like aspects of the "production function"), then the randomization agenda inherits the complete lack of serious claims to policy relevance from its parent, the economics of education. Moreover, taken as a policy-relevant contribution to the traditional economics of education, the randomization agenda as a methodological approach inherits an enormous internal contradiction—that all empirical claims should only be believed when backed by evidence from randomization, excepting, of course, those enormous (and completely unsupported) empirical claims about the impact of randomization on policy. But since randomization is a method and not a movement, it is easily being applied to questions within the accountability agenda by varying not only across inputs (such as textbooks or class size) but also across modes of accountability. An increasing number of experiments are exploring precisely the conditions under which accountability can be effective, and that is a promising direction.

The question of thinking big versus thinking small resonates within development debates on account of the intellectual endeavor called "development." Clearly, "thinking big" has led to centralized, top-down programs of the "big push" variety against which "thinking small" has lashed back, calling for more local variation and experimentation and more market-like mechanisms that would allow the emergent properties of the small to transform the big. But if the system as structured creates no pressures or spaces for the scaling of innovations, then thinking big must attend to systemic issues if the small is to have a chance.

References

Acemoglu, Daron, and James A. Robinson. 2000. "Why Did the West Extend the Franchise: Democracy, Inequality and Growth in Historical Perspective." *Quarterly Journal of Economics* 115, no. 4: 1167–99.

Andrabi, Tahir, and others. 2008. "Learning and Educational Achievements in Punjab Schools (LEAPS): Insights to Inform the Education Policy Debate." Washington: World Bank.

Angrist, Joshua, and Alan B. Krueger. 1991. "Does Compulsory School Attendance Affect Schooling and Earnings?" *Quarterly Journal of Economics* 106, no. 4: 979–1014.

———. 1992. "The Effect of Age at School Entry on Educational Attainment: An Application of Instrumental Variables with Moments from Two Samples." *Journal of the American Statistical Association* 87, no. 418: 328–36.

Angrist, Joshua D., and others. 2002. "Vouchers for Private Schooling in Colombia: Evidence from a Randomized Natural Experiment." *American Economic Review* 92, no. 5: 1535–58.

Basu, Kaushik. 1998. "Child Labor: Cause, Consequence, and Cure, with Remarks on International Labor Standards." Policy Research Working Paper 2027. Washington: World Bank.

Blaug, Mark. 1976. "The Empirical Status of Human Capital Theory: A Slightly Jaundiced Survey." *Journal of Economic Literature* 14 (September): 827–55.

Bourguignon, Francois, and Thierry Verdier. 2001. "The Political Economy of Education and Development in an Open Economy." Discussion Paper 3075. Washington: Center for Economic and Policy Research (November).

Brafman, Ori, and Rod A. Beckstrom. 2006. *The Starfish and the Spider: The Unstoppable Power of Leaderless Organizations.* New York: Portfolio.

Crouch, Louis A. 2000.

Crouch, Louis A., and F. Henry Healey. 1997. *Education Reform Support.* Vol. 1: *Overview and Bibliography.* Washington: U.S. Agency for International Development, Office of Sustainable Development, Bureau for Africa.

Das, Jishnu, Priyanka Pandey, and Tristan Zajonc. 2006. "Learning Levels and Gaps in Pakistan." Policy Research Working Paper, Series 4067. Washington: World Bank.

Duflo, Esther. 2001. "Schooling and Labor Market Consequences of School Construction in Indonesia: Evidence from an Unusual Policy Experiment." *American Economic Review* 91, no. 4: 795–813.

Duflo, Esther, Pascaline Dupas, and Michael Kremer. 2007. "Peer Effects, Pupil Teacher Ratios, and Teacher Incentives: Evidence from a Randomized Evaluation in Kenya." Poverty Action Lab Working Paper. Cambridge, Mass.: MIT.

Epple, Dennis, and Richard E. Romano. 1996. "Public Provision of Private Goods." *Journal of Political Economy* 104, no. 1: 57–84.

Farooqi, Duriya, and Lant Pritchett. 2003. "The Economics of Education Reeducated." Harvard University, John F. Kennedy School of Government and Center for Global Development. Photocopy.

Ferguson, James. 1990. *The Anti-Politics Machine: "Development," Depoliticization, and Bureaucratic Domination in Lesotho.* Cambridge University Press.

Filer, Randall K., and Daniel Munich. 2000. "The Responses of Public and Private Schooling to Voucher Funding: The Hungarian and Czech Experiences." World Paper 360. Ann Arbor, Mich.: William Davidson Institute.

Filmer, Deon, and Lant Pritchett. 1999. "The Effect of Household Wealth on Educational Attainment: Evidence from 35 Countries." *Population and Development Review* 25 (March): 85–120.

Fischel, W. A. 2001. *The Homevoter Hypothesis: How Home Values Influence Local Government Taxation, School Finance, and Land-Use Policies.* Harvard University Press.

Friedman, Milton. 1962. *Capitalism and Freedom.* University of Chicago Press.

Gelbach, Jonah B., and Lant Pritchett. 1997. "More for the Poor Is Less for the Poor: The Politics of Targeting." Development Research Group Policy Working Paper 1799. Washington: World Bank.

———. 2002. "Is More for the Poor Less for the Poor? The Politics of Means-Tested Targeting." *Topics in Economic Analysis and Policy* 2, no. 1: art. 6.

Gradstein, Mark, and Moshe Justman. 2000. "Human Capital, Social Capital, and Public Schooling." *European Economic Review* 44 (May): 879–90.

Hausman, Jerry A. 1997. "Valuation of New Goods under Perfect and Imperfect Competition." In *The Economics of New Goods,* edited by Timothy F. Bresnahan and Robert J. Gordon. University of Chicago Press.

Hoxby, Caroline. 2001. "Ideal Vouchers." Harvard University. Photocopy.

Hsieh, Chang-Tai, and Miguel Urquiola. 2006. "The Effects of Generalized School Choice on Achievement and Stratification: Evidence from Chile's Voucher Program." *Journal of Public Economics* 90 (September): 1477–1503.

Jimenez, Emmanuel, Marlaine Lockheed, and Vicente Paqueo. 1991. "The Relative Efficiency of Private and Public Schools in Developing Countries." *World Bank Research Observer* 6 (July): 205–18.

Kremer, Michael, and Andrei Sarychev. 2000. "Why Do Governments Operate Schools?" Harvard University. Photocopy.

Lanjouw, Peter, and Martin Ravallion. 1999. "Benefit Incidence, Public Spending Reforms, and the Timing of Program Capture." *World Bank Economic Review* 13: 257–73.

Lindert, Peter H. 2004. *Growing Public: Social Spending and Economic Growth since the Eighteenth Century.* Cambridge University Press.

Lott, John R. 1999. "Public Schooling, Indoctrination, and Totalitarianism." *Journal of Political Economy* 107, no. S6: S127–57.

Pigou, Arthur C. 1920. *The Economics of Welfare.* London: Macmillan.

Poterba, James M. 1996. "Demographic Structure and the Political Economy of Public Education." Working Paper 5677. Cambridge, Mass.: National Bureau of Economic Research (July).

Pritchett, Lant. 2003. "When Will They Ever Learn? Why All Governments Produce Schooling." Working Paper 031. Duke University, Bureau for Research and Economic Analysis and Development (June).

Pritchett, Lant, and Deon Filmer. 1999. "What Education Production Functions *Really* Show: A Positive Theory of Education Expenditures." *Economics of Education Review* 18 (April): 223–39.

Pritchett, Lant, and Varad Pande. 2006. "Making Primary Education Work for India's Rural Poor: A Proposal for Effective Decentralization." Social Development Paper 95. Washington: World Bank.

Pritchett, Lant, and Martina Viarengo. 2008. "The State, Socialization, and Private Schooling: When Will Governments Support Alternative Producers?" Harvard University, John F. Kennedy School of Government.

Psacharapoulos, George. 1994. "Returns to Investment in Education: A Global Update." *World Development* 22, no. 9: 1325–43.

Scott, James C. 1999. *Seeing like a State: How Certain Schemes to Improve the Human Condition Have Failed.* Yale University Press.

Spence, A. Michael. 1973. "Job Market Signaling." *Quarterly Journal of Economics* 87, no. 3: 355–74.

Tooley, James, and Pauline Dixon. 2002. *Private Schools for the Poor: A Case Study from India.* Reading, Berkshire: Centre for British Teachers.

World Bank. 2008. "Public-Private Partnerships in the Education Sector" (http://go.worldbank.org/AEGYCFCBG1).

COMMENT BY BENJAMIN A. OLKEN

In his thought-provoking analysis of what evidence is and how evidence plays a role in policy formulation, Lant Pritchett makes three basic claims:

1. That whenever economists do research, they implicitly justify the policy relevance of this research with what Pritchett calls the Normative as Positive (NAP) model of government behavior. This model essentially says that government maximizes social welfare.

2. That this is a silly model or, at the very least, an incomplete model of government behavior. Models that approach government actors and their objective functions much more systematically—that is, political economy models—do a much better job of describing actual government behavior.

3. That if people believe in the NAP model, but it is false, they end up asking the wrong research questions and making incomplete or, worse, incorrect policy recommendations. Pritchett argues that NAP is the policy justification for what he calls the "randomization agenda." So by implication, since the policy justification of the randomization agenda is the NAP model and the NAP model is false, Pritchett argues that the randomization agenda is answering the wrong questions and making incorrect policy recommendations.

In order to evaluate these claims, it is useful to be a bit more precise about what, exactly, Pritchett means by the NAP model. Here is the simplest version of the NAP model I can think of.

Suppose there is some production function for government services, which I denote by $F(P)$, where P is policy and F is the production function. There is some individual utility function over consumption, denoted as x_i, and whatever government services are produced as $F(P)$. This individual utility function is $(u_i(x_i, F(P)))$. The government does not know F; instead, it has some beliefs about what the production function is, which I denote as $\hat{F}$. The government has a social welfare function, which I denote as $SW^G(u_i(x_i, F(P)))$.

NAP says the government chooses policy P to maximize its social welfare function, SW^G, given its beliefs about the production function $\hat{F}$. For example, suppose the government has some beliefs about how to produce school. The government would choose schooling policy to maximize its social welfare function SW^G, given its beliefs about how to produce good school $\hat{F}$. That is the basic NAP model.

The implication of the NAP model is that policy failures come about because the government has the wrong beliefs about F, because if the government knew F, it would choose the correct policy. In this model, evidence like the effect of textbooks, school feeding, class size, and residual tutoring helps improve welfare by moving the government's beliefs about the production function, $\hat{F}$, closer to the true production function, F.

Pritchett argues that NAP is false and therefore that evidence about F does not necessarily improve policy. Instead of discussing whether NAP is true or false, I want to focus on this last point that Pritchett raises—what is the role of learning more about F if in fact NAP does not hold?

Before moving on to this question, it is important to note that NAP is not really the issue, because one does not need to reject NAP to come to the same basic conundrum. In fact, NAP incorporates a wide range of political economy models, since the equilibrium of many political economy models can be written as the solution to maximizing a social welfare function with some set of welfare weights. For example, median voter models turn out to maximize the welfare of the median voter.[1] Similarly, models of collective action problems, such as those of Mancur Olson and George Stigler, have been constructed in which special interests get disproportionate weight in the social welfare function.[2]

The real issue, therefore, is not whether NAP holds per se; rather, the real issue is that the social welfare function that governments maximize, which is the result of these political economy considerations, may not be the social welfare function that "we" want to maximize, whoever "we" are. "We" are more likely to maximize something like a social welfare function with equal welfare weights, or a Rawlsian max-min social welfare function, or something along these lines. Denote the social welfare function that "we" want to maximize as SW^*.

The problem that Pritchett articulates is not NAP per se; the problem is that $SW^G \neq SW^*$, in which case, learning more about F improves SW^G, but not necessarily SW^*.

So where does this leave things? Regardless of whether one believes NAP per se, it is very unlikely that SW^G, whatever it is, is exactly equal to SW^*. In fact, there is a well-established, extensive tradition of political economy models that articulate the myriad ways in which $SW^G \neq SW^*$, and while Pritchett's model is an interesting example of such a model, one does not necessarily need to believe his particular model to believe that $SW^G \neq SW^*$.

In that case, what is the role of evidence? Specifically, under what circumstances might evidence about F improve SW^*? I take Pritchett's point that theoretically improving one's knowledge about F is not guaranteed to improve SW^*; if one improves evidence about F, one improves SW^G, not SW^*. Practically speak-

1. Downs (1957).
2. See Olson (1965); Stigler (1971).

ing, however, improving knowledge about F more often than not moves the world in the right direction. This is not a theorem. This is just a series of intuitive arguments that I think are likely to be true in practice.

Incidentally, one important set of reasons for learning about F that is only indirectly related to improving SW^* and that sometimes gets lost in this debate is that people might care about discovering the truth about the world. They might be scientists and think that learning about F improves their models of human behavior. Indeed, a desire to better understand how the world works is an important and valid motivation for conducting research, even if it only indirectly improves SW^*.

But back to the main argument: why might evidence about F help improve SW^*? The first set of reasons has to do with how the domestic political sphere actually works. To begin with, some group of politicians may actually care about social welfare—in which case, the problem is solved. But even politicians who do not care about social welfare per se probably care about getting reelected. Evidence about F can often help them get reelected.

Consider Indonesia, which is the country I work in most frequently. In 2004 the then presidential candidate, now president, promised during the campaign to reduce poverty by 8 percentage points in five years. Among the many things he has done toward this goal has been to launch a large cash transfer program for the poor. This program is very simple: the government created a list of the 19.2 million poorest households and gave them cash every month for a period of time. Given that they have such a program, the government needs evidence on better ways to target poor households. That may or may not be because the government wants to maximize social welfare per se, but the program—and the need for better evidence on targeting—certainly has to do with the president's reelection. In fact, I have been working with the World Bank and the government of Indonesia to run a randomized experiment on how to improve this type of targeting. Of course, reality intervened, the project timetable slipped, and the results will not be ready until after the 2009 election. Still, this is an example in which reelection might give politicians incentives to adopt better evidence about F and use it to improve social welfare.

Second, evidence about F might help improve SW^* by informing disputes between domestic political groups. The government is not a monolith; it is always composed of many competing groups. Ruling governments, for example, need to justify their programs to parliamentary opposition. Having good evidence about which programs actually work can help keep good programs alive and help reallocate funds away from bad ones. These competing domestic political actors may not be maximizing social welfare per se as "we" see it; they may just be competing to win more political power for themselves. But introducing evidence into their debate can move them in the direction of better policy—and hence of maximizing SW^*.

A third broad role of evidence lies in informing outside advice. Economists, for example, are often asked to give technical advice. In some sense, this is what I mean by "we" when I define the social welfare function that "we" maximize. What should economists—or, even more to the point, external donors who actually have some political power and presumably care about SW^*—push for? What policies should they advocate? Evidence about F can help answer these questions.

One such question is whether to charge user fees for government services, where there appears to be an external donor community with some influence over governments in this regard. In this setting, evidence on user fees (such as that reviewed in chapter 4) would help this external donor decide what it should push for. Knowing F helps the donors—and economists—give answers that will be more likely to increase SW^*.

Of course, I agree with Pritchett that understanding the political economy of reform is critical to implementing reform, but even then, one needs to know what to be aiming for. Evidence about F helps one aim in the right direction.

Fourth, evidence from randomized experiments has a particular role as a rhetorical device. Because of its transparency and quality, randomized evidence can dramatically enhance the rate of diffusion of an idea. Experimental analysis is easy to understand: one just compares treatment and control. Moreover, randomized experiments are methodologically hard to dispute. PROGRESA is a great example of this process, as is the recent work on intestinal worms.[3] The point of this and all the foregoing examples is that good evidence about F can improve social welfare in many situations even if governments are maximizing other things.

I conclude with some comments about the the role of randomization. As Pritchett rightly points out, randomization is a methodology, not an agenda, although he then refers to the "randomization agenda." He takes the "randomization agenda" to mean that randomized experiments are geared to understanding the production function—what is the marginal benefit of class size, textbooks, teachers, and so on—that is, better understanding F.

Since NAP is wrong, says Pritchett, learning about F is the wrong agenda, the right one being the "accountability agenda." The point of this "accountability agenda" is to learn how to improve the system, given that the government is not a monolith and that it is not necessarily using better information about F to maximize SW^*. As I argued earlier, more information about F is likely to improve SW^* anyway, but in any case Pritchett argues that research should be about these accountability ideas instead.

The notion that randomized experiments are only about F, and not about accountability issues, seems a very odd characterization of randomized experiments. This is particularly true in the education realm, where a large number of

3. Miguel and Kremer (2004).

randomized experiments do deal with exactly these types of issues. A mere sampling of the literature shows randomized experiments on how to better monitor teachers, on performance pay for teachers, on performance pay for students, on changing the political structure of local school committees (which is actually under way in Indonesia), and on providing information to villagers.[4] Moreover, a whole range of experiments have focused on vouchers and on the relative effect of private versus public schools and charter schools, as well as experiments such as PROGRESA that have explored increasing demand for education. Many of these experiments are explicitly investigating the "accountability agenda." Although information about the production function can be useful for improving social welfare, this long list of experiments suggests that the methodology can have a much broader application.

References

Banerjee, Abhijit V., Rukmini Banerji, and others. 2008. "Pitfalls of Participatory Programs." Working Paper 14311. Cambridge, Mass.: National Bureau of Economic Research.

Downs, Anthony. 1957. *An Economic Theory of Democracy*. New York: Harper.

Duflo, Esther, Rema Hanna, and Stephen Ryan. 2008. "Monitoring Works: Getting Teachers to Come to School." Cambridge, Mass.: MIT.

Kremer, Michael, Edward Miguel, and Rebecca Thornton. 2009. "Incentives to Learn." *Review of Economics and Statistics*. Forthcoming.

Miguel, Edward, and Michael Kremer. 2004. "Worms: Identifying Impacts on Education and Health in the Presence of Treatment Externalities." *Econometrica* 72, no. 1: 159–217.

Muralidharan, Karthik, and Venkatesh Sundararaman. 2006. "Teacher Incentives in Developing Countries: Experimental Evidence from India." Harvard University.

Olson, Mancur. 1965. *The Logic of Collective Action*. Harvard University Press.

Pradhan, Menno. n.d. "Strengthening School Committees in Indonesia." Jakarta: World Bank.

Stigler, George J. 1971. "The Theory of Economic Regulation." *Bell Journal of Economics and Management Science* 2, no. 1: 3–21.

4. See, respectively, Duflo, Hanna, and Ryan (2008); Muralidharan and Sundararaman (2006); Kremer, Miguel, and Thornton (2009); Pradhan (n.d.); Banerjee, Banerji, and others (2008).

COMMENT BY NANCY BIRDSALL

A research program we are developing at the Center for Global Development is in the thinking big category. It could constitute one response to Lant Pritchett's plea for "a general positive model of schooling policy." Our program focuses on the problem of aid effectiveness and aims to advance knowledge that will allow recommendations for improving education to be grounded in a theory of policy formation that takes into account why, as Pritchett observes, governments provide (and do not just finance) schooling everywhere in the world.

Pritchett wants a theory that explains the government's interest in shaping the nature of education systems. He argues that "normative as positive" (NAP) is the wrong theory of policy formation (or actually rests on the wrong set of assumptions in the absence of any explicit theory). The implication is that in the case of developing countries, NAP fails to provide economists with any guidance on research needed to improve policy. Furthermore, it fails to provide outsiders in general, including donors, with any guidance on how to address the political economy or systemic issues that underlie what Benjamin Olken characterizes as the social welfare function of government (SW^G).

Pritchett's observation is consistent with the fact that across the world it is hard to find an education system in which schooling offsets rather than reinforces inequality of income and wealth. To use Olken's language, the facts are consistent with a world in which the typical implicit social welfare function revealed by government (SW^G) puts less weight on the poor's social welfare than an SW* that is closer to the donor's preferred outcome, SW^D, or some normative optimum, SW^O, for example, with equal weights for all individuals in a society.

Pritchett makes a good point. He is in effect complaining that outside donors who are interested in moving countries dependent on their aid closer to their SW^D are willfully naïve about the reality of an SW^G that is far from theirs. However, his non-NAP characterization of policy formation, as he notes himself, cannot alone explain variation in systems across countries, changes over time within country systems, differences in funding and provision across levels of education (which benefit different income groups differently), the reason reputational risk matters in Indonesia, the reason Mexico has conditional cash transfers, and so on. More research is needed, he implies, in the spirit of public choice models of policy formation (to which he briefly refers) that explicitly model and try to explain government policy (SW^G). Public choice models typically take into account the multiple objectives of different government and other actors that directly influence government policy. Other non-NAP approaches to policy formation might usefully explain changes in policy over time; they might explain, for example, what appear to be the effects of global competitive pressures in moving education policy in countries like India closer to the equivalent of SW^O (that is, closer to an objective of increasing the human capital of the poor majority).

More generally, on the basis of explicitly non-NAP models, donors might be more likely to understand under what conditions, political and otherwise, the SW^G of a government receiving aid moves in the direction of SW^O—or at least toward a social welfare function closer to what they have in mind, SW^D, such as one that encompasses the Millennium Development Goal of universal access to basic schooling of reasonable quality.

The Center for Global Development is proposing a new way for donors to support schooling in developing countries, which is called Cash on Delivery Aid (COD Aid). COD Aid is, we believe, a way to make aid effective and to create an opportunity for research on the determinants of policy formation in a particular setting—research that would be in the thinking big category. The research could shed light on what determines the policies and practices that in large part shape the education system in a particular country

The program's underlying premise is that one can learn about and affect a government's education policies and social welfare function by introducing an incentive designed, as it were, to move a country closer to the implicit social welfare function assumed in the NAP-world. At the same time, it is essential to take into account that neither the donor nor the government may really understand the production function for good-quality schooling/learning. (In the context of the literature on aid, this brings together Pritchett's view that donors are naïve about policy formation and Bill Easterly's view that all outsiders are naïve about "producing" development outcomes such as learning/schooling.)

What motivates COD Aid is the need to link aid to outcomes. In a functional system, taxes buy outcomes. But in aid-dependent countries, there is no citizen scrutiny, and often development or social welfare outcomes of aid spending are limited. In a poor, even perverse, substitute for that scrutiny, donors tend to micromanage inputs, leaving aid without any link to outcomes. To create such a link, we propose that aid pay for progress against a pre-agreed outcome.

This could be done through a binding contract between a donor and a recipient that would guarantee a specific additional payment for specific incremental progress toward an agreed goal—such as $100 per child completing primary school and taking or passing a competency test. The recipient country government would report on progress periodically and agree to an independent third-party audit. The country could spend the money on education supply, demand, or items outside the education sector, without any policy conditions or agreement on inputs or practices.

In the traditional, hands-on approach, donors take many steps, defined in World Bank nomenclature as preparation, preappraisal, appraisal, negotiation, and perhaps but not necessarily (and in fact rarely, as it turns out) actual measurement of outcomes. By contrast, our program's cash on delivery approach skips all those steps and the donor's resulting involvement in specifying inputs, policies, and so on. Instead, cash is delivered on the basis of the validation of measured outcomes by a third party. The donor effectively pays the recipient for moving in the direction of SW^O.

In addition, the citizens play a role in making the government accountable. Under the contract, the government is obliged to publish and make available to the public (a) the number of additional children for which it receives a payment each year, and (b) the test results at least at the country level and more so at the local and school level.

Several donors have expressed interest in trying COD Aid as an aid modality. We believe the approach would help donors implement reforms—such as coordination, alignment with country programs, country ownership—that have by and large eluded them until now.

At present, the center is developing the terms of reference for a research grant that the donor or any other funder would provide to finance a systematic study of the country response to the new and additional incentive. A research grant ought to accompany a COD Aid intervention and would ideally cover the costs of two kinds of research in a country: The first would investigate how a new incentive, COD Aid, affects government policies and programs via political, economic, and institutional channels; it is about SW^G, the political economy of education policy formation—or thinking big. The second would ask how particular education programs that result might generate learning; its objective is to better understand the production function for generating learning, in part through randomized control experiments. As Olken has pointed out, the latter kind of research can change the discourse and affect the former.

The "thinking big" research of level 1 assumes that in most countries, as Pritchett argues, NAP does not constitute the starting point for understanding education policy formation. The starting point is likely to be a set of hypotheses about government policy formation specific to the country receiving COD Aid, to be tested in the light of the new incentive that COD Aid represents. How will the new incentive affect government behavior? In comparison with "thinking small" research, this level has no randomized control trial and no counterfactual. Nor does anyone expect direct attribution of changed outcomes to the new incentive to be possible. Some of its priors are typical of economic models, two being that an adequate incentive will affect behavior, and that information about public policy reduces the cost citizens face in making government accountable.

Subsequent work would have to include a systematic effort to outline political relationships and institutional and bureaucratic arrangements, as well as to compile data on budget relationships and expenditures, management information systems, and accountability relationships (teachers, unions, local versus national, and so on).

Level 1 research would be undertaken by a scholar with a deep understanding of the local context who is perhaps based at a local institution and is probably in partnership with someone having a comparative perspective on the political economy of policy formation. The work would involve systematic tracking over five years of apparent responses of the state and other actors to the additional incentive and would address among other things hypotheses about accountability and other relationships over time.

Level 1 research does not meet any standard that has been discussed, and certainly not the gold standard referred to in the context of randomized controlled experiments. But it is the kind of research that responds to Pritchett's plea to think big about what motivates government's education policies and practices.

6

The Other Invisible Hand:
High Bandwidth Development Policy

RICARDO HAUSMANN

> Little else is requisite to carry a state to the highest degree of opulence from the lowest barbarism but peace, easy taxes, and a tolerable administration of justice: all the rest being brought about by the natural course of things.
>
> —Adam Smith, 1755 Lecture

> The uniform, constant and uninterrupted effort of every man to better his condition, the principle from which public and national, as well as private opulence is originally derived, is frequently powerful enough to maintain the natural progress of things toward improvement, in spite both of the extravagance of government, and of the greatest errors of administration. Like the unknown principle of animal life, it frequently restores health and vigour to the constitution, in spite, not only of the disease, but of the absurd prescriptions of the doctor.
>
> —Adam Smith, *The Wealth of Nations*

> The intensive study of the problem of economic development has had one discouraging result: it has produced an ever lengthening list of factors and conditions, of obstacles and prerequisites.
>
> —Albert O. Hirschman, *The Strategy of Economic Development*

Ever since Adam Smith, economists have been in search of a simple solution to the question of the causes of the wealth of nations and to the challenge of development, but the answer has so far proved elusive. The idea that governments of poor countries need do little to catch up has been a constant refrain in policy

The ideas in this chapter evolved gradually over the past few years. I am particularly indebted to Dani Rodrik and Chuck Sabel, with whom I have been thinking about policy, and to César Hidalgo and Bailey

circles.[1] According to the Washington Consensus, for example, economic success can be achieved through ten relatively straightforward policies.[2]

Yet most governments in the world fill hundreds of thousands of pages trying to legislate policy and call on hundreds of public bureaucracies to implement it. The European common law, the *Acquis Communautaire,* alone takes up 50,000 pages, and its sixth enlargement now contains 35 chapters (see table 6-1). Although the need for each chapter is clearly quite compelling, the sheer bulk of the document makes it hard to imagine how a minimal Smithian state could ever work in a modern society.

The Dimensionality of the Policy Problem

For Adam Smith, the simple, low-dimensional solution to planning the production and allocation of goods in a society lay in a free market. Such a market allows production to self-organize by linking many independent decisionmakers—the producers of eggs, milk, cheese, butter, olives, olive oil, wheat, bread, coffee and sugar, salt, pepper and their inputs (cows, poultry, tractors, seeds, animal feed, gasoline, credit, electricity, transportation, retailing, refrigeration, accounting, advertising, and so on)—and thus enables people to decide to have a cheese omelet, toast, and coffee for breakfast. Nobody has to plan these things centrally.

Economists since Adam Smith have been in awe of the miraculous capacity of the market to solve coordination problems that would be dauntingly complex if they were to be made through the *purposeful* planning of any collection of agencies. The wisdom of the answer took a very long time to sink in. While on the one hand Léon Walras, Kenneth Arrow, and Gerard Debreu were reckoning the conditions under which such an approach would work, socialist economists were seeking an alternative system based on central planning. This was the focal point of debate between the socialists and the liberals from the 1930s to the 1960s.[3] In

Klinger, with whom I have been studying the high dimensionality of the development process. I thank Nava Ashraf and Ross Levine and participants at the Brookings conference that generated this volume for their comments. The errors are mine.

1. For example, as expressed by Roll and Tallbott (2001): "Once a developing country government establishes the rules to a fair game and ensures their enforcement, it would be well advised to stand back and enjoy the self-generating growth." But as discussed in Hausmann, Pritchett, and Rodrik (2005), most growth accelerations are not "self-generating" but peter out after eight years, and this leads to limited convergence of incomes.

2. Williamson (1990).

3. Oskar Lange suggested that central planning could work if a Walrasian auctioneer changed prices in response to excess supply or excess demand. Kornai and Lipták (1971 [1965]) showed that if instead the central planner decided the quantities of goods he wanted made and firms set the price, then a socialist system could achieve a decent general equilibrium very similar to that of a market economy.

Table 6-1. *Chapters of the* Acquis Communautaire, *6th Enlargement*

Free movement of goods	Social policy and employment
Freedom of movement for workers	Enterprise and industrial policy
Right of establishment and freedom to provide services	Trans-European networks
Free movement of capital	Regional policy and coordination of structural instruments
Public procurement	Judiciary and fundamental rights
Company law	Justice, freedom, and security
Intellectual property law	Science and research
Competition policy	Education and culture
Financial services	Environment
Information society and media	Consumer and health protection
Agriculture and rural development	Customs union
Food safety, veterinary and phytosanitary policy	External relations
Fisheries	Foreign, security, and defense policy
Transport policy	Financial control
Energy	Financial and budgetary provisions
Taxation	Institutions
Economic and monetary policy	Other issues
Statistics	

practice, centrally planned regimes, in spite of perpetual reforms to make them more efficient, faced endemic shortages.[4]

The failure of central planning was clearly foreseen by Friedrich Hayek, who pointed out that the information required for the central planner to do a decent job was just too broad and too decentralized.[5] Moreover, no incentive mechanism existed for the central planner to get the requisite information. Decentralization was required to reveal the information that only individuals had about what they wanted and hence were willing to pay for, how much it would actually cost to produce, and what would be the best ways of doing so. The price system in a free market contained that information, whereas the central planner did not.

The central planner could try to use global market prices, but this has two major drawbacks. First, it covers only tradable products. Second, socialism would require that capitalist societies be around to create the international markets from which a successful socialist regime could get the requisite prices for its planning process.[6]

4. Kornai (1992).
5. Hayek (1975 [1935]).
6. As an old socialist joke had it, one day Joseph Stalin announced that the socialist revolution would be victorious everywhere in the world except in New Zealand. So his advisers asked him: why the exception? To which Stalin answered: because we need somewhere to get our prices from. From Kornai (2006).

Furthermore, and most important, the secret of capitalism is not that it is able to clear the market for a set of existing products. Rather, the key is its unending decentralized search for new products and processes.[7] What products are feasible is a rapidly changing set. What products are preferred out of that set is a question that can only be answered by offering them and finding out ex post. This Schumpeterian quest is implicit in the invisible hand.[8] As János Kornai recounts, what impressed him most during his first trips to the West in the 1960s was not the ability of capitalism to balance supply and demand better than socialism, which had been the focus of his research up to then, but the sheer variety and innovation in products, which were nowhere to be seen even in the relatively liberal Hungarian version of socialism.[9]

So the invisible hand is a complex information-processing mechanism cum incentive structure: while having short-run equilibrating properties that tend to balance supply and demand, it also explores a very large and evolving set of new possibilities. Just flip through a thick mail-order catalog or think of what life was like before credit cards, personal computers, cell phones, the Internet, or laser-read code bars at supermarket checkouts to be reminded of how things have changed over the span of a very few years. And consider the alternative under central planning: in March 2008 the Cuban government decided to allow "the unrestricted sale of computers and DVD and video players. . . . Air conditioners would be available next year and toasters in 2010 after a delay caused by limited power supplies."[10]

My central point is that the same complexity characteristic of the development of private products and inputs also typifies public policy. Hence central planning generates similar distortions in both public policy and the market context. First, central planning tends to lead to shortages in the provision of policy solutions. Second, the information requirements regarding evolving obstacles and opportunities that call for policy action are decentralized in society and need to be revealed through some mechanism that addresses the incentive problems faced by participants. This cannot be substituted simply by importing international best practice (the counterpart of international prices).[11] Third, the system requires a Schumpeterian capacity to constantly evolve new solutions: concerning, for example, property rights in the electromagnetic spectrum, cap-and-trade regimes

7. The typical supermarket carries about 45,000 different types of products or stock-keeping units (SKUs). The total number of SKUs in a modern economy is probably in the billions. See Beinhoecker (2006).

8. Schumpeter (1949 [1934]).

9. Kornai's research had up to then been centered on the question of why socialism tended to create shortages of goods in economies characterized by full employment (Kornai [2006]).

10. Mark Frank, "Cuba Lifts Ban on Computers and DVD Player Sales," Reuters, March 13, 2008.

11. This, by the way, suffers from the same critique as the joke quoted by Kornai: if everybody imports the best practice, whom would they be copying? Does one also need to have a New Zealand that the rest can copy?

for contaminants, the ability to sell music over the Internet, e-commerce, and the certification of clinical trials.

Much of the policy debate surrounding development has focused on discovering the few important elements that require prioritized attention. Instead, more attention should be given to the bandwidth that the policymaking process can cope with and the information it can produce in each area of concern.

Does the Invisible Hand Require a Complex Institutional Setting?

Does the invisible hand imply policy's irrelevance ("the absurd prescriptions of the doctor"), as the Smith quotations at the beginning of this chapter suggest? Can the system work simply with the provision of "peace, easy taxes and a tolerable administration of justice"? If so, why is it burdened by hundreds of thousands of pages of legislation and hundreds of government agencies? Why this complexity?

Economists are split on this issue. Some would argue that the primary motivation for government intervention is rent-seeking.[12] Industry can use the state's capacity to coerce for its own gain. Bureaucrats and politicians create regulations in order to extract rents, and incumbents use them to keep competitors out.[13] The world would be better off with a minimal state.

Furthermore, because collective action is only possible if the gains cannot be obtained by just free-riding on the efforts of others, participants in the policy process favor the provision of private, not public goods, which ultimately limits growth.[14] But consumers obviously need assurance that food, medicine, air travel, banks, and work are safe so that they can confidently transact in markets. Recall what happened to the meat market when a few animals came down with "mad cow" disease. Formulating regulation that assures consumers in a world of rapidly changing products and technologies is a highly complex process.

Others would say the key reason for government involvement in economic institutions is the desire to lower transaction costs.[15] As economic agents interact, they face specific transaction costs of different sorts. In response, they organize private-order institutions to find solutions to these costs. Some solutions are self-enforcing or rely on ad hoc outside enforcement.[16] But many are not self-enforcing, so agents turn to the government, whose comparative advantage is precisely its enforcement capacity. When it steps in, however, the government may use (and abuse) its position to extract rents. This makes government involvement less

12. Stigler (1971); Krueger (1974).

13. For example, Djankov and others (2002) state that the evidence on the regulation of entry of firms "is inconsistent with public interest theories of regulation, but supports the public choice view that entry regulation benefits politicians and bureaucrats."

14. Olsen (1965, 1982).

15. Williamson (1975, 1985); and North (1990). Greif (2005) is also particularly enlightening on this subject.

16. Dixit (2004).

attractive to the private sector unless coercion-constraining institutions such as elections and the separation of powers exist to limit the rapacity of the government.

Hence policy complexity may be due to quite constructive reasons. Take the simple case of the real estate market.[17] In this market, assets already exist. They just need to change hands. Buyers need to find out what properties are for sale and what their specific characteristics are. Sellers need to transmit that information to buyers. So a market of real estate brokers develops to achieve these goals. Now, not all the characteristics of a house or apartment are easily visible to a naked untrained eye. A house may have hidden defects that the owner knows about and has an interest in concealing from the buyer. This creates an asymmetric information problem that is addressed through a market for inspectors. These inspectors are licensed by some entity to assure their customers that they know what they are doing. They are hired by the buyer to report on the conditions of the property and its compliance with the building code. Then it is important to know whether the seller has full rights to the property and whether there are liens or other impediments on his right to sell. Otherwise a buyer may find after paying that others have a legal claim on the property too. Such circumstances call for a system of property registries that can track financial and tax claims on individual properties. But it may be inefficient for the buyer to bear the risk of any surprises or defects in the ownership rights, so a market for title insurance is helpful. Also, public authorities may have imposed some easements on that property to secure some public interest, or the municipality may be planning changes nearby that may significantly affect the property's value. Then, too, the buyer needs finance to purchase the home, for which he needs a market for loans. To address willingness-to-pay and other incentive and information problems in this market, it is convenient to be able to pledge the house as collateral to a lender endowed with a set of rights in case the buyer does not abide by the mortgage contract. A legal system needs to define these rights and enforce them. The lender may also require insurance against fire, storms, and other events, lest the collateral go up in smoke. Hence a home insurance market is needed. To complicate matters further, the sale takes time because after an initial agreement has been reached, the inspection needs to take place and the buyer needs to secure financing, title insurance, and home insurance. But many unexpected events may occur during that process, so it is important to be aware of how to deal with them, say, through a deposit, a down payment, or an escrow account for contractual problems, which would have to be handled by a real estate lawyer. The real estate lawyer in turn needs to be accredited (by some body) to carry out these functions. If the property is an apartment in a condominium, the rights and obligations of the apartment owner compared with the rest of the condominium must be clearly established and understood.

17. This example first appeared in Hausmann and Rodrik (2006).

This property sale shows just how complex a seemingly simple transaction actually is, with its multiple connections to a network of interrelated markets and institutional arrangements. It involves not just a market for homes, but also a market for brokers, mortgage loans, inspections, title and home insurance, and lawyers. It also involves registries, municipal rules, accreditation of the different specialized agents, rules on creditor rights and condominiums, and so on. And this is just part of what trade in existing homes entails. Urban development and construction adds more complexity.

Note that the public sector's role here is closely related to the specific transaction costs. Its role is legitimate and sector-specific. It is not driven by rent-seeking per se, and it cannot be carried out through horizontal mechanisms that apply across all sectors. Interventions are sector-specific because the transaction costs they are designed to address are also specific. The government acts not because it is "picking winners." It is simply providing the necessary complementary inputs to one of myriad activities in the economy.

The interaction between markets and policy is clearly high-dimensional and interactive. Hence the way the market for insurance is organized, for example, affects the way the market for mortgages works. And the way every page of a country's voluminous legislation is written can affect all the other pages of legislation. These interactions make the system orders of magnitude more complex than a mere list of its components would suggest. This inevitably makes interventions context-specific.

Development economics is slowly recognizing that a successful economy requires a complex policy framework, but is also trying to elude the complexity by hiding it. In my view, the right approach is to embrace complexity and deal with it in the same way Smith dealt with the problem of the cheese omelet, toast, and coffee. That is to say, the policy process must be treated as something that looks more like the "invisible hand" rather than central planning.

Smith's Policy Simplicity: "We're Not in Kansas Any More"

If the prerequisites of development were not so complex, they could be benchmarked with a few indicators, as in Larry Summers's often-cited suggestion:

> The rate at which countries grow is substantially determined by three things: their ability to *integrate with the global economy* through trade and investment; their capacity to *maintain sustainable government finances and sound money*; and their ability to put in place an institutional environment in which *contracts can be enforced and property rights can be established*. I would challenge anyone to identify a country that has done all three of these things and has not grown at a substantial rate. And I would challenge anyone to identify a country that for any significant period has been held

back either by excessive trade links with the global economy, overly sound public finances, or property rights and contracts that are excessively enforced.[18]

That is to say, growth requires openness, sound money, and property rights. In a simple low-dimensional interpretation, this quotation implies that an index of the level of restrictions to trade and investment, the rate of inflation, the public debt ratio, and an index of property rights and contract enforcement are what matter to a country's ability to grow.[19] But the World Economic Forum recently concluded from its study of competitiveness that "the determinants of competitiveness are *many* and *complex*."[20] The forum's Global Competitiveness Index measures twelve areas or pillars considered key to a country's competitiveness: institutions, infrastructure, macroeconomic stability, health and primary education, higher education and training, goods market efficiency, labor market efficiency, financial market sophistication, technological readiness, market size, business sophistication, and innovation. Each of these areas is a composite of many others. For example, the institutions pillar is composed of eighteen elements (table 6-2).

Thus more than 100 indicators underpin the forum's twelve pillars. But many of these indicators are systemic properties, not fundamental areas of policy, as in the case of public trust in politicians, transparency of government policymaking, or wastefulness in government spending. These are outcomes of a system packed with many agencies and rules and perceived by many constituencies. What causes most of these outcomes is unclear, and therefore it is difficult to tell which actionable variables should be adjusted to improve performance in these areas. In all likelihood, the requisite policy actions constitute an even longer list, with its own complicated sets of interactions.

The World Bank faces a similar situation in its attempt to measure the quality of the investment climate through its *Doing Business Report*. The index it uses for this purpose consists of ten elements: starting a business, dealing with licenses, employing workers, registering property, getting credit, protecting investors, paying taxes, trading across borders, enforcing contracts, and closing a business. Each component has many dimensions. For example, employing workers is the product of six other indexes, which measure the difficulty in hiring and in firing and rigidities in the workday and in employment, as well as non-wage and firing costs. Each of these is in turn an aggregation of several sub-subindexes. In total, this

18. Summers (2003).

19. A higher-dimension interpretation of this quotation would instead put the emphasis on the words "ability" or "capacity," which Summers uses three times: the ability to integrate with the global economy, the capacity to maintain sound money, the ability to put in place an institutional environment. These abilities may be high-dimensional and may not be captured just by the level of tariffs or the inflation rate. They could be very complex and context-specific. See Rodrik (2007) for a discussion of this point.

20. World Economic Forum (2007–08, p. 3).

Table 6-2. *Components of the Institutions Pillar of the Global Competitiveness Index*

Intellectual property	Diversion of public funds
Protection of property rights	Strength of auditing and reporting standards
Transparency of government policymaking	Business costs of terrorism
Judicial independence	Efficacy of corporate boards
Efficiency of legal framework	Ethical behavior of firms
Favoritism in decisions of government officials	Business costs of crime and violence
Presence of organized crime	Wastefulness of government spending
Protection of minority shareholders' interests	Reliability of police services
Public trust of politicians	Burden of government regulation

index comprises more than 100 variables. How is one to handle this high-dimensional space?

Attempts at Collapsing the High-Dimensional Space

The simple policy world that Adam Smith envisioned has turned out to be one with a multitude of rather complex dimensions. In reality, the dimensionality is orders of magnitude larger than indicated by the *Global Competitiveness Report*, for example, but this fact is suppressed through a set of assumptions that project the complexity into a few dimensions, even to a single dimension consisting of country rankings.

One such mechanism reduces dimensionality by applying the same label to many different real phenomena. This is more of a linguistic than a practical device. Under the Global Competitiveness Index, for instance, the term "burden of regulation" should in theory encompass food safety standards, environmental controls, phytosanitary permits, capital adequacy requirements, zoning rules, tax administration, labor market regulations, and so on. Similarly, "property rights" applies to various categories of rights: the right of a person to an apartment in a condominium, of a company to the mineral resources underground, of a bank to a loan, and of a musician to a song. These rights are defined in different legal texts and enforced by different agencies. It is as if all men in the world were lumped into categories based on their first names (John, George, Joseph, Peter, Daniel, William, and so on), even though the individuals assigned to each group have few traits in common other than their name. When performance has to be improved, however, high dimensionality comes back into play as each individual in the group requires different treatment.

A second strategy to reduce dimensionality is to suppress sector specificity. For example, the *Doing Business Report* tries to measure the time and cost of licenses by looking only at those required to set up a warehouse. Similarly, the measures for enforcing contracts are benchmarked to those used in collecting a loan granted to a hotel. Although these may be interesting points of comparison among countries, licenses for a warehouse entail very different considerations from those for registering a drug, getting a concession for a TV channel, obtaining rights over natural resources, or procuring phytosanitary permits. The basic assumption here seems to be that if a country is bad at licensing a warehouse, it must be hopeless at dealing with any other specific area requiring a license. But sector-specific dimensions are highly relevant to the investment climate, the quality of which depends heavily on addressing issues at the right level of specificity.

Moreover, improving the licensing process is more than just a matter of cutting through red tape. Licenses must take into account important trade-offs, such as consumer safety, environmental protection, urban conditions, network effects, labor safety, intellectual property, and the like. Each licensing process is a distinct transaction, often based on a different law, run by a different agency, and addressing a host of issues. Consider the environmental concerns, right-of-way questions, network effects, urban spillovers, natural monopolies, tax issues, labor and consumer safety standards, and many other issues specific to agriculture, power, telecommunications, mining, ports, or the pharmaceutical industry. In order to provide an adequate investment climate in each of these areas, societies must squarely face the problem of high dimensionality. Making the licensing of a warehouse an expeditious catchall will not do, because high dimensionality cannot simply be glossed over.[21]

Another means of reducing dimensionality is to base indexes on linearity and separability.[22] Linearity assumes that the dimensions of an index are substitutes. Suppose an index averages the number of licenses required with the number of days it takes to get them and the formal fees that have to be paid. Accordingly, underperformance on one of these elements can be made up by overperforming on the others. In real life, these elements are more likely to be complements than

21. For example, in a critical assessment of the Doing Business (DB) Index, the World Bank's Independent Evaluation Group states that "the indicators have been highly effective in drawing attention to the burdens of business regulation, but cannot by themselves capture other key dimensions of a country's business climate, the benefits of regulation, or key related aspects of development effectiveness. . . . Since regulations generate social benefits as well as private costs, what is good for an individual firm is not necessarily good for the economy or society as a whole. Therefore, policy implications are not always clear-cut, and the right level and type of regulation is a matter of policy choice in each country." It concludes that "the Bank Group, by prominently recognizing DB's highly ranked countries, may be inadvertently signaling that it values reduced regulatory burdens more than other development goals." See "Doing Business: An Independent Evaluation" (http://siteresources.worldbank.org/EXTDOIBUS/Resources/exec_summary.pdf [2008]).

22. In a study of linearity and separability in the context of cross-country growth regressions, Rodriguez (2007) finds that the data do not support these assumptions.

substitutes: problems in one area can kill off all investments in a sector; it is not compensated by overperformance along other regulatory dimensions.

Separability means that the impact of improvements in one dimension is independent of the state of other dimensions. In other words, mapping between each dimension and performance is increasing monotonically in all dimensions, all the time. This is highly unlikely to be the case. Second-best interactions are bound to be very important. The benefit from having fewer licenses, say, has to be traded off against the benefit of assuring consumers that products are safe and banks are sound. The benefit of having low license fees must be traded off against the cost of having cash-strapped licensing offices because, in the absence of adequate fees, they depend on a weak central government budget. Low labor taxes in the United States go hand in hand with little public provision of health services, leaving more of the burden of health insurance on corporate balance sheets while making labor mobility riskier for workers.

If in real life things were linear and separable, then good countries would be choosing good policies and bad countries choosing lousier ones along the dimensions described by the index. However, the median cell in the correlation matrix of the Doing Business Index is just 0.16.[23] The best performers are clearly not going to a corner in each of the chosen dimensions. They are optimizing along some complicated internal solution, and different countries find very different configurations.

Economic theory often does away with the high dimensionality of the policy space by assuming that government action consists of a set of taxes and subsidies, in the Pigovian manner. The idea is that market distortions create a wedge between private and public returns, so the role of policy is to create the Pigovian taxes or subsidies to bring these two returns into line. This approach may work for a limited set of interventions, a good example being the cap-and-trade approach to environmental problems such as acid rain. However, most public policy issues call for concrete action by the public sector—whether it be a specific regulation, infrastructure change, or some other move—not a tax or a subsidy. The point is that compensating the private sector financially for the absence of a road or an appropriate solution to a transaction cost is inferior to solving the problem. Furthermore, the set of interventions that can effect a solution is much larger than the simple provision of money, which affirms that the policy action space itself is high-dimensional.

Because of this high dimensionality, recent development thinking has been coming up with an ever-expanding set of indicators. But to make the plethora of dimensions tractable, it has opted for low-dimensional representations of that space that assumes away the inherent complexity. Simple competitiveness or

---

23. To take into account the fact that some correlations are expected to be positive and others negative, I take the absolute value of the estimated correlations to calculate these numbers.

investment climate rankings do not imply a relatively simple list of best practices that any government can follow. Fixing the policy environment for development is a high-dimensional and evolving space with many context-specific interactions. Just as with the case of products, it will be very hard for a central planner to keep all these considerations in mind when charting a course of action, or for countries wedded to a central planning approach to avoid the policy equivalent of shortages and lack of innovation.

Complexity in Production

Under capitalism, Joseph Schumpeter has pointed out, development and sustained economic growth require the constant introduction of new products. This means, says Robert Lucas, "A growth miracle sustained for a period of decades . . . must involve the continual introduction of new goods, not merely continual learning on a fixed set of goods."[24]

But this process is rife with market failures, due by and large to three classes of problems: coordination failures, information spillovers, and labor-training externalities.[25] Coordination failures occur when markets are incomplete, with the result that the return to one investment depends on whether some other investment is also made: building a hotel near a beautiful beach may only be profitable if somebody builds an airport in the same vicinity. The opposite may also be the case. Yet there may be no way for the market to coordinate both investments.[26]

Information spillovers relate to self-discovery, which is the process of finding out the cost structure of an economy for the production of new goods.[27] The first mover will find out whether something is profitable or not; if it is, she will be copied by other entrants. But if she fails, she bears the whole loss. Therefore the private returns from engaging in this type of innovation are lower than the social benefits, and the market incentives for self-discovery are inefficiently low. The typical policy implication is that a subsidy may be needed to bring the private returns in line with the social returns.

Labor-training externalities can be equally troublesome. A firm that trains its labor force provides a potential benefit to other firms through the poaching of its workers. This dampens the incentives to provide the optimal amount of training for fear of losing the investment. Although labor mobility may not entail a social

24. Robert Lucas (1993, p. 263).
25. Hausmann and Rodrik (2006).
26. A typical solution is for the government to provide a guarantee to both investors. If done well, this will be costless for the government ex post as the investments will be profitable when they both take place. If the guarantee is not credible, then the government can just build the airport and the hotels will follow.
27. Hausmann and Rodrik (2003). Structural transformation is not really about inventing new products. It is about identifying which of the products that exist in the world could be profitably produced by a particular country. It is not a discovery of a product but of a national capability; hence the term.

loss, in that workers can deploy their skills elsewhere, a company cannot appropriate these benefits while incurring the training cost. Given inadequate investment in labor training, the policy solution is to subsidize it.

These three problems are clearly more acute for new activities than for already established ones. In the first place, coordination is impeded by the proverbial chicken-and-egg question: new activities are hard to develop unless their suppliers are present, but why would the suppliers exist if they have nobody to sell to? Second, by definition, new activities must incur self-discovery costs. And third, new activities cannot find workers with the relevant experience since the activities have not been in existence before and hence have not been hiring and training workers.

How, then, could structural change ever take place? One way forward is to find new activities that can use the factors and capabilities already developed for other purposes in the economy. That is why product discoveries tend to favor "nearby" goods, as measured by the probability that these goods are simultaneously exported in other countries.[28] The product space is very irregular, with some goods having many nearby products and others being quite isolated. Countries differ markedly in the availability of nearby goods to move to, and this affects their capacity to introduce new products, upgrade their product mix, and grow.[29]

In this sense, the development process is a coevolution of products and capabilities. Products require capabilities, which only accumulate in the expectation that someone will demand them. A country does not develop a cold-storage logistic system unless there is a market for it, but there will be no market unless products require it. To reiterate, countries move to nearby goods because they share similar capabilities with the ones already in place. Development is a sequence of stepping-stones that justify the accumulation of an increasing number of ever more complex capabilities.[30]

Coevolution implies a great potential for coordination failures, as it is hard to synchronize the development of a capability with the demand for it. Moreover, because capabilities are numerous and coevolve locally, finding out how to do things in a given context involves costly self-discovery, which in turn entails information externalities.[31]

---

28. Hausmann and Klinger (2006).

29. Hidalgo and others (2007) use network science to graph the product space and show that the shape of the product space may explain the lack of global income convergence. To be able to diffuse through the product space, countries must be able to "jump" distances that are statistically infrequent in the data. Hausmann and Klinger (2007) show that countries better positioned in the product space, in terms of the proximity to other products, tend to upgrade their exports faster.

30. This is very much in the spirit of Hirschman's (1958) backward and forward linkages. However, he emphasized what could be interpreted as input-output relationships. The emphasis here is on the similarity of the requisite inputs.

31. Hausmann and Rodrik (2003). Acemoglu, Antras, and Helpman (2005) have a model with strong complementarities of inputs and limited contractability. Countries with better contractual envi-

What Role for Policy in a High-Dimensional World?

If this description reflects the development process, what is the role for policy? How should a government decide which of the hundreds of thousands of pages of legislation to revise or which of the hundreds of agencies to reform? How should it assess the impact of any reform in any area of legislation on the performance of other areas of activity and other second-best interactions? How should it balance the costs and benefits of different changes? How should it choose between fighting foot-and-mouth disease and building new rural roads, certifying dentists and real estate brokers, or prohibiting child labor and environmental degradation?

How can actual governments cope with the large bandwidth of requisite information and decisions? Stated this way, the problem seems as hopeless as that of my earlier example: making an omelet with toast and coffee. The latter was solved with the aid of Adam Smith's invisible hand. Central planning could not work, yet policy thinkers have tended to look for central planning solutions because they have ignored the high dimensionality of the problem. Can Adam Smith come to the rescue again?

The invisible hand works because information about social wants and possibilities is highly decentralized in society, so decisions have to be delegated to where the information exists: that is, among the suppliers and demanders of products and services. Similarly, information about productive possibilities and obstacles is widely disseminated in society, as is the capacity to see how one policy idea, often designed for one purpose, may have unintended consequences in other sectors. Therefore a more decentralized approach may actually work for the provision of public policies as well.

However, the policy problem differs from the market problem in an important respect: markets have three elements at their disposal that the policy process lacks. First, *prices* give them *information* about relative costs and willingness to pay. Second, *the profit motive* provides the *incentive* to respond to prices. Third, the *capital market* takes care of *mobilizing resources* to areas that are expected to show good profit opportunities. Hence the market has an information, incentive, and resource mobilization system to solve the coordination problem. The market is not expected to get everything right instantaneously and without waste. It is

---

ronments avoid ex post renegotiations, are thus better able to solve the coordination problems, and can produce goods that require more inputs. This would explain the division of labor across countries as a function of their contractual environment. It is an empirical question whether the requisite coordination of capabilities and products has been effectively addressed through legal enforcement of contracts or whether the world has relied on other forms of coordination. An alternative model would make the *liquidity* of input markets the mechanism that protects investors against opportunistic ex post behavior. For new inputs, liquidity is bound to be low, exacerbating hold-up problems and slowing down structural transformation.

expected to figure things out over a reasonable period of time as imbalances show up and force agents to change their plans.

In the provision of public inputs, all three dimensions are lacking: an article of law has no affixed price that reflects the costs and benefits it provides. Even if it did, why would the political process respond to that price, as it is not in the business of maximizing profits? And, of course, no capital market is present to move resources to where the promise of return is highest.

But could the policy process mimic an "invisible hand" approach to the problem? Can it address the information, incentive, and resource mobilization problem? To see how this might be done, one needs a more detailed account of the interaction between policy and production. Production in a market economy requires three types of inputs: market tradable, market nontradable, and public inputs. Market tradable items can be imported, so their firms need not exist in the given economic area. However, even here rules about trading across borders, requirements of product registration, copyrights, safety standards, logistics, other transaction costs, and many additional details come into consideration, all of which are provided by governments. By contrast, nontradable market inputs must exist in situ if production is to take place. Here coordination failures and holdup problems can complicate things greatly. Faced with these transaction problems, agents would have the incentive to form private-order entities and to involve the government in solutions, as discussed earlier.[32] The success of this process will most likely depend on the costs of private association—which are affected by free-riding, trust, and social capital among other things—and the political institutions that limit government rapacity and facilitate public involvement in solutions.

The rules, norms, infrastructure, and other public actions that emerge from this process become inputs in the production process and affect the efficiency with which the latter operates. Call them *public inputs*. For some products, these public inputs determine whether they are at all feasible. So production depends not just on private inputs provided by markets but also on public inputs generated by a different process. Public inputs are strong complements of private inputs in that the more people have of one, the more they demand of the other. This also means that investors in a particular field are bound to benefit from a greater provision of the requisite public inputs. Their willingness to pay for an improvement in the provision of the public inputs is not independent from the social return to that input. This creates incentives to participate in the policymaking process. Note that this does not need to involve unproductive rent-seeking. In a competitive world, the initial gains from improved provision of public inputs to firms already in the industry will be dissipated through competition and will benefit society at large. However, without at least some temporary benefits to petitioners, there would be no incentive to participate in the policymaking process.

32. See Greif (2005).

Public inputs, just like private inputs, are very high-dimensional. However, public inputs—for example, Article 00 of Law X—typically do not have a price, so no decentralized system arises to deliver information about what is demanded, and it is very hard for governments to know what changes in norms or infrastructure would deliver the biggest bang. Even if the government had that information, it would still face an incentive problem: even if the government knew that there was a problem with Article 00, it is not clear what incentives would lead it to change that article. And even if the government had the information and the incentive to provide a certain public input, how it could mobilize the resources is unclear, since each public entity does not have ready access to the capital market.

How Does the World Deal with High Dimensionality? The U.S. Example

Somehow the world has been able to cope with the high-dimensional policy problem. How it does so is not a question that development economics has addressed in any significant way for a large sample of countries. A little is known about how things take place in the United States, though it is likely to be a unique case. Nevertheless, it merits a closer look.

The U.S. Congress has 435 elected members in the House of Representatives and 100 in the Senate. Contrary to practice in many other countries, these officials act independently and frequently do not vote along party lines. They can initiate legislation (something that is restricted to the executive body in many systems) and at times may attach their names to pieces of legislation, which creates an incentive for political entrepreneurship. In addition, as opposed to a parliamentary system, the U.S. system does not guarantee the executive a majority in Congress. As a result, the private sector must lobby Congress, not just the executive, to press for its interests.

According to the Center for Responsive Politics, the United States has more than 20,000 registered lobbyists, and they spent 2.8 billion dollars on their activities in 2007 (double the amount spent in 1999).[33] What are these lobbyists about? In the standard economist story, they are about pure rent-seeking.[34] In the framework I have laid out, lobbyists play a much more productive role. They provide information to members of Congress regarding legislation that may benefit them or that may be harmful to their interests and they want to impede. Lobbyists influence policymakers not just through information, but also through analysis and campaign contributions. They operate much like market makers in finance.

The stated mission of the lobby group Good Government, for example, is "to effectively impact the development of legislation and regulation important to the

33. See Center for Responsive Politics (http://www.opensecrets.org/lobby/index.php). Interestingly for my example, the National Association of Realtors is the eleventh largest spender in lobby activities. See also Grossman and Helpman (2001, esp. chap. 1).

34. Krueger (1974).

mortgage lending industry, working for laws that protect consumers and keep mortgage capital available to them on fair and affordable terms, in ways consistent with responsible corporate citizenship and Good Government."[35] The group defines a good lobbyist as one who

—Convinces politicians to vote on legislation by demonstrating that doing so is in the politicians' interest.

—Meets with legislators and provides information they would not otherwise have received.

— . . . Educates legislators with support documentation (charts, graphs, polls, reports).

—Sits down with legislators and helps them draft legislation.[36]

In other words, lobbyists define their role in terms of information and incentives. According to one theory of lobbying, policymakers face two basic needs: to adopt policies preferred by their voters and to finance their campaigns.[37] Their response to lobbyists will therefore depend on the cost of deviating from their voters' preferences and the benefit in electoral funding. Since lobbyists far outnumber legislators, many are present on opposite sides of most issues. This creates an adversarial system, much like the judicial system. The idea is that by having each side put its best arguments on the table, the system reveals much more information than one open only to experts informed by "best practices."

Put simply, the U.S. system reveals information and creates incentives for policymakers to respond to that information. To facilitate their response, the legislative agenda is decentralized through committee work. This open architecture permits many channels of communication to develop between the private sector and government and many policy processes to operate in parallel.

At the same time, the U.S. approach to policymaking generates significant distortions. For example, free-riding affects activities differentially.[38] Concentrated interests or those in which the capacity to cooperate is enhanced for other reasons are bound to be overrepresented. Members of Congress have to fund their own reelection every two or six years, which makes their sensitivity to contributions quite high. And the public's capacity to follow the many fine points of policy tends to be limited.

Clearly, this process must be far from optimal, compared with what could be achieved by an omniscient and benevolent social planner. The same can be said of the market compared with an omniscient central planner. However, omniscience is not for mortals.

---

35. See www.oomc.com/GoodGovt/index.shtml.

36 See www.oomc.com/GoodGovt/Civics/whatalobdoes.shtml.

37. Grossman and Helpman (1994).

38. See Olsen's (1965) seminal work on this subject.

Is It Only about the Rents, or Are Rents Part of the Solution?

Ample evidence has been put forth to illustrate that the lobbying process is a pure rent-seeking game.[39] Yet the fact that rents are present does not mean that this is what the entire process is about. I would emphasize the complementarity between public inputs and private production, along with the information and incentive constraints that lobbying is a response to. Given the varied participation constraints that the different players face—especially free-riding on the part of the public—it makes sense for participants to expect some rents from the process. This does not mean rent-seeking is the only motive. People lobby to prohibit abortion and stem-cell research, to curb the emission of greenhouse gasses, to create the legal infrastructure to sell music on the Internet and protect copyrights, to curb acid rain, to save the whales, and so on. Looking at this as a simple rent-seeking game is like recounting Hamlet without the prince.

Needless to say, the tension between enacting policies that are good for voters and policies that are good for contributors may not be well balanced. Moreover, productivity-enhancing and rent-seeking motivations may coexist with a greater presence of the latter, which can be borne out by countless anecdotes. I am not aware of any study that has looked at the relative presence of either. Productivity-enhancing measures are bound to have larger constituencies in their favor or fewer opponents as they create value that can then be distributed among stakeholders. So if the political process is fairly open, such measures would tend to be favored. Pure rent-seeking is bound to survive only in less transparent environments as most other participants would oppose such interventions since they do not stand to gain from it. But rents are needed to justify participating in the process and avoid free-riding. It is not clear what the benchmark for an appropriate balance between productivity enhancement and rents would be in the absence of an omniscient and benevolent social planner.

The Policymaking Process in Developing Countries

The point is that economists barely understand how the system that matches the demand for and the supply of public inputs actually works in the United States, let alone how it works in most developing countries.[40] In some countries, parliaments play a small role in policymaking, essentially rubber-stamping the initiatives of the executive. Even when parliaments do play a role, decisions are often

---

39. See, for example, Stigler (1971).

40. One important recent study of the policymaking process in a developing country context is by Stein and others (2006). The authors look at political institutions and the institutional setting of the different actors to assess aggregate performance in terms of stability, adaptability, coordination and coherence, and efficiency of policies in general. Unfortunately, they do not deal with the supply of and demand for highly dimensional public policies.

made by political parties rather than by individual members of parliament. Campaigns are often financed by the party, not by individual candidates. The lobbying game must shift accordingly. In some countries, the relationship between the political elite and the needs of the business sector is quite dysfunctional and riddled with distrust. In others, the relationship is dominated by a sense of shared interests. In countries with a highly concentrated private sector, the coordination may involve few players. For example, the Korean policymaking framework under President Park Chung-hee was based on a deal with the country's chaebols (business conglomerates) making them responsible for creating export jobs in exchange for a supportive public policy. A relatively independent bureaucracy and foreign competition kept the system fairly honest. The nature of the public inputs system can determine how different market failures are addressed, how the provision of public inputs can be improved, and how animal spirits are affected once investors learn how the future provision of public inputs will be decided.

Little evidence is available on the potential importance of the expected provision of public inputs in explaining growth, but some investigations are suggestive. A study of growth acceleration in India based on policy reforms and their dates shows that growth began picking up about a decade before the major liberalizing reforms often credited with the upswing, such as trade reform. The cause of this acceleration is thought to have been "an attitudinal shift by the government in the early 1980s" that turned in favor of the established business interests (as opposed to potential new entrants, say).[41] This attitudinal shift was expressed in many small decisions but no major reforms. The vigorous response of established interests suggests that they had been constrained by an inadequate provision of public inputs that could be improved with small changes. If existing businesses can expect to get their issues resolved, their animal spirits will respond quickly, and productivity can rise dramatically, as it did.

The alignment of incentives between investors and policymakers often takes forms that are hard to present in polite society. What matters, some say, is not a government's policy actions but the expected mapping of future states of the world in relation to the policy actions they would trigger.[42] Private sector behavior today will be responsive to what agents expect that mapping to be in the future. For example, the government of Indonesia could be trusted to provide the right public inputs when the Suharto clan was adequately represented in the ownership structure of the firm, but when Suharto's health started to fail and his sons got into a political quagmire, the mechanism broke down, and animal spirits flew out the window.

Consider, by contrast, the traditional modus operandi of an International Monetary Fund program or a World Bank policy loan. Typically, conditionality is more

---

41. Rodrik and Subramanian (2004).
42. Pritchett (2008).

or less secretly negotiated with minimal social input. Officials from the Bretton Woods institutions base their views on international best practices with little knowledge of the local specificities that would naturally emerge from a more democratic process. The priorities for reform come from the fashions of the day in the development community, such as trade liberalization, financial reform, privatization, or conditional cash transfers. The solutions are considered relatively obvious and are derived from first principles, with the policy problem often defined as the lack of "political will" or "appetite for reform." Note that the rest of society is uninvolved in identifying either policy priorities or alternative solutions.

Randomized Trials and Benchmarking Clubs in a High-Dimensional World

Another method that loses its appeal in a world of high dimensionality is the randomized trial. A typical program—whether a conditional cash transfer, a microfinance program, or a health intervention—can easily have fifteen relevant dimensions. Assume that each dimension can take only two values. Then the possible combinations are 2^{15} or 32,768 possible combinations. But randomized trials can only distinguish between a control group and one to three treatment groups. Hence many of the design or contextual features are kept constant while just one or three are varied. This means that the search over the design space is quite limited, and the external validity of the experiments reduced by the fact that many of the design or contextual elements are bound to change from place to place. For the majority of design elements, then, policymakers must decide on many design criteria without support from randomized trials, which will necessarily play a secondary role in practice.

High dimensionality is more amenable to an "evolutionary" treatment. Since the search space is so large, the optimum is just too difficult to find. An alternative is to organize many searches and have a mechanism for selecting the most promising options. In biology, the searches are by and large random, but if the selection mechanism is effective, the system will constantly pick those variations that improve performance. Humans should be able to search more efficiently, but they will need an effective selection mechanism.

Such a mechanism exists and is used effectively in the private sector: it is benchmarking, a practice that was started in the auto industry but has spread to many other areas. Units of production are given operational flexibility, but their performance is meticulously measured and compared. The feedback from repeated comparative measures is meant to facilitate the decentralized open-ended search for improvements. In education, the search for improvements would rely on school autonomy and feedback from repeated standardized tests, which are rather different from randomized trials that try to assess the impact that class size, teaching materials, deworming, micronutrients, toilets, or incentives for teacher attendance may have on school performance. Clearly, the impact of any of these interventions is bound to be highly context-specific: class size will matter little if the teacher does not attend school, and micronutrients are likely to be ineffective if nutrition is adequate. Decentralized experimentation and benchmarking of outcomes is likely to be a more effective and dynamic way of making progress.

Both the Global Competitiveness Index and the Doing Business Index represent attempts to use benchmarking in policymaking. In principle, each country tries to make progress in its own way, and its performance is measured and compared as in a benchmarking club. Other countries provide information on feasible outcomes, and this may help each country assess its own performance. Defined in this way, indexes may add value as feedback that informs the search process by pointing out what outcomes are achievable, without pretending to specify how they could be improved in any particular context.

But to play this role, an index must actually convey information about relative performance in the relevant areas. Instead, such indexes are often a mixture of policy inputs and performance measures, which complicates their interpretation. For example, the Doing Business Index calculates the time it actually takes on average to get a permit—a clear measure of performance—along with the number of permits and their cost, which are policy variables. To play their role in the feedback loop, they should include only performance measures, while it should be up to the decentralized decisionmakers to figure out if the process would be more efficient with fewer complex licenses or with more simple ones. Also, calculating averages of averages of indexes does not provide a clear metric of anybody's performance. Finding the right measure of performance is often more important than compiling a plethora of poor measures in the expectation that the error terms of each bad measure will be orthogonal to the true measure so that they cancel out.

Setting Priorities versus Increasing the Bandwidth

One approach to the high dimensionality of the policy space is to set well-defined priorities so as to focus on what is really important, to the detriment of secondary goals or problems. The question is, who sets such priorities, what set of wants informs their decisions? Another approach is to enable the policy process to deal with more issues, that is, to operate at a higher bandwidth. This can be done by multiplying the channels through which priorities are expressed and policies are produced and by enriching the informational environment in which the policy process takes place. As Charles Lindblom has pointed out:

> Because policy makers learn through trial and error, we should not ask that today's policies be consistent with yesterday's. Because policy makers learn through trial and error about goals and means, we should not ask that

today's policies not waver or alter in their objectives; we should hope instead that they do. Because in a pluralist, complex society, social goals are not a tightly knit harmonious structure, because we value openness in goal structure, and because we keep the social peace by permitting conflicting interests to pursue conflicting goals, we do not even want to reject such apparent inconsistencies as—to take a common example—subsidizing some farmers to restrict output, and others to expand it.[43]

As Friedrich Hayek had highlighted about markets, the requisite information required for public inputs is decentralized in society, and one should focus on the mechanisms that allow societies to reveal it and to evaluate different courses of action. For Dani Rodrik, "participatory and decentralized political systems are the most effective ones we have for processing and aggregating local knowledge. We can think of democracy as a meta-institution for building good institutions."[44]

Policy Designs for Higher Bandwidth

To increase the bandwidth of policymaking, societies need a means of searching the space of opportunities and obstacles. Here, as with the market versus central planning, the problem is that information is highly dispersed in society, so that revealing information becomes a central activity of the policy process. This problem can be addressed through an open architecture approach to economic policymaking.[45] This means meeting the government's need for information about the space of possibilities and obstacles by creating mechanisms to motivate the private sector to provide the information and to build the government's capacity and desire to respond effectively.

First, an *open architecture* approach imbues many *self-organizing bodies* in society with the initiative for action.[46] These bodies exist because they share interests in a set of public or club goods. If, instead, the government structure parses society into predetermined groups that must reach agreement, information about the missing public goods will not necessarily be revealed, and policymaking will focus on whatever shared interest constitutes a common denominator, which often is a subsidy or a tax holiday rather than a more specific and productive intervention.

Second, if a public or club good is particularly productive, the private sector should in principle be willing to *co-finance*. Therefore willingness to co-pay may be a good screening device.

43. Lindblom (1968, p. 109).
44. Rodrik (2000).
45. See Hausmann and Rodrik (2006); Hausmann, Rodrik, and Sabel (2007).
46. Romer (1993) proposes self-organizing industry investment boards to allocate research and development expenditures.

Third, the rest of society must view the relationship between the private and the public sectors as a legitimate one—and not as a means of serving the already rich. Therefore the system must operate on principles of transparency, which will not only limit the types of requests that the private sector will be willing to make but will also discipline the public response.

Fourth, the government should evaluate its actions for their impact on productivity, not just profitability. Profitability can be increased by transferring income from the rest of society (for example, by buying inputs cheaper or selling output at a higher price), but unless there is an externality, this does not provide a rationale for action. By contrast, improved productivity increases the total amount of resources that a society can generate.

Fifth, solutions should be designed from universalist criteria and should not constitute an ad hoc remedy for a particular plaintiff. That way, the policy dialogue will generate positive spillovers to other activities, not just the ones asking for treatment.

Mechanisms of intervention should also take into account the likelihood that existing activities are overrepresented compared with activities that could exist but do not because the right public inputs and other capabilities are not present. It is essential to think of mechanisms that could search into more distant parts of the product space. Institutions such as development banks and industrial zones can play a significant role in exploring these outer confines of the feasible product space and can facilitate the provision of the requisite public inputs. They do so by offering something—finance in one case and good infrastructure in the other—so that potential entrepreneurs enter into a relationship that reveals information about their plans. Since the relationship is potentially win-win, both parties have incentives to identify opportunities and obstacles and work to remove them. The government can view these institutions as arranging organized searches and as helping to identify initiatives that create opportunities and remove obstacles in ways that would facilitate future entry. While this is not the way these institutions are formally set up, they often do play this role in practice, and it would be beneficial to formalize such a role.[47]

Embracing Complexity: Reinterpreting Adam Smith

Little is gained from disregarding the high-dimensional nature of the development process and its requisite public inputs. Instead of focusing on a small number of potential silver bullets, an effective development strategy will seek the mechanisms that increase a society's capacity to process information and ideas, that is, to increase bandwidth. The alternatives for policymakers are clear: either embrace and deal with high dimensionality or hide from it. Embracing it implies working not

47. See Hausmann, Rodrik, and Sabel (2007) for a discussion of this issue.

only on individual policy actions that may be required but more importantly on the meta-structures whereby problems are identified and addressed. This is what will ultimately allow societies to deal with their inherent complexity.

Adam Smith said that "the uniform, constant and uninterrupted effort of every man to better his condition . . . is frequently powerful enough to maintain the natural progress of things toward improvement." Maybe Smith could be reinterpreted a bit to acknowledge that part of man's effort to better his condition lies in participating in the collective search for public policies that can seize opportunities and overcome obstacles. Letting that invisible hand operate to improve policies may be the appropriate way to deal with the high dimensionality of the real world.

References

Acemoglu, Daron, Pol Antras, and Elhanan Helpman. 2005. "Contracts and the Division of Labor." Working Paper 05-14. Cambridge, Mass: MIT Department of Economics.

Beinhoecker, Eric. 2006. *The Origin of Wealth*. Harvard Business Press.

Dixit, Avinash. 2004. *Lawlessness and Economics: Alternative Modes of Governance*. Princeton University Press.

Djankov, Simeon, and others. 2002. "The Regulation of Entry." *Quarterly Journal of Economics* 117 (February): 1–37.

Greif, Avner. 2005. "Commitment, Coercion, and Markets: The Nature and Dynamics of Institutions Supporting Exchange." In *Handbook of New Institutional Economics*, edited by Claude Ménard and Mary Shirley, pp. 727–86. Netherlands: Springer.

Grossman, Gene M., and Elhanan Helpman. 1994. "Protection for Sale." *American Economic Review* 84, no. 4 (September): 833–50.

———. 2001. *Special Interest Politics*. MIT Press.

Hausmann, Ricardo, and Bailey Klinger. 2006. "Structural Transformation and the Patterns of Comparative Advantage in the Product Space." Working Paper 128. Harvard University Center for International Development (August).

———. 2007. "The Product Space and the Evolution of Comparative Advantage." Working Paper 146. Harvard University Center for International Development (April).

Hausmann, Ricardo, Lant Pritchett, and Dani Rodrik. 2005. "Growth Accelerations." *Journal of Economic Growth* 10, no. 4: 303–29.

Hausmann, Ricardo, and Dani Rodrik. 2003. "Economic Development as Self-Discovery." *Journal of Development Economics* 72 (December): 603–33.

———. 2006. "Doomed to Choose: Industrial Policy as Predicament." Harvard University. Photocopy.

Hausmann, Ricardo, Dani Rodrik, and Charles Sabel. 2007. "Reconfiguring Industrial Policy: A Framework with an Application to South Africa." Harvard University. Photocopy.

Hayek, Friedrich A. 1975 (1935). *Collectivist Economic Planning: Critical Studies on the Possibilities of Socialism*. Clifton, N.J.: A. M. Kelly.

Hidalgo, César, and others. 2007. "The Product Space Conditions the Development of Nations." *Science* 317 (July): 482–87.

Hirschman, Albert. 1958. *The Strategy of Economic Development*. Yale University Press.

Kornai, János. 1992. *The Socialist System: The Political Economy of Communism*. Princeton Paperbacks.

———. 2006. *By Force of Thought*. MIT Press.

Kornai, János, and Tamás Lipták. 1971 (1965). "Two-Level Planning." In *Selected Readings in Economic Theory,* edited by Keneth J. Arrow, pp. 412–40. MIT Press.

Krueger, Anne O. 1974. "The Political Economy of the Rent-Seeking Society." *American Economic Review.* 64 (June): 291–303.

Lindblom, Charles E. 1968. *The Policy-Making Process.* Englewood Cliffs, N.J.: Prentice-Hall.

Lucas, Robert E., Jr. 1993. "Making a Miracle." *Econometrica* 61 (March): 251–72.

North, Douglas. 1990. *Institutions, Institutional Change and Economic Performance.* Cambridge University Press.

Olson, Mancur. 1965. *The Logic of Collective Action: Public Goods and the Theory of Groups.* Harvard University Press.

———. 1982. *The Rise and Decline of Nations: Economic Growth, Stagflation, and Social Rigidities.* Yale University Press.

Pritchett, Lant. 2008. "Reform Is Like a Box of Chocolates: An Interpretive Essay on Understanding the Pleasant and Unpleasant Surprises of Policy Reform." Harvard University. Photocopy.

Rodriguez, Francisco. 2007. "Cleaning Up the Kitchen Sink: Growth Empirics When the World Is Not Simple." Wesleyan University (http://frrodriguez.web.wesleyan.edu/docs/working_papers/cleaning_up_the_kitchen_sink.pdf).

Rodrik, Dani. 2000. "Institutions for High-Quality Growth: What They Are and How to Acquire Them." *Studies in Comparative International Development* (Fall).

———. 2007. *One Economics, Many Recipes.* Princeton University Press.

Rodrik, Dani, and Arvind Subramanian. 2004. "From 'Hindu Growth' to Productivity Surge: The Mystery of the Indian Growth Transition." Working Paper. Washington: International Monetary Fund.

Roll, Richard, and John Talbott. 2001. "Why Many Developing Countries Just Aren't." University of California at Los Angeles.

Romer, Paul. 1993. "Implementing a National Technology Strategy with Self-Organizing Industry Investment Boards." *Brookings Papers on Economic Activity: Microeconomics,* no. 2, pp. 345–99.

Schumpeter, Joseph A. 1949 (1934). *The Theory of Economic Development: An Inquiry into Profits, Capital, Credit, Interest, and the Business Cycle.* Harvard University Press.

Stein, Ernesto, and others. 2006. *The Politics of Policies.* Economic and Social Progress Report. Washington: Inter-American Development Bank.

Stigler, George J. 1971. "The Theory of Economic Regulation." *Bell Journal of Economics and Management Science* 2 (Spring): 3–21.

Summers, Lawrence H. 2003. "Godkin Lectures." Harvard University, Kennedy School of Government.

Williamson, John. 1990. *Latin American Adjustment: How Much Has Happened?* Washington: Institute for International Economics.

Williamson, Oliver. 1975. *Markets and Hierarchies: Analysis and Antitrust Implications.* New York: Free Press.

———. 1985. *The Economic Institutions of Capitalism: Firms, Markets, Relational Contracting.* New York: Free Press.

World Economic Forum. 2007–08. *Global Competitiveness Report 2007–2008.* Geneva.

COMMENT BY NAVA ASHRAF

Drawing broadly, from Adam Smith to Arthur Pigo and the history of physics, Ricardo Hausmann argues that economists tend to oversimplify the world. The simple policy prescriptions of Smith, the International Monetary Fund (IMF), or the World Bank hardly match the complexities of economic transaction on the microlevel, says Hausmann. Understanding the development process requires a better understanding of the social structures between the economically active individual and the macromeasures of a given country. Each sector has different, sometimes competing, requirements, and politicians will hardly be able to meet these requirements with incomplete information and misaligned incentives. Thus a system of discovery must be established whereby "high-bandwidth" policies—policies that acknowledge and address the multidimensional nature of their context—can surface and be applied.

Hausmannn is right: economists do like to simplify, perhaps to the detriment of important contextual richness. As he says, they should "embrace complexity and deal with it," rather than hide from it. They need to look for high-bandwidth policies instead of one-dimensional silver bullets. It is hard to disagree with this. Even "tolerable administration" (Adam Smith) and an "institutional environment where contracts can be enforced and property rights established" (Larry Summers) are much more complex and context-specific to actually achieve. Indeed, "institutions"/"property rights"/"government quality" are hard to measure, as attested by the large institutional literature on the challenge and complexity of policy evolution, interacting with legal origins and education, for example.[1] I was surprised not to see more discussion of this. In fact, not even Adam Smith would disagree with the high dimensionality of the invisible hand.[2] So it seems that while a reminder to eschew lists of standard policy prescriptions is helpful, Hausmann's discussion makes its main contribution in clarifying the conditions that guide economists to discovering high-bandwidth policies.

1. On policy evolution, see Lipset (1960); on legal origins, Acemoglu, Johnson, and Robinson (2001).
2. See Grampp (2000) for what Smith originally meant by the invisible hand; and Ashraf, Camerer, and Loewenstein (2005), for Smith's emphasis on trust, reciprocity, and particularly justice for the well-functioning of the market.

Indeed, the chapter raises an important challenge. It asks if there is a way to create a decentralized market for policies that can draw from the simplicity of the invisible hand but embrace the complexity of context. Hausmann's response to the challenge is a provocative one: a system in which entrepreneurs directly provide politicians with the requisite information and convince them of the benefits of reform—in other words, something like the U.S. lobbying system, which gives private citizens incentives to inform politicians. One could call this the "visible hand(out)."

This is an intriguing take on lobbying, which is too often seen simply as rent-seeking. However, it is unclear that formally allowing or encouraging people to talk to (bribe) politicians leads to greater market efficiency. In addition, it is hard to know how to generalize this, since, as Hausmann points out, such a system is unique to the United States. Thus in the spirit of Hausmann's challenge, I would suggest economists look for other means of fostering the discovery of high-bandwidth policies.

To this end, I was inspired by Hausmann to return to Smith for ideas on how effective economic practices may come about. Smith writes, for example, of the "many advantages" derived from the division of labor, which "evolved slowly as the consequence of the propensity to truck, barter, and exchange."[3] Hausmann asks how to accelerate this evolution.

He describes the three features of a market that allow for aggregation of information: prices, which give information about relative costs and willingness to pay; the profit motive, which provides incentives to respond to prices; and capital markets, which ensure that resources will mobilize to high-return areas. The objective, then, is to look for the "policy market equivalent" of capital, prices, and profit motive—features that are deceptively simple and hard to engineer but not impossible to identify.

By way of example, Hausmann points to the systematic discovery of best practices in business through benchmarking/trial and error, with competitive measures and feedback loops. He refers to this as a kind of experimentation that can accommodate the reality of high dimensionality, in contrast to randomized experimentation, which "loses its appeal in a world of high dimensionality" since "many of the design or contextual features are kept constant while just one or three are varied." Hausmann is right that randomized experiments, by their nature, control for all other elements, while varying only a few. However, that in itself is not inconsistent with high dimensionality.

A randomized experiment can take on a high-dimensionality topic such as the determinants of fertility or increasing the productivity of the agricultural sector while systematically seeking to understand each dimension by itself and how all dimensions interact. An excellent example of this comes from the rigorous testing

---

3. Smith (1981 [1776], p. 25).

of alternative hypotheses for the lack of fertilizer adoption among farmers in Kenya.[4] Here randomized experimentation provides innovative solutions to previously undocumented challenges to adopting technology, such as a product that helps farms save for inputs. In determining randomization's ability to contribute to the discovery of good policy, it is important not only to recognize that randomized experiments control for various dimensions but also to understand the numerous dimensions themselves in every field and to prioritize which dimensions to study. I would argue that, within field experiments, substantial qualitative research that guides design can shed light on the dimensions, while theory can inform the task of identifying the dimensions to prioritize and therefore make it possible to generalize beyond the specific experiments and context.

But beyond the input of randomized experiments, how can system-wide market mechanisms aid in the discovery of high-bandwidth policies? At least two fields offer some lessons in this regard. The social entrepreneurship sector, for one, has aimed to use the market mechanisms of price or other forms of customer feedback (for example, vouchers) to aggregate feedback, and to use social venture capital, a rapidly growing tool, to send resources where they have greatest social returns. The dual motive of "doing good while doing well" encourages entrepreneurs to meet a need in society. This sector, working very much from the ground up, has received surprisingly little attention from development economists and policymakers, with some notable exceptions, as in the work on vouchers as a mechanism for aggregating customer feedback.[5]

The second promising field, one that economists are generally familiar with, is that of market design, which stresses the importance of complexity.[6] The leaders here are designing markets with all the benefits of the invisible hand for domains previously organized in a more centralized fashion, from medical residency and kidney exchange to school choice. Research here has already recognized the importance of details and context, and one can imagine how much can be learned as it ventures forward to design markets for other domains.

However, both of these emerging fields—social entrepreneurship and market design—deal mainly with domains in which units can be *commoditized*. Social entrepreneurs provide products and services, as illustrated in Muhammad Yunus's groundbreaking work in Grameen microfinance and technology applications, while market design focuses on units such as slots in schools and hospitals. It is much harder to think about how to design markets for *regulation*.

Much of what eventually turns into regulation has been discovered as best practice earlier through other means. Yet, as Hausmann points out, people live in a complex world, and it is essential to take into account that complexity. Even so, economists can still learn systematically. Although it is important to foster systems

4. Duflo, Kremer, and Robinson (2008).
5. See Kremer, Angrist, and Bettinger (2006).
6. See Roth (2008).

of learning that allow excellent ideas for development ("public inputs") to emerge—systems that facilitate feedback from recipients, appropriate incentives for providers, and efficient capital-flow mechanisms—I still find it difficult to accept lobbying as one of these systems. Rather, I would rely more on inputs from randomized experiments, systems set up in the social entrepreneurship sector, and lessons from the growing field of market design for greater insight into high-bandwidth best practices for development.

References

Acemoglu, Daron, Simon Johnson, and James A. Robinson. 2001. "The Colonial Origins of Comparative Development: An Empirical Investigation." *American Economic Review* 91, no. 5: 1369–1401.

Ashraf, Nava, Colin F. Camerer, and George Loewenstein. 2005. "Adam Smith, Behavioral Economist." *Journal of Economic Perspectives* 19, no. 3: 131–46.

Duflo, Esther, Michael Kremer, and Jonathan Robinson. 2008. "How High Are Rates of Return to Fertilizer? Evidence from Field Experiments in Kenya." *American Economic Review* 98, no. 2: 482–88.

Grampp, W. D. 2000. "What Did Smith Mean by the Invisible Hand?" *Journal of Political Economy* 108, no. 3: 441–65.

Kremer, Michael, Joshua Angrist, and Eric Bettinger. 2006. "Long-Term Educational Consequences of Secondary School Vouchers: Evidence from Administrative Records in Colombia." *American Economic Review* 96, no. 3: 847–62.

Lipset, Martin S. 1960. *Political Man: The Social Bases of Politics.* New York: Doubleday.

Roth, Alvin E. 2008. "What Have We Learned from Market Design?" Hahn Lecture, *Economic Journal* 118: 285–310.

Smith, Adam. 1981 (1776). *An Inquiry into the Nature and Causes of the Wealth of Nations*, edited by R. H. Campbell, A. S. Skinner, and W. B. Todd. Indianapolis: Liberty Fund.

Comment by Ross Levine

The discussion by Ricardo Hausmann is characteristically imaginative, provocative, and substantive. Perhaps because of the complexity of the topic, however, I am not sure whether his points coalesce into a clear, novel message. Consequently, I address only two points that he raises.

Should External Policy Advisers Embrace Complexity?

Baseball provides a useful springboard to discuss this question. Think about coaching a child to hit a baseball. The basic advice would be: eat healthy foods and get plenty of rest to build strong muscles and an alert mind; practice, in order to develop good eye-hand coordination; watch the ball when the pitcher throws it, and hit the ball with your bat.

Now, think about a scientist studying a child trying to hit a baseball. The scientist might want to build a model of this process. The complexity would be enormous. The optics, physics, and geometry of gauging the speed, spin, and location of the ball are exceptionally complex. Designing a robot to get the bat in the right place, at the right time, with the right force entails multidisciplinary scientific challenges. Moreover, the environment keeps changing. Each pitch has a different speed, curvature, and trajectory. Each moment has different lighting, wind, humidity, and atmospheric pressure. Building such a high-dimensional, complex model may be fascinating and perhaps necessary for understanding the science of hitting a baseball, but how can this science translate into advice that will raise the child's batting average?

My point is this. Economists, as scientists, should delve into the dynamic complexities of institutions, policies, and the processes of economic development. But as policy advisers are they really going to do much better than outline some broad strategies for policymakers, such as those advanced by Adam Smith and more recently by Larry Summers, as quoted by Hausmann?

On a recent trip to Israel, I was asked to review the country's different financial regulations and laws and to explain how these interacted with tax policies, nonfinancial sector regulations, corporate law, and securities law. As an outsider with both a limited understanding of Israel in particular and the details associated with the full range of financial laws and regulations in general, the complexity of this task was beyond my capabilities.

Rather, I discussed financial sector policies with a multidisciplinary, cross-department team of Israeli experts. On the basis of my broad experiences in other countries and from my reading of the research literature, I posed basic, tangible questions about how to get a loan, change banks, obtain information about borrowers and collateral, open a bank, acquire an existing bank, and so on. The answers—and discussion among the Israelis— yielded information on an array of factors hindering the effective functioning of the banking system. I could never have anticipated—nor produced—the insights emerging from the discussion because of the intricacy and breadth of the themes.

This example illustrates some advantages of Adam Smith's strategic approach in comparison with Hausmann's high-dimensional complexity approach. I am not arguing for a simple three-point plan to create nirvana. Rather, I am merely suggesting that policy formation and reform can benefit from strategic approaches based on experience and sound research.

Institutions Form and Evolve for a Reason

It appears that Hausmann and other experts are embracing complexity and trying to figure out which institutions to recommend to encourage countries to adopt growth-enhancing policies. I believe that the ability of policy advisers to materially change the rules of the game through persuasive arguments or even through multilateral conditionality is far more limited than they may realize.

Let me return to baseball to illustrate that institutions are frequently formed and reformed through the unintended consequences of technological innovation. Consider an institution that has exerted a profound influence on the North American continent for about 500 years: racial discrimination against African Americans.

As is well known, the first black player in major league baseball was Jackie Robinson, who was hired by Branch Rickey, the white owner of the Brooklyn Dodgers. After Robinson broke the color barrier, many African American players were hired by other major league teams. In view of the current focus on institutional change, one might conclude that enlightenment among certain individuals was responsible for the decision to eliminate the degrading institution of racial discrimination within baseball.

Nobel economist Gary Becker might argue, however, that it was competition. Basically, from Becker's analysis, competition among the Dodgers, Giants, and Yankees spurred Branch Rickey to hire the best players, not the best white players. Rickey gambled that he could spur profits by having a better baseball team, even if it meant breaking the color barrier. More generally, Becker argued, competition would increase the costs associated with satisfying a taste for discrimination, implying that intensified competition would boost the demand for black workers, reducing the premium paid to white workers.

Without getting too deep into what motivated Rickey, this little snippet from baseball raises a question about institutional change. Is institutional change—such as breaking the color barrier in baseball—driven by the enlightened choices of society's decisionmakers or by prices and economic incentives?

In the field of banking, the driving force appears to have been technological innovation, which induced reforms to bank regulation. These reforms then intensified competition throughout the economy.

Following the ratification of the U.S. Constitution, which banned states from taxing interstate commerce, states began collecting revenues from the chartering of banks. Since states received no chartering fees from banks incorporated in other states, their legislatures prohibited the entry of out-of-state banks. These restrictions created local monopolies, thereby protecting inefficient banks from competition and creating a powerful constituency for maintaining and strengthening restrictions on bank competition.

In the last quarter of the twentieth century, however, technological innovations diminished the economic and political power of protected banks. With the invention of automatic teller machines (ATMs), for example, the geographical link between banks and their clientele weakened. Furthermore, improvements in telecommunications made it easier to use distant banks, further eroding the power of local banking monopolies. Finally, the increasing sophistication of credit-scoring techniques and improvements in information processing reduced the informational advantages of local bankers. These technological innovations reduced not only the power of local banks but also their incentives to lobby for continued restrictions on competition.

Thus from the mid-1970s to the mid-1990s states deregulated restrictions on interstate banking, not because the regulations were considered bad for banking efficiency or economic growth or social welfare, but because profit-motivated technological changes reduced the economic power of those supporting the bank regulations. Bank deregulation had several striking effects. Competition among banks increased. Moreover, competition among nonfinancial sector firms increased because deregulation made it easier for start-up firms to obtain capital. This facilitated the entry of new firms and corporations.

With the increasing competition in the nonfinancial sector, the economic incentives of firm owners changed, and discrimination against blacks declined throughout the economy. I show this in a recent paper with Alex Levkov and Yona Rubinstein.[1] Put differently, technological innovation, including the invention of

---

1. Levine, Levkov, and Rubinstein (2009).

the ATM machine, reduced the effects of a prominent, pervasive, and enduring institution: racial discrimination. Policies and institutions are created for reasons, and they change when those underlying reasons change.

This relates to complexity and policy advice. If the experts are smart enough to understand the multidimensional complexity underlying the formation of institutions, they should also know that it is impossible to change major institutions without altering the reasons underlying their creation and maintenance.

Reference

Levine, Ross, Alex Levkov, and Yona Rubinstein. 2009. "Racial Discrimination and Competition." Brown University. Photocopy.

7

Big Answers for Big Questions: The Presumption of Growth Policy

ABHIJIT VINAYAK BANERJEE

D on't we know that all that matters for reducing poverty is growth, especially after China? And therefore we development economists should focus on the things that make growth happen: macropolicy and creating the right institutional environment? And not bother with the microevidence?

No, no, and, as the expression goes, no. Every step of that syllogism is wrong, and, I argue in this essay, each step is probably more obviously wrong than the previous one. But before I come to that, let me make an important clarification: none of what I am about to say denies the fundamental usefulness of the macromode of thinking—of what might be the single most important insight of the field of economics—that you have to be aware of the fact that everything is connected to everything else and that things need to add up. This chapter is about growth policy, implicitly defined as those high-level, broad-brush actions that purportedly promote growth, in opposition to the many micromanipulations of policy that development economists spend their time studying.[1] And in particular about the evidence base of growth policy.

With that, back to our syllogism.

I am grateful to Angus Deaton, Bill Easterly, and Peter Klenow for their comments. One of Klenow's comments in particular made me change the title from "The Presumption of Macroeconomics" to the current one.

1. This is not to deny that some broad-brush actions are important—you need markets and trade, businesses should be run by the private sector, and so on. The point is that there is substantial agreement at this

Growth Is All You Need

The one claim among the three that is both the most controversial and the least obviously false is the first one (this says something about the nature of macroeconomic debates). Not because it is actually true—but at least the starting point is a claim that at least has a chance of being right.

What the cross-country evidence does seem to show (though this is disputed, and I am no expert on the nuances of cross-country data) is that there is *no evidence* for a trade-off between growth and poverty reduction. Poverty goes down by more in countries that grow faster, and indeed even the elasticity of poverty reduction with respect to growth does not go down significantly in countries that grow faster.

This is certainly a useful correlation to know, especially given the amount of sententious rubbish that gets written justifying bad macroeconomic policies in the name of poverty reduction. But by itself it tells us very little about what we should or shouldn't do. One could, for example, read it to say that countries that do poverty reduction more effectively grow faster. Isn't that much less plausible than the opposite, you might say? After all, it is hard to imagine fast growth not reducing poverty. But how about a mixture of the two: policies that cause poverty reduction make growth happen, which in turn brings about more poverty reduction? As Roland Benabou and others have shown, countries that redistribute more grow faster (though of course, the causality could be running from growth to redistribution).[2]

Or how about a third view: that growth that is not accompanied by substantial poverty reduction is unsustainable (for political or other reasons) and therefore the episodes of sustained growth that we observe in the data are actually exactly the episodes where growth came with poverty reduction? In the relevant sense, therefore, it is poverty reduction that determines growth, and not the other way around.

Moreover, as Martin Ravallion has emphasized, the fact that on average countries that grow faster reduce poverty more is in some ways less interesting than the fact that the effect of growth on poverty is so much greater in some countries than in others.[3] The point is that there is no reason to assume that this entire difference is just random. Indeed, it is well recognized that the impact on poverty reflects the way the income was initially distributed—growth moves more people across the poverty line if there are more people near it to start with. But there are also some more interesting reasons why countries differ that have to do with policies, the

---

level, at least within the economist community and much of the policy community. Where there is a disagreement is at the next level—over the kind of market economy we would want to be.

2. Benabou (1996).

3. Ravallion (2001).

initial distribution of skills and other endowments (which may be the result of policy as well), or both. Even in China, which is everyone's favorite example of poverty reduction through growth, a very substantial part of the massive poverty reduction that happened in the 1990s was a result of one-off changes in the taxation of agriculture and the pricing of agricultural products.[4]

Hence Development Economists Should Study Growth

The problem with this claim comes down to basic economics. The one thing that everyone learns in their first economics class is that it all comes down to where your *marginal* product is highest. Even if growth were the best way to reduce poverty, we economists might want to focus on poverty reduction through other means if we think that is where we have the highest marginal product.

The reason why this is more than just a debating point is that we know precious little about how to make growth happen. Even in terms of just accounting for growth, the remarkably optimistic results of Gregory Mankiw, David Romer, and David Weil claiming that differences in savings rates, rates of investment in human capital, and population growth rates can explain nearly 80 percent of the variation in gross domestic product (GDP) levels have now been replaced by a more pessimistic position, summarized in Francesco Caselli, which suggests that nearly two-thirds of the variation remains unexplained.[5] The difference comes mainly from replacing the Mankiw, Romer, and Weil measure of investment in human capital (a fraction of the population who have some secondary schooling) with a more continuous measure that gives weight to primary and tertiary schooling as well.[6]

However, even if we were able to explain away all the cross-country differences, it would tell us relatively little about how to narrow the existing differences. Savings rates, human capital investment rates, and population growth rates are at least as much symptoms of the problem as their cause, and the challenge is in part to figure out how to move them in the right direction. For this, we need to be able to identify proper causal factors.

The challenges of identifying causal factors using cross-country data are well known. There is the fact that almost everything at the country level is a product of something else—educational investment, for example, to take one factor that was emphasized in the early cross-country literature,[7] is clearly in part a product of the effectiveness of the government as a provider, which presumably has other effects as well, and in part a result of people's expectations about growth itself.[8] Moreover,

4. Chen and Wang (2001).

5. See Mankiw, Romer, and Weil (1992); and Caselli (2005).

6. Klenow and Rodríguez-Clare (1997).

7. Barro (1991).

8. Bils and Klenow (2000).

both countries and country policies differ in so many ways that, in effect, every cross-country regression runs the risk of working with negative degrees of freedom. That is to say, there are so many different ways one could run the regression that one could more or less guarantee that some of those regressions show significant "causal" effects, even in a world where policy is entirely irrelevant.

That does not mean that we have not learned anything from this literature. In particular, some of the more remarkable findings in the literature are convincing because, a priori, they seem so entirely implausible. The most striking of these is almost surely the finding in Daron Acemoglu, Simon Johnson, and James Robinson showing that countries in which in the initial years of European colonization settler mortality was high tended to be places that are still doing badly.[9] Moreover, it is not because these places were somehow handicapped from the start. There was actually what they call a "Reversal of Fortune": the countries that were the most prosperous at the time of colonization (at least measured by population density) actually ended up at the bottom of the heap.

Acemoglu, Johnson, and Robinson argue that this reflects the power of institutions. The places that were empty to start with and where settler mortality was low (which tended to be the same places, for fairly conventional epidemiological reasons) were the places where the Europeans settled in large numbers and that got the institutions that the Europeans were then developing, which would eventually provide the basis of modern capitalism.[10]

It is certainly true that settler mortality is an excellent predictor of the quality of contemporary institutions at the country level, measured by, say, the risk of capital being expropriated in that country. It is also true that these institutions as predicted by settler mortality are extraordinarily powerful in predicting the economic status of the country today. While this does not prove that it is these institutions that are responsible for growth (could be culture or political traditions, for example), it does say that some very long-run factors have a lot to do with economic success.

What does all this tell us about policy? We learn that institutions matter (perhaps) but not whether it would help to set up a particular set of institutions today. The evidence emphasizes the part of the difference in institutional quality that is attributable to things that happened over several hundreds of years. Does that mean that institutions need to be developed over several hundred years for them to be effective (after all, the U.S. Constitution of today, strict constructionists notwithstanding, is a very different document than it was when written, enriched by two hundred years of jurisprudence, public debate, and popular involvement)?

What is more worrying is that once we control for the cross-country variation in institutional quality predicted by differences in settler mortality, the standard

---

9. See Acemoglu, Johnson, and Robinson (2001, 2002).
10. Acemoglu and others (2001, 2002).

measures of macroeconomic policy (monetary policy, trade policy, government involvement in the economy) have little or no effect on how fast countries grow.[11] This implies not quite that policy does not matter, but at least that there is no evidence that the variations in policy that we see between countries of similar institutional quality make any difference to growth. In other words, conventional notions of macropolicy might matter, but perhaps only when the relevant variation in policy is the kind that we see when we compare the Singapores of the world with the Sudans. It is only the hyperinflations, the large-scale nationalizations, and the civil wars that are obviously contraindicated.

This does not say anything about unconventional forms of macropolicy. It will probably surprise no one that no two episodes of sustained fast growth have been exactly alike and each successful country has pursued its own idiosyncratic policies as a part of its development strategy. In each of these cases the debate has been whether growth happened because of the particular deviant policy (industrial policy in Korea and Japan, massive government involvement in factor markets in China as well as an undervalued exchange rate, forced savings in Singapore) or in spite of it. And in each case, predictably, the discussion has been inconclusive, though everyone seems to agree that there are other things these countries could have done that are worse.

Does that mean that they just lucked out? Or is there actually a lesson to be learned from their success? The problem is that we do not know of a way to even begin to answer that question on the basis of the standard empirical methodologies used in the growth literature—let alone actually have something reliable to say about it—since these are essentially unique events and it is not clear what we could compare them to. I return to this methodological challenge later in the chapter.

By contrast, we know a significant amount about many specific strategies that can help improve the lot of the poor, and perhaps more important, we know how to go about learning more. One great advantage of randomized trials is that we can often start from a specific policy question and then look for the evidence. While it is not always feasible to get an implementing organization to implement the exact experiment that you want, there is so much going on these days, especially in the world of nongovernmental organizations (NGOs), that opportunities to do something closely related are easily found. The fact that experimental work has now acquired a certain currency helps very much here—we observe much less resistance to the idea now outside academia than there was ten years ago, which makes for many more opportunities.

Moreover, there is little dispute that a carefully designed experiment gives an unbiased estimate of the impact of the particular intervention being studied. To use the accepted jargon, experimental results are internally valid. This is in contrast to most forms of empirical research, where the internal validity is never conclusive,

11. Rodrik, Subramanian, and Trebbi (2004).

the one exception being certain natural quasi-experiments, where it is clear that some accident of fortune generated something very close to a real experiment.

The concern is with external validity. Many experiments are based on variation that is essentially local. In part this reflects the scope of the implementing organization, in part the fact that it is managerially easier (and therefore cheaper) to collect high-quality data in a relatively small area.

The concern that this creates is whether the results from the experiment can be applied to settings other than the one in which they were generated. There are really two parts to this objection. The first is environmental dependence: the results may be specific to the setting in which the experiment was carried out. This is, of course, an old concern with all forms of empirical reasoning, as Scottish economist and philosopher David Hume pointed out more than two centuries ago.[12] But it may be more serious here than in many other instances because we know that the setting matters and we only observe the result from one very particular setting. One claimed advantage of cross-country research and macroempirical research more generally (comparing regions within the same country, for example) is that the "treatment" effect is an average across a large number of settings and is therefore more generalizable.

However, this is not necessarily true, even though it seems that it ought to be. Part of the problem comes down to what it means to be generalizable: it means that if you take the same action in a different location you would get the same result. But what action? When we talk about comparing educational investment or road construction or labor laws across large jurisdictions, what makes us believe that we are comparing the same action? After all, some of those investments that we see might defy all logic (institutes of higher study where almost no one has been to college, roads to nowhere, and so on) and unless we believe, like Hegel, that we are fated to make the same mistakes over and over again, there is no reason to reason to believe that the results of those particularly disastrous investments tell us anything about what would happen if we were to invest, now that we know what obvious mistakes to avoid. In other words, most large-area studies end up having to trust that what the data gatherers chose to put under the same label (miles of roads constructed, number of teachers hired, and so forth) indeed represents reasonable alternative implementations of the same "treatment." By contrast, in most microdata-based studies we actually know exactly what the intended action/actions looked like, and it is much more plausible that the unplanned variation in the treatment that we observe is really beyond anyone's control.

There is also a more subtle point about generalizations. The fact that a program evaluation uses data from a large area does not necessarily mean that the estimate of the program effect that we get from that evaluation is an average of the

12. Hume (1993 [1772]).

program effects on all the different types of people living in that large area (or all the people who are plausible program participants). The way to estimate the program effect in such cases is to first try to control for any observable and unobservable differences between those covered by the program and those not covered (say, by matching like with like) and then to look at how those in the program perform compared with those who are not. But it is possible that once we match like with like, either almost everyone who is in a particular matched group is a program participant or everyone is a nonparticipant. Then these people are going to be very little help in figuring out the program effect. The estimate will be entirely driven by the subgroups in the population, in which, even after matching, there are both lots of participants and lots of nonparticipants, and these subgroups could be entirely nonrepresentative.

The point is not that generalizability is not an issue for the experimental/ quasi-experimental approach, but that it is not obviously less of an issue for any other approach, and may well be more of an issue. Despite this, there seems to be a presumption in some quarters (see chapter 2 in this volume, for example) that there is a certain kind of symmetry between the more micro, experimental/quasi-experimental studies and the more macro-style studies in which the identification is assumed to come from having included enough controls: the former tend to be better identified, while the latter are more easily generalized.[13] Hence there is no reason to privilege one kind of evidence over another—cross-country regressions may teach us more or less than an experimental estimate—and the evidence on growth policy is no worse than the evidence on specific strategies to fight poverty.

To see why this is misleading or at least overstated, consider a scenario in which we are worrying about generalizing from a certain experimental result. Say, we suspect that there are locations in which a particular treatment may seem a priori appropriate but does not actually work. The point is that this hypothesis is entirely testable: all we need to do is to carry out additional experiments in different locations—indeed, continue to experiment until we are either satisfied that the treatment effect is reasonably stable or find that it is not and therefore need to rethink the generalizablity of the treatment. If we have a theory that tells us where it might break down, we focus the extra experiments there. If not, we choose random locations within the relevant domain.

This is more than an articulation of a principle. A number of experiment results have been replicated. For example, Gustavo Bobonis, Edward Miguel, and Charu Sharma get the same kind of impact of deworming (treatment for intestinal helminths) on school attendance in North India that Miguel and Michael Kremer found in Kenya, and Hoyt Bleakley finds similar results with a natural

13. "Generalize what?" you may ask, given that it is not clear what we are estimating. But someone who takes this position typically takes a more Bayesian view, arguing, quite reasonably, that we do learn even when certainty is entirely not an option. ("Does she love me, does she not"—lovers through the ages have tried to figure out, often aided by not much more than a single sideways glance.)

experiment approach using data from the U.S. South in the early part of the twentieth century.[14] Other results turn out not to be replicable: an information campaign that mobilized parents' committees on issues around education and encouraged them to make use of a public program that allows school committees to hire local teachers where the schools are overcrowded had a positive impact on learning outcomes in Kenya but not in India.[15]

The claim is not that every experimental result generalizes, but that there is always (at least in principle) a clear process that can inform us about the generalizability of a given result. Whether or not that process gets followed depends on a variety of practical concerns, such as the cost of doing another experiment and the cost of a potential delay, and it may not always happen, but if we cared enough about being right, we could always do it. Contrast this with the results from a cross-country regression. Suppose we suspect that the relation between women's literacy and fertility rates estimated from a cross-country regression is contaminated by the fact that women's literacy is correlated with many other unobserved aspects of women's literacy. Running the same regression in different data sets many times over (regions within the same country, comparing the same region over time) may not help here, because every one of these results may be biased by the presence of the same unobservable. The only way to solve this problem is to look for variation in women's education that is quasi-randomly or randomly assigned. There is, however, a second, less obvious, problem with microexperimental results.

Consider what would happen if we tried to scale up a program that shows, in a small-scale experimental implementation, that economically disadvantaged girls who get vouchers to go to private schools end up with a better education and a higher income. When we scale up the program to the national level, two challenges arise: one is that there will be crowding in the private schools, and the other is that the returns to education will fall because of increased supply. For both reasons, the experimental evidence would overstate the returns to the vouchers program.

These so-called general equilibrium effects pose a problem that has no perfect solution. We could try to do experiments at a larger scale so that these kinds of spillovers are internalized within the experimental units. But this is expensive and often infeasible. However, there are clearly many instances in which this is only a problem if we are not careful in interpreting the results of our experiments. For example, the results of an experiment that says that in the current state of the health system a particular intervention can increase immunization rates by x percent tells us what we would get if we universalized the intervention *under the assumption that nothing else changes in the immunization* environment. In other words, the government is not allowed to say that it wants to boost immunization

---

14. Bobonis, Miguel, and Sharma (2006); Miguel and Kremer (2004); Bleakley (2007).
15. See Banerjee and others (2009) for the India study, and Duflo, Dupas, and Kremer (2008) for the Kenya study.

rates without spending an extra penny, or rather, if that it is what it wants, then the relevant interventions may have to be very different.

The real problem arises when keeping the environment constant is not directly an option. For example, while the government could presumably solve the problem of the supply of private schools that I brought up earlier by making it sufficiently lucrative to set up schools, the experiment tells us nothing about the price it would have to pay for that. The difference with the immunization case comes from the fact that the unit cost of expanding immunization is likely to be more or constant at least in the relevant range (immunization does not require that much extra manpower, and it is easy to procure more vaccines on the world market given enough lag time). Or it may be that it does not make economic sense to keep the environment constant. The fact that the price of skill goes down when the supply goes up may be exactly what makes the program socially desirable.

The response to this, however, is not less microevidence but more. The problem arises because we do not know the relevant elasticities of supply and demand, and more generally, the production functions. Had we known them, we would have mapped the increase in demand for private schooling and the rise in the supply of skills through them, to infer the true social benefits of the intervention. Simply implementing the intervention without doing that obviously runs the risk of a disaster, but the alternative of not doing anything because we do not know these elasticities seems unnecessarily pessimistic. For the long haul, we clearly need more carefully designed experimental/quasi-experimental studies that will give us the relevant elasticities.

The point once again is not that the experimental/quasi-experimental route always offers an answer, but that it offers a process by which we should be able to converge to usable evidence. Of course, there is a long way to go, but the process is relatively well defined, and we know where we are headed. And while the ambition is limited, it may be achievable: we might soon know enough in certain domains (health, education, the environment) to be fairly confident that lives are being saved and people are living better lives because of the evidence we have.

Studying Growth Means Studying Macroevidence

This is the illusion of commensurability: big questions must have big answers. Growth is surely the biggest question that we economists tackle. Hence the evidence that can inform growth policy must be evidence about big things

There are at least two senses in which this is misleading. First suppose the conclusion from the macroevidence is that reducing corruption is vital for promoting growth. But reducing corruption how? And what forms of corruption are worth fighting the most?

One very simple reason why we cannot use macroevidence to answer these kinds of questions is that no comprehensive data set on corruption exists, because while many data sets record the impression of corruption (usually among businessmen) associated with particular countries, this evidence does not sort between the various sources of unhappiness among the victims of corruption (coercion, unnecessary delays, meaningless procedures).[16] But even more important, it says little about the many costs of corruption that are not observed by the individual businessman (misallocated resources, biased decisionmaking, lost government revenues, lobbying and other forms of rent-seeking, investments that did not happen). Therefore we need microdata to tell us which of these forms of corruption are the most costly.

The situation with respect to how to fight corruption is even worse. There are no macrodata on fighting corruption, for the simple reason that different countries have chosen their own distinct ways to deal with corruption. To make matters even more complicated, the evidence from the experimental work suggests that the effectiveness of anticorruption strategies turns very much on the details. Research by Ben Olken in Indonesia finds that a strategy of inviting villagers to a meeting where village road construction expenses were discussed reduced "missing" expenditures by a third or so when the invitations to the meeting were distributed to school children (to take home to their parents), but not at all when the village head got to distribute them.[17] Olken plausibly interprets this as an effect of popular participation: the village heads managed to make sure that the meetings were stacked when they controlled the invitations, but not when it was taken out of their hands.

There is obviously no way one would pick up this fact from macrodata, simply because this type of fine variation never shows up there. And while the conclusion seems plausible ex post (of course it is better to distribute the invitations in school), how did we know that the head could not discourage/intimidate people enough to keep them out of the meeting even when they had been invited? After all, the meetings were always open to the public, but no one showed up except when they were specifically invited.

The same point can be made, mutatis mutandis, about many other dimensions of growth policy: investment in education (where? at what level? through better teacher training or greater parental involvement?), investment in health care, more effective capital markets, and so on. In the end, details matter too much for it to be possible to make effective growth policy without experimental/quasi-experimental data.

The second reason why macrodata tell us little about how to do growth has already been discussed. Countries seem to vary enormously in their performance even after we control for differences in standard macrofactors such as capital, human capital, and demographics, and differences in macromeasures of policy do

---

16. This is where the World Bank's "Doing Business" reports have been a useful innovation.
17. Olken (2007).

not help much here either, at least once we control for differences in institutional quality.

How do we enter the black box of differences in total factor productivity (TFP)? Why does India in the 1990s seem to have a TFP level that is about half of that in the United States, if we use Lucas's Cobb-Douglas model of GDP?[18] One answer to this question that was proposed in the growth literature is that the TFP differences are the result of spillovers from human capital investments. Human capital investments are worth much more than standard growth models (like the one Esther Duflo and I used) have given them credit for, because they also benefit everyone in the country. Therefore relatively small differences in human capital can explain big differences across countries.

The problem with this theory is that it fails the quasi-experimental test. Acemoglu and Joshua Angrist as well as Duflo—who look at this question using microdata from credible natural experiments in the United States and in Indonesia, respectively, which led to expansions in high school attendance and completion rates—find that if there are spillovers, they are swamped by the standard diminishing returns effects.[19]

Another standard theory of growth attributes the TFP difference to differences in access to effective and appropriate technologies. Yet as Duflo and I argue, once again the microdata get in the way: we argue that if the entire twofold difference in TFP between India and the United States has to be fully explained by technological differences, then, given the 1–1.5 percent growth rate of TFP in the United States, India in 2000 should have been using technologies developed in the 1950s.[20] In fact, the best Indian firms use technologies that are entirely contemporary, and a recent McKinsey report concludes that upgrading very close to the latest technologies would be profitable at the current factor prices in India. Hence it is not access to viable technological improvements that seems to be the constraint on the average Indian firm.[21]

At least a part of the answer to the TFP puzzle seems to come from massive misallocation of resources within the same economy, something that is not picked up by any of the macroaggregates that are used in growth accounting exercises. These misallocations are not the product of any one distortion but rather the cumulative effect of many, many individual distortions resulting from both government failures and market failures. Duflo and I described the evidence for these distortions in some detail, drawing on a range of microstudies. We then carried out a heuristic exercise to assess whether the extent of observed misallocation is large enough to explain away the Indo-U.S. TFP differences. Our answer, which we proposed quite tentatively, since what we did was no more than a finger exercise, is yes: if we

18. Banerjee and Duflo (2005).
19. See Acemoglu and Angrist (1999); and Duflo (2004).
20. Banerjee and Duflo (2005).
21. McKinsey Global Institute (2001).

are willing to assume a model in which there are some increasing returns at the firm level, the fact that the medium firms in India are too small and too numerous compared with what they would be in an efficient economy can actually explain the entire TFP gap.

Peter Klenow and Chang-Tai Hsieh used data from firm-level annual surveys from the United States, China, and India to carry out a much more empirically founded version of the same exercise.[22] They calibrated a model of monopolistically competitive differentiated firms based on these data and showed that the allocation of resources across firms within the same industry is indeed much more distorted in both India and China than in the United States, and that in particular it is the most productive firms that are too small in both those countries. If these countries could achieve a U.S. level of efficiency in the allocation of resources within the same industry, they calculate, TFP would go up by 30–45 percent in China and 45–50 percent in India. Clearly, there may also be misallocation across industries, which would presumably add to this total.

This is all based on microevidence but not necessarily data from any experiment/quasi-experiment (though there are those too). Indeed, a lot of the data are simply descriptive and do not require a causal interpretation. However, anyone looking at the economy through a macrolens would miss them.[23]

This research is too new to have many specific implications for policy. But it suggests a very different view of what we are looking for. The range of distortions is so diverse that it is hard to imagine that we would not want to address them separately, and they seem specific enough that we can at least think of addressing them through policy. In this sense, Dani Rodrik is right in insisting in chapter 2 that there is a certain commonality between this view of growth and the growth diagnostics approach: both favor an ecumenical view and resist the idea that there is necessarily something called growth policy that lives independently of the country context. Where they do not always line up is in their view of how to go about identifying the appropriate policies.

To see an example of the approach to a policy question being suggested here, consider the fact that fertilizer seems massively underused in much of Africa: the question is to what extent this is a result of an unwillingness to take risks, the unavailability of credit, the lack of the right internal or external incentives for long-range planning, distortions in the land market, or a lack of understanding of the benefits of fertilizer. This is the kind of problem that is probably best ad-

---

22. Klenow and Hsieh (2007).

23. Peter Klenow (personal communication) has suggested that most macroeconomists today would agree with this position, and in this sense I am being unfair to the community of macroeconomists. My view is that he is speaking from the cutting edge of the field, where this is probably truer than in the work that is more directed toward policymakers. Moreover, at least as recently as the time when the articles in the *Handbook of Growth Economics*, edited by Philippe Aghion and Steve Durlauf (2005), were written, the conceptual frame of growth economics was clearly one in which the primary thinking was at the level of a few aggregates.

dressed by a combination of theoretical thinking and experimental work, exemplified by the work of Duflo, Kremer, and Robinson on fertilizer adoption in Kenya.[24] In the first of their experimental treatments, they worked with some randomly chosen farmers to apply fertilizer to their plots. The returns on this fertilizer use were massive (always over 100 percent and sometimes over 500 percent). But even after the farmers saw these spectacular results, neither they nor their neighbors (who observed their success) showed much change in their behavior: left to themselves, less than 40 percent of them used fertilizer. This, the authors concluded, suggests that it is not lack of knowledge that is holding them back; nor does it seem likely that it is risk aversion, since the evidence suggested that they would always make more money.[25] On the other hand, the authors also found that a simple contract that offers the farmers the option of forward-buying fertilizer at harvest time for delivery at the time of planting was enthusiastically taken up by over three-quarters of the farmers. This suggested that a lack of credit could not be the entire story either, because the farmers did have money to buy fertilizer at harvest time, as demonstrated by their willingness to take up the contracts they were being offered. At least part of the problem had to be the inability to commit to a long-range plan.

This is, quite possibly, only part of the answer: And it is possible (though hardly obvious—Kenya is, after all, famous for its many NGOs) that Kenya lacks the implementation capacity to provide the needed contract to everyone. On the other hand, once the need is well understood, I see no obvious reason why the market would not start to offer it. This is a possibility that Duflo, Robinson, and Kremer are now investigating.[26]

Beyond this, there is the concern that in a relatively fragile state like Kenya, there may be no point in trying to do anything about agricultural productivity because all gains will eventually be destroyed by some form of civil conflict. This is both much too pessimistic—Kenya has been growing quite fast for the past few years—and potentially self-fulfilling, since it may be precisely the lack of any economic progress that will eventually lead to civil conflict.

This brings me to my last, most radical, thought: it is not clear that the best way to get growth is to do growth policy of any form. Perhaps making growth happen is ultimately beyond our control. Maybe all that happens is that something goes right for once (privatized agriculture raises incomes in rural China) and then that sparks growth somewhere else in the economy, and so on. Perhaps we will never learn where it will start or what will make it continue. The best we can do in that world is to hold the fort until that initial spark arrives: make sure that there is not too much human misery, maintain the social equilibrium, and try to

24. Duflo, Kremer, and Robinson (2008).
25. There is still the possibility that what the farmers are worried about is a small probability of a huge disaster, which is something that is always hard to detect in the data.
26. Work in progress by Duflo, Robinson, and Kremer.

make sure that there is enough human capital around to take advantage of the spark when it arrives. It is not impossible that social policy may be the best thing that we can do for growth to happen, and microevidence on how to do it well could turn out to be the key to growth success.

References

Acemoglu, Daron, and Joshua Angrist. 1999. "How Large Are the Social Returns to Education? Evidence from Compulsory Schooling Laws." Working Paper 7444. Cambridge, Mass.: National Bureau of Economic Research.

Acemoglu, Daron, Simon Johnson, and James Robinson. 2001. "The Colonial Origins of Comparative Development: An Empirical Investigation." *American Economic Review* 91 (December): 1369–1401.

———. 2002. "Reversal of Fortune: Geography and Institutions in the Making of the Modern World Income Distribution." *Quarterly Journal of Economics* 117 (November): 1231–94.

Aghion, Philippe, and Steven Durlauf, eds. 2005. *Handbook of Economic Growth.* Amsterdam: Elsevier.

Banerjee, Abhijit, and Esther Duflo. 2005. "Growth Theory through the Lens of Development Economics." In *Handbook of Economic Growth,* edited by Aghion and Durlauf, vol. 1a, pp. 473–552. Amsterdam: Elsevier.

Banerjee, Abhijit, and others. 2009. "Pitfalls of Participatory Programs: Evidence from a Randomized Evaluation in Education in India." *American Economic Journal: Economic Policy,* forthcoming.

Barro, Robert J. 1991. "Economic Growth in a Cross Section of Countries." *Quarterly Journal of Economics* 106 (May): 407–43.

Benabou, Roland. 1996. "Inequality and Growth." *NBER Macroeconomics Annual,* edited by Ben Bernanke and Julio Rotemberg, pp. 11–74. MIT Press.

Bils, Mark, and Peter Klenow. 2000. "Does Schooling Cause Growth?" *American Economic Review* 90 (December): 1160–83.

Bleakley, Hoyt. 2007. "Disease and Development: Evidence from Hookworm Eradication in the American South." *Quarterly Journal of Economics* 122 (February): 73-117.

Bobonis, Gustavo, Edward Miguel, and Charu Sharma. 2006. "Iron Deficiency Anemia and School Participation." *Journal of Human Resources* 41, no. 4: 692–721.

Caselli, Francesco. 2005. "Accounting for Cross-Country Income Differences." In *Handbook of Economic Growth,* edited by Aghion and Durlauf. Amsterdam: Elsevier.

Chen, Shaohua, and Yan Wang. 2001. "China's Growth and Poverty Reduction Trends between 1990 and 1999." Policy Research Working Paper 2651. Washington: World Bank.

Duflo, Esther. 2004. "The Medium-Run Consequences of Educational Expansion: Evidence from a Large School Construction Program in Indonesia." *Journal of Development Economics* 74, no. 1: 163–97.

Duflo, Esther, Pascaline Dupas, and Michael Kremer, 2008. "Additional Resources versus Organizational Changes in Education: Experimental Evidence from Kenya." MIT. Photocopy.

Duflo, Esther, Michael Kremer, and Jonathan Robinson. 2008. "How High Are Rates of Return to Fertilizer? Evidence from Field Experiments in Kenya." *American Economic Association Papers and Proceedings* (May).

Hume, David. 1993 (1772). "An Enquiry Concerning Human Understanding. " Cambridge, Mass.: Hackett.

Klenow, Peter, and Chang-Tai Hsieh. 2007. "Misallocation and Manufacturing TFP in China and India." *Quarterly Journal of Economics*. Under revision (July).

Klenow, Peter, and Andrés Rodríguez-Clare. 1997. "The Neoclassical Revival in Growth Economics: Has It Gone Too Far?" *NBER Macroeconomics Annual,* edited by Ben Bernanke and Julio Rotemberg, pp. 73–102. MIT Press.

Mankiw, N. Gregory, David Romer, and David Weil. 1992. "A Contribution to the Empirics of Economic Growth." *Quarterly Journal of Economics* 107 (June): 407–37.

McKinsey Global Institute. 2001. "India: The Growth Imperative." Washington (September).

Miguel, Edward, and Michael Kremer. 2004. "Worms: Identifying Impacts on Education and Health in the Presence of Treatment Externalities." *Econometrica* 72, no. 1: 159–217.

Olken, Ben. 2007. "Monitoring Corruption: Evidence from a Field Experiment in Indonesia." *Journal of Political Economy* 115 (April): 200–49.

Ravallion, Martin. 2001. "Growth, Inequality and Poverty: Looking beyond Averages." *World Development* 29 (November): 1803–15.

Rodrik, Dani, Arvind Subramanian, and Francesco Trebbi. 2004. "Institutions Rule: The Primacy of Institutions over Geography and Integration in Economic Development." *Journal of Economic Growth* 9 (June): 131–65.

COMMENT BY PETER KLENOW

As Abhijit Banerjee acknowledges in his provocative and compelling chapter, the most important questions in development are often "macro" ones, such as how to boost growth in the fashion of China and India in recent decades. But, he emphasizes, economists do not know very much about how to do this despite lots of research effort. So he suggests abandoning macrodevelopment research for the most part and concentrating on microdevelopment questions such as the effect of randomized interventions in health and education. Banerjee's position can be summarized as follows.

$$\frac{\partial \text{Welfare}}{\partial \text{Research}} = \frac{\partial \text{Welfare}}{\partial \text{Knowledge}} \cdot \frac{\partial \text{Knowledge}}{\partial \text{Research}}$$

	$\frac{\partial \text{Welfare}}{\partial \text{Research}}$	$\frac{\partial \text{Welfare}}{\partial \text{Knowledge}}$	$\frac{\partial \text{Knowledge}}{\partial \text{Research}}$
Micro	>0	High	Low
Macro	≈0 ?	Low	High

I wholeheartedly agree with the "micro" row in this representation, so need not say any more about it. Instead I want to defend the value of doing macrodevelopment research. Since I consider myself at the microdata end of the macrospectrum, I do this without feeling particularly defensive.

A useful analogy to begin with concerns the potential micro versus macro divides in medicine and biology. "Micro" researchers in medicine who do carefully controlled clinical trials and lab work might disdain "macro" medicine, which looks at trends in life expectancy, heart disease, cancer, autism, and so on. Their skepticism may extend to epidemiological studies (reduced-form regressions) that relate individual outcomes to a variety of other individual observables. Microresearchers may rightly say they learn little about causality and effective treatments from such macrostudies. Similarly, one can imagine a conflict between microbiologists (who study molecular biology, genetics, neuroscience, immunology, embryology, and so on) and macrobiologists (who study whole ecologies, that is, populations and how their traits and numbers evolve and interact).

A common element in macromedicine, macrobiology, and macrodevelopment is that each motivates and guides a lot of the microwork that is done. In medicine, macroevidence has documented an obesity epidemic in the United States, and epidemiological evidence has related obesity to heart disease, diabetes, and other ailments. This macrowork has motivated a myriad of microexperiments on what sorts of diet, exercise, and drug interventions might best prevent or treat obesity and its complications.

In biology, macroresearch has documented the vanishing diversity of species and related it to macrofactors such as deforestation, pollution, and global climate change. As a result, biologists are studying the consequences of global warming for agriculture and animal populations. Some of these studies take the form of microexperiments, either natural or controlled (unnatural).

Robert Sapolsky, a famous biologist who does both macro- and microwork, has spent many summers in Kenya studying baboon populations.[1] He combines field observations with blood work to document social and individual correlates with stress hormones. He devotes the rest of his research year to lab work. He says his fieldwork is critical for studying normal social interactions, as opposed to contrived lab environments. The fieldwork motivates much of the lab work he does.

Again, macroresearch identifies the disease, its severity, and its symptoms. Macrowork indicates where randomized trials are most urgently needed. In macrodevelopment, the extent of the disease is the difference in incomes between some African economies and those in the Organization for Economic Cooperation and Development (OECD). The symptoms/correlates are low life expectancy, low investment rates in physical and human capital, high fertility rates, political instability, and so on. This macroresearch has presumably helped spur the microexperiments on health and education in Africa.

My own recent work with Chang-Tai Hsieh on China and India has been driven by macroevidence.[2] China and India are poor and populous but growing fast. Macrodevelopment accounting leaves unexplained a nontrivial portion of their initial poverty and subsequent growth. Hsieh and I use microdata on manufacturing plants to assess the potential contribution of allocative efficiency. This particular hypothesis was also inspired by macroevidence, namely, that growth took off in China and India in the wake of a series of policy reforms (privatization, trade liberalization, and foreign direct investment, among others) designed to improve allocative efficiency.

Both macro- and microwork is also being done on Indian manufacturing firms, whose productivity on average is lower than in firms in OECD countries. Important differences in managerial practices of Indian and U.S. firms have been documented with regard to monitoring (for example, how well they are tracking, whether they are hitting their performance targets), targets (whether the targets are realistic, aimed for, and economically rational), and incentives (whether people are

---

1. Sapolsky (2002).
2. Hsieh and Klenow (2009).

promoted primarily on tenure or performance).[3] These macrofindings have led others to embark on a randomized evaluation of whether management consulting services can improve productivity in Indian firms.[4] Again, macroevidence is usefully motivating microexperimental work.

I have mentioned growth and development accounting several times. Banerjee suggests this macroevidence contains an unhelpfully wide range of estimates. But this assessment is inaccurate. A macroconsensus exists on many points, such as that rising workers per capita account for one-fifth of the growth in much of East Asia;[5] physical capital intensity accounts for one-fifth of income differences across countries;[6] much of China's growth has come from productivity growth in agriculture and the movement of workers out of agriculture;[7] and productivity differences between rich and poor nations are concentrated in agriculture and investment sectors.[8]

Beyond accounting, macroanalysis has contributed a slew of robust correlations that help guide microexperimental work. Correlation need not imply causality, of course, but certainly does not rule it out. Many correlations are later confirmed to be causal in various ways (as with lung cancer and smoking, earnings and education, life expectancy and income). Here are a few of the facts emphasized by recent macrodevelopment research: developing countries import most of their equipment, particularly from the United States, Japan, and Germany;[9] the local-currency return on reproducible capital is no higher in poor than in rich countries;[10] the skill premium increases with liberalization of trade and FDI;[11] and poor countries exhibit greater dispersion of average products of capital and labor across firms within industries.[12] It is up to theorists and microexperimentalists to flesh out the causal mechanisms behind these correlations.

On the issue of causality, there *are* some macroinstruments. Climate (rainfall, temperature, wind speed and direction), geography (distance to the other land masses, ruggedness of terrain), and accidents (such as natural deaths of dictators) have been deployed in the past decade. Another strategy is to have common shocks interact with different initial conditions. For example, some have examined how the epidemiological transition interacts with different initial disease burdens to study the effects of reduced mortality on populations and incomes.[13] Similarly, many researchers have studied the effects of trade liberalization using

3. Bloom and van Reenen (2007).
4. Bloom and others (2008).
5. Young (1995).
6. Mankiw, Romer, and Weil (1992); Hall and Jones (1999); Caselli (2005).
7. Young (2003); Brandt, Hsieh, and Zhu (2008).
8. Caselli (2005); Hsieh and Klenow (2007).
9. Eaton and Kortum (2001).
10. Caselli and Feyrer (2007).
11. Goldberg and Pavcnik (2007).
12. For example, Hsieh and Klenow (2009).
13. See Acemoglu and Johnson (2007).

the differential effect of a country's World Trade Organization entry on tariffs across its industries.

Macrodevelopment research consists of much more than cross-country growth regressions, however. Much of the work is not even particularly empirical.[14] Banerjee readily (and predictably!) concedes that random evaluations must be combined with theorizing. Economists will always need general equilibrium models to fill in the gaps between the results of randomized trials and to do welfare analysis.

In the past decade, the overwhelming majority of papers presented at the National Bureau of Economic Research Summer Institute Growth Meeting have been neither empirical nor theoretical, but what might be called "quantitative theory" (to use Edward Prescott's phrase). This literature typically identifies exogenous driving forces (such as observable policy distortions documented by the World Bank's Doing Business studies), then calibrates a model to obtain a quantitative sense of how these driving forces might affect aggregates (income, investment, schooling, and so on) across time or countries. Like strictly theoretical work, such quantitative theorizing is a vital complement to microempirical research.

To sum up, I agree with everything Banerjee says about the positive value of microempirical work in development. But I am less sympathetic with his nihilism toward macrodevelopment research. Macroresearch remains enormously valuable alongside more definitive but narrower microresearch.

References

Acemoglu, Daron. 2009. *Introduction to Modern Economic Growth*. Princeton University Press.
Acemoglu, Daron, and Simon Johnson. 2007. "Disease and Development: The Effect of Life Expectancy on Economic Growth." *Journal of Political Economy* 115 (December): 925–85.
Aghion, Philippe, and Peter Howitt. 1992. "A Model of Growth through Creative Destruction." *Econometrica* 60 (March): 323–51.
Brandt, Loren, Chang-Tai Hsieh, and Xiaodong Zhu. 2008. "Growth and Structural Transformation in China." In *China's Great Economic Transformation*, edited by Loren Brandt and T. G. Rawski. Cambridge University Press.
Bloom, Nick, and John van Reenen. 2007. "Measuring and Explaining Management Practices across Firms and Countries." *Quarterly Journal of Economics* 122 (November): 1351–1408.
Bloom, Nick, and others. 2008. "Management as a Technology: Evidence from India." Stanford University. In progress.
Caselli, Francesco. 2005. "Accounting for Cross-Country Income Differences." In *Handbook of Economic Growth*, edited by Philippe Aghion and Steven Durlauf. Amsterdam: Elsevier.
Caselli, Francesco, and James Feyrer. 2007. "The Marginal Product of Capital." *Quarterly Journal of Economics* 122 (May): 535–68.

14. Examples include the classic growth theories of Lucas (1988), Romer (1990), Grossman and Helpman (1991), and Aghion and Howitt (1992), as well as the more recent work of Acemoglu (2009), Jones (2008), and others.

Eaton, Jonathan, and Samuel S. Kortum. 2001. "Trade in Capital Goods." *European Economic Review* 45 (June): 1195–1235.

Goldberg, Pinelopi K., and Nina Pavcnik. 2007. "Distributional Effects of Globalization in Developing Countries." *Journal of Economic Literature* 45 (March): 39–82.

Grossman, Gene M., and Elhanan Helpman. 1991. *Innovation and Growth in the Global Economy.* MIT Press.

Hall, Robert E., and Charles I. Jones. 1999. "Why Do Some Countries Produce So Much More Output per Worker than Others?" *Quarterly Journal of Economics* 114 (February): 83–116.

Hsieh, Chang-Tai, and Peter J. Klenow. 2007 "Relative Prices and Relative Prosperity." *American Economic Review* 97 (June): 562–85.

———. 2009. "Misallocation and Manufacturing TFP in China and India." *Quarterly Journal of Economics* 124 (November).

Jones, Charles I. 2008. "Intermediate Goods, Weak Links, and Superstars: A Theory of Economic Development." Stanford University. Photocopy (February).

Lucas, Robert E., Jr. 1988. "On the Mechanics of Economic Development." *Journal of Monetary Economics* 22 (July): 3–42.

Mankiw, N. Gregory, David Romer, and David N. Weil. 1992. "A Contribution to the Empirics of Economic Growth." *Quarterly Journal of Economics* 107 (May): 407–37.

Romer, Paul M. 1990. "Endogenous Technological Change." *Journal of Political Economy* 98 (October): S71–S102.

Sapolsky, Robert M. 2002. *A Primate's Memoir: A Neuroscientist's Unconventional Life among the Baboons.* New York: Scribner.

Young, Alwyn. 1995. "The Tyranny of Numbers: Confronting the Statistical Realities of the East Asian Growth Experience." *Quarterly Journal of Economics* 110 (August): 641–80.

———. 2003. "Gold into Base Metals: Productivity Growth in the People's Republic of China during the Reform Period." *Journal of Political Economy* 111 (December): 1220–61.

COMMENT BY WILLIAM EASTERLY

M y first reaction to Abhijit Banerjee's chapter is defensive: "Hey, you are only allowed to make fun of our macrogrowth ethnic group if you yourself are a member of the group!" However, in the end, I agree with Banerjee's radically skeptical microconclusion about aggregate growth research: "Perhaps making growth happen is ultimately beyond our control. Maybe all that happens is that something goes right for once (privatized agriculture raises incomes in rural China) and then that sparks growth somewhere else in the economy, and so on. Perhaps we will never learn where it will start or what will make it continue."

But I am not persuaded of this conclusion by Banerjee's own arguments. His point that growth observations "are essentially unique events, and it is not clear what we could compare them to" is so generic that it could apply to virtually any empirical research in economics.

At the beginning of the new wave of empirical research on growth about two decades ago, economists hoped to establish at least some robust partial correlations between government policies (or other factors) and economic growth. Moreover, growth theory gave some clear predictions about such variables as tax rates (or any other policy analogous to a marginal tax on income or investment), human capital, physical capital investment, and population growth. And indeed, extremely high values of inflation, sharply negative real interest rates, extreme overvaluation of the currency, or a very high black market premium (all pretty much acting like indirect marginal taxes), separately or in combination, did predict poor growth performance.[1] Although these results did not address causality, even mere correlations have some usefulness (see chapter 1).

So a strong correlation between extreme policies and growth was at least a little informative. These extreme policy results were relevant to a far from trivial number of countries in Latin America and in Africa. Of course, the most empirically successful results were also the least theoretically necessary—most macroeconomists already knew that such extreme policies were bad and could have predicted that Robert Mugabe's expropriation of Zimbabwe's most productive farms and then printing of money like crazy would result in negative economic

1. Easterly (2005).

growth, regardless of whether there was regression evidence to inform such a prediction.

Similar results could have held for more moderate values of policy, informing a much larger number of policy questions on which there was less a priori knowledge. Alas, it was not to be. The extreme results were only robust for the extreme values.[2] For virtually all other growth determinants, there has clearly been a generalized failure to establish even correlations.

Ross Levine and David Renelt prefigured this early on, with their finding that virtually "nothing was robust."[3] Remarkably, much empirical growth research was done even after they predicted it would fail. In retrospect, though, it was probably necessary to go through all this research simply because the demand for explanations of growth was so intense. One had to show that all attempts at such explanation did in fact fail.

In the parade of ignorance about growth, 145 variables were "significant" in growth regressions.[4] Since a cross-section regression has about 100 observations, Banerjee rightly notes that growth researchers work with negative degrees of freedom. Some attempted to reduce the set to a much smaller number of robust variables using Bayesian model averaging, which raised hopes briefly.[5] But this approach gave completely different "robust" variables for different equally plausible samples.[6] More than Banerjee acknowledges, macroeconomists have earned their ignorance the hard way.

Why are the coefficients in growth regressions so unstable and not very robust? One contributing factor was probably the "law of small numbers" problem—that is, researchers tried to infer too much from too few observations.[7] One would think that a decade or two would be enough to average out the random noise on growth (which probably included severe measurement error), but surprisingly enough it was not. There is an astonishingly high amount of transitory variance in growth rates, which swamps the much smaller permanent growth differences between countries (see chapter 1), and most of the candidate explanatory variables are relatively permanent country characteristics.

Of course, the "law of small numbers" problem has an easy solution—get more numbers! One simple way to get to *very* long-run averages is to run regressions for the log level of per capita income, which is the cumulative sum of log growth rates since the dawn of time. This has been the tendency in cross-country research over the past decade. These level regressions are also far from perfect as a way to infer

2. Ibid.
3. Levine and Renelt (1992).
4. Durlauf, Johnson, and Temple (2005).
5. Doppelhofer, Miller, and Sala-i-Martin (2004).
6. Ciccone and Jarociński (2008).
7. The term comes from Kahneman, Slovic, and Tversky (1982).

anything. Still, even with some rather shaky attempts at identification, they have been at least modestly useful for making assertions about the importance of institutions in development (stimulating much further research), and then debating the relative role of human capital versus institutions in development.[8] (Inexplicably, Banerjee makes no distinction between growth regressions and level regressions.)

Aside from regressions, there are other uses of aggregate data, most notably in testing models of overall growth and development. Stylized facts about per capita income, capital flows, skilled and unskilled migration, and goods trade, for example, all reflect poorly on the neoclassical model in which development differences are primarily due to differences in the level of physical and human capital.[9] Alternatively, they could be due to productivity differences. Banerjee's discussion of the micro-macro collaboration that has helped enter the "black box" of productivity is excellent, but he fails to mention that the topic originated from stylized facts in aggregate data.

Perhaps the levels' stylized facts do salvage something from the wreckage of growth regressions. And perhaps the robust result that the no-growth result is robust is itself useful, something that macroeconomists can use to shoot down amateur attempts to explain growth, which usually feature hefty doses of confirmation bias, ex-post rationalization, and circular reasoning. Macroeconomists seem to have given Banerjee a lot of (mostly unacknowledged) cover for his courageous statement cited at the beginning of this comment.

How about Banerjee's alternative? Those who are aggressively skeptical about one alternative are going to be held to a high standard when offering another alternative (as I know from personal experience). Does the randomized evaluation (RE) literature also have a problem with the law of small numbers? The usual complaint is that any finding that "X works to improve Y" is highly context-specific, dependent on many other factors in the experimental situation that will vary both over time and across settings.[10] In response, Banerjee would say, do many replications in other contexts. But how many replications would be enough? According to Banerjee, all one needs to do is continue to experiment in different locations "until we are either satisfied that the treatment effect is reasonably stable or find that it is not and therefore need to rethink the generalizability of the treatment. If we have a theory that tells us where it might break down, we focus the extra experiments there. If not, we choose random locations within the relevant domain."

But Banerjee does not explain how many replications are necessary to produce satisfaction and how that number is affected by a focus on where their effect

8. See, for example, Glaeser and others (2004); Acemoglu, Johnson, and Robinson (2005).

9. Klenow and Rodríguez-Clare (1997); Easterly and Levine (2001).

10. For well-articulated discussions of this complaint, see chapter 2 in this volume and Deaton (2009).

"might break down." Nor can I recall seeing *any* attempt in the RE literature to address this issue. Without an answer to this question, the usefulness of a given (usually small) number of replications is unclear, and Banerjee's claim about the generalizability of a given result does not hold up. Perhaps it is impossible to determine how many replications are enough, but saying a problem is impossible to solve does not make it go away.

Banerjee makes his own ambitious suggestion that social policy and microevidence on how to do it well may be the key to make growth happen:

> The best we can do in that world is to hold the fort until that initial spark arrives: make sure that there is not too much human misery, maintain the social equilibrium, and try to make sure that there is enough human capital around to take advantage of the spark when it arrives. Social policy may be the best thing that we can do for growth to happen, and microevidence on how to do it well may turn out to be the key to growth success.

These statements obviously cannot be tested with Banerjee's own RE methodology (a contradiction that appears frequently in the RE discussion and that has already been noted by many others). How is RE going to discover the set of actions that "maintain the social equilibrium," that keep "enough" human capital to "take advantage of the spark" and thus get growth? Where did this theory of "social equilibrium" and complementarity between human capital and sparks come from, and how would one test it? On what evidence is the preference for social policy based (compared with building roads and ports, for example)? Most ambitious of all, how will one know if "the microevidence on how to do social policy" is or is not "the key to growth success?" All of these are aggregate growth questions, and Banerjee says he does not accept the methodology that addresses aggregate growth questions (probably correctly, as argued here).

What Banerjee is really offering as an alternative is treatment effects of very small interventions in particular settings (which, as just argued, are of uncertain applicability to other settings). There is nothing wrong with very small interventions, but (even if they generalized) their marginal effect on overall economic growth and development would be very small and hard to discern in *any* methodology. A process in which rigorous testing of many different small interventions is multiplied by a huge order of magnitude could perhaps achieve some kind of sizable impact. However, the prospects that such a system would come to pass are close to nonexistent, and even if it did, there would be huge questions of unintended general equilibrium effects (see chapter 1)—and these effects would *not* be subject to testing with the RE methodology itself. So RE does not really offer a serious alternative to how to achieve "growth success." Banerjee's doubts about whether making growth happen is actually within "our control" apply even more forcefully to RE than to what he correctly criticizes as the macro "presumption of growth policy."

References

Acemoglu, Daron, Simon Johnson, and James A. Robinson. 2005. "Institutions as the Fundamental Cause of Long-Run Growth." In *Handbook of Economic Growth*, edited by Philippe Aghion and Steven Durlauf. Amsterdam: North-Holland.

Ciccone, Antonio, and Marek Jarociński. 2008. "Determinants of Economic Growth: Will Data Tell?" Working Paper 852. Frankfurt am Main, Germany: European Central Bank.

Deaton, Angus. 2009. "Instruments of Development: Randomization in the Tropics, and the Search for the Elusive Keys to Economic Development." Working Paper w14690. Cambridge, Mass.: National Bureau of Economic Research.

Doppelhofer, Gernot, Ronald Miller, and Xavier Sala-i-Martin. 2004. "Determinants of Long-Term Growth: A Bayesian Averaging of Classical Estimates (BACE) Approach." *American Economic Review* 94 (September): 813–35.

Durlauf, Steven N., Paul A. Johnson, and Jonathan Temple. 2005. "Growth Econometrics." In *Handbook of Economic Growth*, vol. 1A, edited by Philippe Aghion and Steven Durlauf, pp. 555–677. Amsterdam: North-Holland.

Easterly, William. 2005. "National Policies and Economic Growth: A Reappraisal." in *Handbook of Economic Growth*, edited by Philippe Aghion and Steven Durlauf. Amsterdam: North-Holland.

Easterly, William, and Ross Levine. 2001. "It's Not Factor Accumulation: Stylized Facts and Growth Models." *World Bank Economic Review* 15, no. 2.

Glaeser, E. R., and others. 2004. "Do Institutions Cause Growth?" *Journal of Economic Growth* 9 (September): 271–303.

Kahneman, Daniel, Paul Slovic, and Amos Tversky, eds. 1982. *Judgment under Uncertainty: Heuristics and Biases.* Cambridge University Press.

Klenow, Peter, and Andrés Rodríguez-Clare. 1997. "The Neoclassical Revival in Growth Economics: Has It Gone Too Far?" *National Bureau of Economic Research Macroeconomics Annual 1997*, vol. 12, pp. 73–103.

Levine, Ross, and David Renelt. 1992. "A Sensitivity Analysis of Cross-Country Growth Regressions." *American Economic Review* 82, no. 4: 942–63.

Contributors

Nava Ashraf
Harvard Business School

Abhijit Vinayak Banerjee
Massachusetts Institute of Technology

Nancy Birdsall
Center for Global Development

Peter Boone
London School of Economics,
  Centre for Economic
  Performance (CEP)

Anne Case
Princeton University

Jessica Cohen
Harvard University,
  School of Public Health

William Easterly
New York University

Ricardo Hausmann
Harvard University,
  Center for International
  Development

Alaka Holla
World Bank

Simon Johnson
Massachusetts Institute of Technology

Peter Klenow
Stanford University

Michael Kremer
Harvard University

Ross Levine
Brown University

Sendhil Mullainathan
Harvard University

Benjamin A. Olken
Massachusetts Institute of Technology

Lant Pritchett
Harvard University, Kennedy School

Martin Ravallion
World Bank

Dani Rodrik
Harvard University, Kennedy School

Paul Romer
Stanford University

David N. Weil
Brown University

Index